THE THEORY AND PRACTICE
OF HELL

"The best of the many books on Nazi concentration camps and the society behind them."
—C. Wright Mills

"Kogon omits nothing and spares no one. His account, magnificently controlled and dispassionate . . . achieves a devastating impact."
—*The Nation*

"Here is a book so chilling in its catalogue of barbarism as to shock even the most calloused . . . "
—John Barkham
Book of the Month Club News

"Urgently recommended for public and college libraries!"
—*Library Journal*

THE THEORY AND PRACTICE OF HELL

The German Concentration Camps
and the System Behind Them

EUGEN KOGON

Translated from the German by
Heinz Norden

BERKLEY BOOKS, NEW YORK

Translated by Heinz Norden from the German,
Der SS Staat.

THE THEORY AND PRACTICE OF HELL

A Berkley Book / published by arrangement with
Farrar, Straus and Giroux, Inc.

PRINTING HISTORY
Farrar, Straus and Cudahy, Inc., edition published 1950
First Windhover edition / March 1958
Berkley mass market edition / February 1980
Berkley trade paperback edition / July 1998

The Penguin Putnam Inc. World Wide Web site address is
http://www.penguinputnam.com

ISBN: 0-425-16431-4

BERKLEY®
Berkley Books are published by
The Berkley Publishing Group, a member of Penguin Putnam Inc.,
200 Madison Avenue, New York, New York 10016.
BERKLEY and the "B" design are trademarks
belonging to Berkley Publishing Corporation.

PRINTED IN THE UNITED STATES OF AMERICA

10 9 8 7 6 5 4 3 2 1

CONTENTS

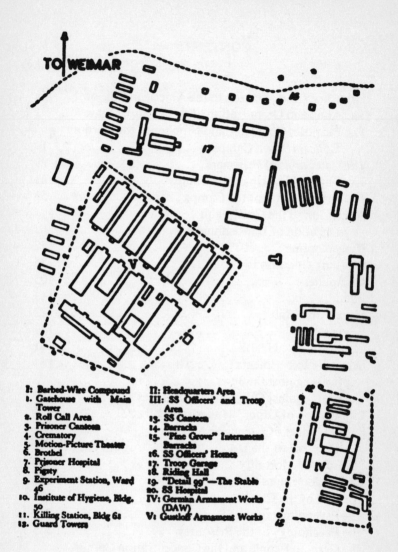

TO WEIMAR

I: Barbed-Wire Compound
1. Gatehouse with Main Tower
2. Roll Call Area
3. Prisoner Canteen
4. Crematory
5. Motion-Picture Theater
6. Brothel
7. Prisoner Hospital
8. Pigsty
9. Experiment Station, Ward 46
10. Institute of Hygiene, Bldg. 50
11. Killing Station, Bldg 61
12. Guard Towers

II: Headquarters Area

III: SS Officers' and Troop Area
13. SS Canteen
14. Barracks
15. "Pine Grove" Internment Barracks
16. SS Officers' Homes
17. Troop Garage
18. Riding Hall
19. "Detail 99"—The Stable
20. SS Hospital

IV: German Armament Works (DAW)

V: Gustloff Armament Works

SITE-PLAN OF BUCHENWALD
CONCENTRATION CAMP

MURDER PLANT
LOCATED IN THE BUCHENWALD STABLE

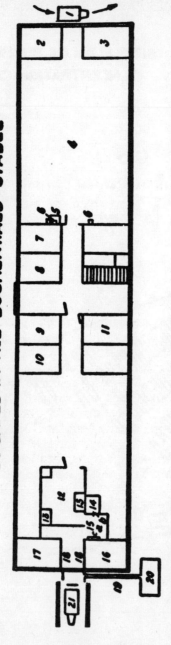

1. Incoming Truck with Prisoners
2. Storage Space for Straw
3. Storage Space for Feed
4. Undressing Room for the Prisoners
5. Table for Valuables and Dog-Tags
6. Loudspeaker
7. Radio Room
8. SS Dressing Room
9. SS Mess Hall
10. SS Dayroom
11. Latrine
12. So-Called Medical Room
13. Table with Medical Instruments
14. SS Shooting Stand with Embrasure
15. Killing Room
   a. Drain for Blood
   b. Wooden Screen for SS Man with Hose
   c. Curtain Screening Bullet Impact Wall
16. Storage Space for Sawdust
17. Storage Space for Straw
18. Bodies Piled Here
19. Drainpipe for Blood
20. Cesspool
21. Truck for Carrying off Bodies

Publishers' Introduction to the American Edition[1]

Dr. Eugen Kogon was born on February 2, 1903, in Munich. After graduating from a humanistic *Gymnasium*, he studied economics and sociology at the Universities of Munich, Florence and Vienna. Until early 1934 he lived in Austria, a writer and editor, and later a trustee of a private trust company whose operations extended over several countries. He took advantage of repeated trips in Germany, England, France, Italy, Switzerland, Czechoslovakia, Hungary and Austria to engage in intensive anti-Nazi activities, in the course of which he was twice arrested for brief periods in 1937. Immediately after the Germans marched into Austria, during the very night of March 11 to 12, 1938, he was finally arrested as one of the first opponents of the regime. Without possibility of court proceedings he spent eighteen months as a prisoner of the Gestapo.

In September 1939, he was taken to the Buchenwald concentration camp where he was at first a common laborer, then a blacksmith; after the fall of 1940, a tailor's assistant. For

[1] Based on the introductory material to the first and second German editions.

two months in the spring of 1943 he was clerk in the "Pathology Section." During these weeks three different orders from the Reich Main Security Office were received, assigning him to Auschwitz for death in the gas chamber. With the aid of a few influential friends in the camp it proved possible to delay his shipment three times. On June 6, 1943, Kogon voluntarily and with the approval of his comrades assumed the position of so-called "First Medical Clerk" in Building 50 (Institute of Hygiene, Division for Serum Production), under SS Major Ding-Schuler, who was at the same time chief of the laboratory where human experiments were conducted. By circuitous means a teletype message from the Reich Main Security Office was effected which ordered Kogon's "liquidation" postponed until the end of the war.

Following Buchenwald's liberation on April 11, 1945, Dr. Kogon settled, after seven years in prison camp, near Frankfurt-on-Main with his wife, his two sons and his daughter. Since April 1946, together with his friends Walter Dirks and Clement Münster, he has been publisher and editor of a literary and political monthly, the *Frankfurter Hefte*.

2

On April 16, 1945, five days after the first American armored units had arrived, an Intelligence Team from the Psychological Warfare Division visited the Buchenwald concentration camp. Its mission was to study the situation and to prepare a comprehensive report for Supreme Headquarters, Allied Expeditionary Forces (SHAEF). The report was to show how a German concentration camp was organized, what role was assigned to it in the Nazi State and what happened to those who were sent to the camps by the Gestapo and detained there by the SS.

Buchenwald was the first big concentration camp to fall into the hands of the western allies intact. It was to serve as the key to an understanding of the system behind the concentration camps as a whole.

Under the direction of Lieutenant Albert G. Rosenberg, the members of the team, Max M. Kimental, Richard Akselrad,

Alfred H. Sampson and Ernest S. Biberfeld, began to lay the groundwork for an objective and conclusive report. Their own work in helping to dissolve the camp quickly made them realize that it was quite impossible for outsiders to gain even an approximately accurate picture of the complex situation within the camp and to evaluate its true significance. Such a task could be carried out only in close collaboration with a few reliable camp inmates who had no axe to grind. Kogon was asked to take over this job.

The initial report was completed in Weimar within about a month. Constant liaison was maintained with the camp and the numerous groups of former prisoners, and rather formidable difficulties had to be overcome, as will become evident from many of the chapters in this book. The first report comprised some 400 typewritten pages, single-spaced. There was a main report of 125 pages which Kogon himself had dictated, and approximately 150 statements from individual prisoners who, by virtue of their experience, had been asked to give their views on various facts, incidents, persons and phases. Kogon's chief collaborators were the Socialist writer Ferdinand Römhild; Heinz Baumeister of Dortmund, a Social Democrat; and Stefan Heymann, an orthodox Communist editor with whom Kogon was on excellent terms, although Heymann had been detailed by the Communist leadership in camp to serve as a check on him.

Kogon consulted further with Dr. Werner Hilpert, former leader of the Catholic Action in Saxony and chairman of the Catholic Center party in Saxony, as well as with the radical leftist writer Franz Hackel. Except for Stefan Heymann, Kogon had long been on terms of close friendship with all these men. Each of them had wide experience in camp, their minimum term of detention being five years. They had "come up from below." Under circumstances that were often very difficult they had slowly risen to positions that afforded them insight and influence. Both had always involved danger, especially since none of these men belonged to the "big shot" group in camp. None of them was soiled by corruption or other camp misdeeds.

To dispel certain apprehensions that the report might become a kind of indictment of leading camp inmates, Kogon read all but two of the twelve chapters—all that was finished at the time—to a group of fifteen men early in May 1945. All fifteen had been leaders of the camp underground, or were representative of certain groups of political prisoners. Their verdict was that the contents of the report were objective and accurate.

Meanwhile the Austrian engineer Gustav Wagerer (today editor-in-chief of Vienna's Communist daily), a good friend of Kogon's to whom he and many other non-Communist comrades owe much, had begun to compose a kind of Buchenwald chronicle, for which he likewise solicited special contributions. Kogan and he exchanged carbon copies of important records of this nature. In addition, Stefan Heymann, with the full approval of Kogon, furnished the camp information office with a copy of every record that came before him for editing.

Thus occasional passages from the wealth of material (such as the stories of the German Air Force experiments on Dachau inmates, of certain incidents that occurred in the camp prisons, etc.) have appeared word for word, although with source unacknowledged, in a pamphlet entitled *KL BU* (the German abbreviation for Buchenwald concentration camp) which has been published in the Russian Zone of Occupation.

One copy each of the finished report was transmitted by way of the Rosenberg Intelligence Team to the Psychological Warfare Division, SHAEF, Paris, and the headquarters of the Twelfth United States Army Group at Bad Nauheim. Subsequently this material repeatedly served as a basis for investigations by the War Crimes Commission at Nuremberg and Wiesbaden, and by the Military Intelligence Service Center of the United States Forces, European Theater.

Mr. Crossman of Oxford, today a Labor party member of the British House of Commons, at the time working for the British Broadcasting Corporation with the Psychological Warfare Division in Paris, was the first to recommend that the report, which was addressed to an official agency rather than to the public, be reworked into a book. The chief of the Psychological Warfare Division, later to become the Information Control Division, Brigadier-General Robert A. McClure, agreed to the proposal, and upon returning from Paris Kogon went to work.

The present book is a new manuscript, although here and

there sections of the original text have been used. Instead of Buchenwald as an individual case, the system of the German concentration camps is set forth as a whole. The style has been sharply modified. Important new documentary material has been added. The earlier individual reports written at Kogon's suggestion have all been carefully and critically worked over. In a few outstanding cases they have been quoted verbatim. In other cases, when he felt justified in assuming the responsibility for doing so, Kogon has used them as sources for the narrative. At no point is there any conflict between the earlier report and the present book.

In his introduction, Kogon expresses sincere gratitude to all his friends who encouraged, advised and helped him whenever the task bogged down, some of them even financially. He thanks, in particular, his friends Walter Dirks of Frankfurt-on-Main and Hermann Frühauf, M.D., of Offenbach; also the City of Oberursel, under its former and present mayors, which generously offered to him and his family a new home, where he was able to work. And on the American side, he thanks Captain Albert G. Rosenberg (now of New York City), Captain Daniel Lerner (of the same city), Mr. Richard Akselrad (Fulda), Captain Richard Gutman (Military Intelligence Service Center, Oberursel), and Mr. H. H. Blake (now of Boston).

Yet Kogon alone answers for the book. None of these gentlemen shares any part of the responsibility for it. Nor is it associated with any German or foreign propaganda agency, nor with any party or other office or other person.

The book was written between June 15 and December 15, 1945. In the second German edition, of which the American edition is a translation, the text was in places condensed, and in places cut, and in certain sections expanded. Its sense, however, was not altered. Some factual corrections of minor details proved necessary as Kogon had prophesied in the preface to the first edition they would be. But the core of the narrative remains the same, and is neither a history of the German concentration camps nor a compendium of all the atrocities that were committed. It is, as it was intended to be, primarily a sociological study and its verified contents can, as its author says, claim outstanding significance from a human, political and moral aspect.

By its very nature, this is not a pretty book. Yet the mirror that it holds up to mankind reflects no nameless monsters. The image in the glass is familiar. There, but for the grace of God, go you and I. It is a pageant of horror to make even the sturdiest blench. Indeed, it may so deeply shock even upright men and women that they will be tempted to put the book aside. But its author could not allow this contingency to temper his account of human—and German—depravity. The entanglements of collective guilt are too sinister. They reach far beyond the borders of Germany. They enmesh even those who can honestly claim ignorance.

National Socialism has left behind in the world a foul heritage of arrogance, violence, arbitrary power and hate. Even while the battle was still on, the victors were inexorably dragged down to the level of the enemy. Since the liberation there have been "Christian Soldiers"—the exception, happily, rather than the rule—who were easily the match of the SS, and not in battle alone. Below a news picture of the battered skeleton of a Japanese bus, crushed by the atomic bomb, runs the caption: "They found a swift way to join their ancestors." "I am not persuaded," observes Kogon, "that this does credit to the better world, the world that won victory. But I take heart from the fact that I am permitted to say this, that the world does not turn a deaf ear."

The voluminous concentration-camp literature of the past twelve years, the profuse propaganda engaged in by press and radio when some of the camps had been liberated—all this was virtually straight atrocity-reporting. As a result, no one seems to know even now *what a German concentration camp was really like*.

It was a world unto itself, a state within a state, a society without law. Men were flung into it to fight for their naked lives, for mere survival. They fought with all the virtues and vices at their command—and usually there was more vice than virtue. Was the SS alone the enemy? Far from it. Inmate fought fellow inmate with the same tenacity, if not even more bitterly! Traditional behavior patterns were utterly disrupted, moral values strained to the bursting point. The human tragedy ran its full gamut.

The despair of those compelled to recognize to what extent

certain SS practices were emulated in the ranks of the victims, was only deepened after the liberation, when they saw a credulous world invest injustice and brutality with an aura of heroism. Those survivors who battened on the despair of their fellow prisoners will take small comfort from this book, which makes short shrift of false haloes. There are certain telling questions that anyone who has read this book can ask: What was your camp? Your group? Your job? Your identifying color? Your party membership? How long did you serve?

Kogon is quite aware that it is a somber burden he has taken on his shoulders. He knows that the book may be exploited for one-sided propaganda purposes, or for purposes of sensationalism, both of which he despises—sensationalism even more than propaganda. The objective interpretation of these unspeakable events may be perverted, by those more monstrous than the criminals themselves, merely to satisfy esoteric tastes and tickle jaded palates. Or it may merely make a pleasant shudder run down the spines of the smug—and guiltiest of all are the smug, to whom the sufferings of others are no more than a foil for their own well-being. They are the rotten soil from which spring the argument and sophistry justifying any wrong done in the name of authority, any suppression of the challenge of morality.

Sometimes, moreover, Kogon asked himself whether, in his efforts to dissect the system dispassionately, to point out its every strength and weakness, he was not actually rationalizing it, offering a ready-made blueprint for tyrants yet to come. On several occasions he was tempted to burn the whole manuscript. At other times he thought he might evade responsibility by remaining anonymous.

But he found himself unable to take either way out. He feels that among the few who escaped the hellish system alive, he brings peculiar qualifications to the task in hand. He is a man of religion as well as of politics, a sociologist as well as a writer. For certain reasons he was able, even at the moment when he himself was the victim of utter degradation, to keep a sense of detachment, to remain a critical witness, to estimate the sphere and significance of events, to trace motivations and reactions in the perverted and violated minds about him, to tell the general from the specific. One of the inexorable consequences is that his name is likely to remain linked to this gloomy and controversial document.

It is his hope that this book may help to keep Germany from ever again surrendering to the powers of evil, that it may warn the rest of the world of the fate awaiting those who do surrender. The purge to which he offers this contribution is a necessary step toward victory, lest in the end the facts become so twisted that the gnawing sense of guilt be stilled, indeed, lest the unregenerate use the facts as a screen for renewed plotting. There is a duty to attempt clarification now, when facts and motives, already growing dim, are not yet obscured. The world, and above all Germany, must pause for self-analysis. A factual report, not of personal history or of atrocities, but covering every aspect of the German concentration camps may well serve to start this process of catharsis. What is needed is not merely a mosaic of many fragments, of individual experiences, but a picture of the system as a whole. This is the answer to the objection that too much has already been said and written about the German concentration camps. *The truth alone can set us free.*

Chapter One

THE AIMS
AND ORGANIZATION OF
THE SS SUPER STATE

Late in the fall of 1937, in Frankfurt, I had occasion for an extended discussion with a leading SS man from Vogelsang Castle—a discussion that continued over several afternoons.

It should be noted that Vogelsang, in the Eiffel Mountains, was one of three castles—*Ordensburg* is the German term—where the new Nazi elite was to be incubated. *Ordensburg* really describes a castle belonging to a medieval order, such as the Knights Templar—and that is how the Nazis thought of their elite. At the *Ordensburg*, young men chosen with care were trained for several years under an austere regimen of consecration.

My discussion with the SS officer was very frank on both sides. It dealt with such questions as the meaning of German history, the role of the Third Reich, and the racial theories of the SS. The contrast between the views expressed was, of course, extreme and gave me a wealth of insight, confirming much that I had already suspected. The SS officer was by no means stupid, indeed he had a superior intellect, for all that he was a thoroughgoing fanatic. He made three remarkable statements:

1

"What we trainers of the younger generation of Führers aspire to is a modern governmental structure on the model of the ancient Greek city states. It is to these aristocratically run democracies with their broad economic basis of serfdom that we owe the great cultural achievements of antiquity. From five to ten per cent of the people, their finest flower, shall rule; the rest must work and obey. In this way alone can we attain that peak performance we must demand of ourselves and of the German people.

*"The new Führer class is selected by the SS—in a positive sense by means of the National Political Education Institutes (*Napola*) as a preparatory stage, of the Ordensburgen as the academies proper of the coming Nazi aristocracy, and of a subsequent active internship in public affairs; in a negative sense by the extermination of all racially and biologically inferior elements and by the radical removal of all incorrigible political opposition that refuses on principle to acknowledge the philosophical basis of the Nazi State and its essential institutions.*

"Within ten years at the latest it will be possible for us in this way to dictate the law of Adolf Hitler to Europe, put a halt to the other wise inevitable decay of the continent, and build up a true community of nations, with Germany as the leading power keeping order."

I shall not here cite the arguments I marshaled against these propositions. If there was any need for further incriminating evidence against me, this incident earned me a place of honor on the first Gestapo black list when the Germans marched into Austria on March 12, 1938. What is of importance here is merely the extraordinary precision with which an SS leader was able to set forth the true aims of the Nazi State.

It is the *Schutz-Staffel*[1] of Heinrich Himmler that must be regarded as the preordained guardian of the Nazi spirit, the elite on whom was to rest the ultimate exercise of Nazi power.

---

[1] *Schutz-Staffel* literally means "Defense Echelon." The term was universally abbreviated to SS, but the abbreviation could not be written in ordinary Roman or even Gothic letters. It was written as a double lightning flash, *z/z*, in imitation of ancient runic characters. Ultimately even German typewriters had to carry this symbol on a special key.—*Tr.*

Himmler, the son of a Bavarian official and a failure as a schoolteacher, had risen from the ranks of the "Artamans," an obscure branch of the German youth movement, dedicated to the glorification and arming of the German peasantry. Even then the Nazi symbols of blood, soil and the sword were foreshadowed. Looking at Himmler's features, moreover, it is not surprising to find that his man was to become the disciple, the henchman and finally the most dogged protagonist of Adolf Hitler's obsessions. Pince-nez clamped before his cynical eyes and rather stupid face, he was certainly not the prototype of the non-existent and thus all the more exalted "Teutonic race." None of the principal Nazi leaders were. Certainly not Alfred Rosenberg, a man without a drop of German blood, who yet presumed to play the part of the great German philosopher; nor Joseph Goebbels, about whose skull formation, stature and clubfoot few words need be wasted; nor the bloated Hermann Göring; nor, especially, their lord and master himself, Adolf Hitler, one of the receding forehead type, of whom his one-time press agent, the cynical "Putzi" Hanfstaengel, once told foreign correspondents that at least the hair in his armpits was fair.

What Himmler, Hitler's policeman, lacked in intelligence, he made up in unwavering pigheadedness. His character exhibited two essential German qualities, quite dissociated from each other: brutality, and a romantic streak. He was able to alternate them like shirts. He was fond of displaying the mystic rigmarole of his "Sworn Fellowship" before the counterfeit bones of King Henry I, founder of medieval German power in the East, at the midnight consecrations of SS ensigns in the Quedlinburg Cathedral. But daybreak might already see him at some concentration camp, watching the mass whippings of political prisoners. From the symbolism of the sun wheel, the path of the swastika led straight to the smoking furnaces of Auschwitz.

The SS was an organization that served a specific and quite realistic purpose, true, but from the outset Himmler had conceived and created it as a sacred order. He never intended to turn it into a mass army. Only the general trend of the Third Reich itself drove him in this direction. To the last, he tried time and again to maintain a basic core that should enable him some day to return to his original purpose. That purpose was to develop and protect with all the methods of power a German system of rule, based on race. That this meant guarding the person of its Messianic preincarnation, the so-called Führer, was understood.

The very qualifications for SS candidates were unusual. They had to be at least five feet, eleven inches tall. (Later on this qualification was largely waived, and even the halt and the lame found their way into the SS, until the "elite guards" bore little resemblance any longer to the supposed ideal of "Teutonic braves.") Their pedigrees had to be traced back to 1750 and to be of pure "German blood." Their character—in the Nazi sense—had to be impeccable.

For the purpose of suppressing political opposition, however, Himmler needed bullies and strong-arm men who were also fanatics. The members of the elite guard in actual fact, therefore, were necessarily capable of reacting to but two extremes: the Führer—that meant *Sieg Heil*; while the "enemy" meant *Nieder* (down). On the one side was the personified symbol of a world of radiance—and significantly enough it did not matter in the least that their idol in no way corresponded to any ideal concept of the Teutonic race, for neither did they themselves. On the other side were the Jews, the Marxists, the Free Masons, the Jesuits—all of them undifferentiated blanket images of the foe, absurdly primitive in character. The SS was predominantly composed of unemployed from every class, men who had come to accept it as convenient and grand to serve the nationalist upsurge with brass knuckles and revolver.

There is some question whether the rank and file which joined the SS in the course of the years, voluntarily or by compulsion, had any real knowledge of the true aims of Himmler and his immediate staff. It is a question of no great moment in judging the blueprint of the SS super state, considering the system of authority that prevailed in the organization. The SS leadership, at any rate, did pursue such a plan, consistently, step by step, at any cost. Each partial objective was sought with a degree of ruthlessness completely transcending ordinary concepts. The testimony and documentary evidence since the end of the war have established the inner structure of the SS for all the world to see.

The SS was established in 1929 as Hitler's black-uniformed

bodyguard. Originally it numbered but 250 men. Its chief, Heinrich Himmler, was under the command of Ernst Rohm, the chief of the SA.[1] A significant sidelight on Himmler's plans, which even then far transcended the protection of Hitler's person, is thrown by the fact of the simultaneous establishment within the SS of a "Race and Settlement Office," later to acquire ominous significance. Eventually it guarded the purity of the original ideal of a sacred order, protected the elite character of the SS, conducted a continuous process of selecting the master class for the super state and, by means of extermination, resettlement and land distribution, buttressed its rule throughout Germany and Europe.

The recruitment appeal of the General SS was directed primarily to the aristocracy, the intelligentsia and the scions of the wealthy middle class. This by no means meant that the "consecrated fellowship of the SS" was to be turned into a fashionable gentlemen's club. The General SS was merely to furnish the leaders of the SS with broad connections, money and prestige among the German people—a facade behind which true SS aims could be realized all the easier. It was a transition phase. When it had served its purpose it was allowed to wither away without fanfare though it was never formally abolished. By 1939 its only remaining role was to serve as the vehicle for the summary calling up of many of its members to the SS Reserve. These were then simply assigned to such SS units as suffered from a shortage of enlisted men or officers.

Many a German in this way paid dearly for the social privileges of former membership in the General SS, being swept into the doom that engulfed the SS as a whole. In the early days it was counted as a fine thing to be permitted to belong to what was looked on as the national elite! Propaganda was centered on the proposition that the General SS was to become the equivalent of the old Guard and Corps units. The SS leaders made it easy for new members. There was little work even for men on active duty. They could simply look on themselves as lords of the realm engaged in

---

[1] The *Sturm-Abteilungen*, the brown-shirted storm troops, Hitler's private army of bully boys who really swept the Nazi movement into power.—*Tr.*

aristocratic pastimes—such as prancing about on horseback in the Mounted SS. All that so-called "Sponsoring Members" had to do to wear the black pin with the runic symbol of the SS was to pay a monthly contribution. There was no trace of any hardheaded theoretical or political indoctrination to make them fit for the "sacred order."

These tactics skillfully exploited prevailing trends. "Sponsoring Members" saw in their financial contributions a cheap way of evading all other Nazi organizations and compulsions while yet being "insiders." Active Nazis, who recoiled from the Storm Troops as no more than an organized rabble, gained distinction over the general run of the people by wearing the fabulous black uniform—a perfect job of tailoring which was not issued but had to be paid for at fancy prices from one's own pocket. The uniform made it possible to strut about in the spirit of the German military tradition, reaping the prestige due a crack outfit.

From the outset, Himmler boasted the title of Reichsführer SS, and the spread of his organization across the German Reich was relatively rapid. By 1930 there were two thousand members; a year later, ten thousand. But the general Nazi upsweep soon created such a wealth of opportunity for careers involving prestige and financial remuneration—in the government, the foreign service, the army, industry—that there was no longer any question of consolidating the General SS in the direction of ideals of "consecration." The Blood Purge of June 30, 1934, and the ensuing terror caused many members to sever even their outward connection with the SS. But many others stayed in as a matter of form. Essentially their membership was no more than participation in a loose kind of association for the mutual promotion of social and professional ambitions. Yet precisely such an organization fitted in well with the intelligence needs of the Security Service chief, Heydrich, and with the financial needs of the SS leadership. The dregs of the aristocracy, the intelligentsia and the bourgeoisie who were caught up in the General SS—men who for some reason had failed to make a career in government, the army or industry, or who were especially attracted by the SS ideals—this negative elite, as it were, readily found its way from the General SS into the real SS cadres.

Until the purge of June 30, 1934, it was the SA, however,

that stood in the foreground of Nazi activity, far outdoing the SS in undisciplined terror. The SA was, according to Hitler's plan, the couter-balance to the German army. Hitler intended to build his state upon those two pillars. The purge was skillfully stage-managed by the General Staff of one of these props, the German army, against its rival, the SA, and especially against the chief of the SA, Röhm. But it gave the SS, Himmler and his lieutenants, the long-awaited opportunity for the clean-up for which they had prepared. At last they were able to put their blueprint into effect. For weeks and months after the purge, the SS cleaned house. Opposing SA leaders, high Nazi officials, any political leaders at all who offered opposition or could not be controlled, were ruthlessly disposed of. In the end the SA stood stripped of all its power.

But it is highly significant that down to 1944 the Army General Staff stubbornly resisted pressure to accord Himmler any form of recognition whatever. Long after Himmler's divisional commanders as well as his high police officials had been confirmed by the army as officers, he himself, the all-powerful ruler of the SS, was denied the privilege of calling himself a general. Himmler never forgave this slight, and after the plot of July 20, 1944, when he rose to the position of "commander-in-chief of the home army," he wreaked bitter vengeance.

By 1936 Himmler had become not only supreme head of the SS but chief of the German police, and by 1944, had become also commander-in-chief of the German replacement forces. He was at the head of the whole machine, the many diversified branches of which often enjoyed considerable degrees of independence, for all that they were attuned to each other. All the threads ran together in his hands. At his beck and call were the SD (the Security Service); the Reich Main Security Office; the SS troops; the SS Main Economic and Administrative Office; the Personal Staff of the Reichsführer SS; and the Operational Main Office.

To guard against the rapid growth of the SS and safeguard his own objectives, Himmler had created in 1931 the SD (*Sicherheits-Dienst*), his own personal Security Service. It was a harmless sounding name. It did not then partake of the terror its very mention was to spread only two years later even in the ranks of the Nazi party itself. No less a personage than

Hitler's powerful deputy, Rudolf Hess, took part in setting up the SD. He called it the "nerve center of party and state." Actual organizer and chief of this nerve center was a young ex-naval lieutenant, Reinhard Heydrich, a man of diabolical cast.

The original sphere of the SD was the Nazi party rather than the German people. It became a kind of "shoo-fly squad" with an elaborate system of stool pigeons. Heydrich's slogan was: "It's all right if you know about it—but you've got to know."

Of the members of the SD, Himmler expected all the virtues implicit in his sacred order. They had to be incorruptible and blindly loyal to himself and to their group. They had to be as hard on themselves as they were expected to be on others. Their family life must be above suspicion. In short, what was wanted was the full embodiment, not necessarily with any deep moral roots, of those "Prussian virtues" that have become notorious throughout German history. This is a code that unquestionably has validity, or at the very least contains elements of real morality. Unfortunately it has always shown a readiness to let itself by misused for the most ignoble social and political purposes. The SD had its own Courts of Honor to watch over its adherence to the true and narrow path. Violators were subject to the swift action of a special "Flying Squad." Its death sentences were at that time largely confined to the ranks of the SD.

It was Heydrich and the SD alone that enabled Himmler to establish the power of the SS and to keep that power once it was established. Remember that the early days of Nazi power, from 1932 to 1937, were a welter of intrigue, cross-currents and struggle within the Party. Without the strong network of the upper SD echelons, which extended clear across Germany, the SS could hardly have established its will. During and after the purge of June 30, 1934, the flying squads of the SD worked overtime until their gun barrels and brass knuckles grew hot.

The SD, under Heydrich and his deputy, Dr. Werner Best—after Heydrich's assassination in Czechoslovakia, under Ernst Kaltenbrunner—was organized into seven (later twelve) administrative districts, which largely coincided with the corps areas of the German army.

The vast machine of the SS could never have functioned successfully had it not gained police power and had that power not been completely severed from any constitutional basis, and especially from the judiciary. From the moment of the Nazi seizure of power in 1933, Himmler had been out to become chief of the German political police. He succeeded only in Bavaria. Prussia, some two-thirds of Germany, remained Göring's dominion. On March 4, 1933, Göring had said: "Mine not to do justice, but to destroy and exterminate." He soon carried his threat into effect. By June 1933, the old political police had become the Gestapo (abbreviated from *Geheime Staatspolizei*, Secret State Police), with headquarters in Berlin's Prince Albrecht Street.

Chief of the Gestapo at the time was thirty-three-year-old Rudolf Diels, a product of the old Prussian State Police, and a member of neither the Nazi party nor the SA nor the SS. This close confidant of Göring agreed fully with Himmler, however, that the terrorism of the SA must be curbed. Behind the scenes Himmler, together with Heydrich and Dr. Werner Best, who became Heydrich's deputy late in 1933, worked systematically. By 1934 they succeeded in taking over for the SS one provincial police force after another in Germany. Prussia alone, with its Berlin Gestapo, held out, though there too Heydrich had his SD men in key positions, enabling him, as early as March 1934, to take over the heart of the Gestapo, the so-called Gestapa or central office.

Complete organization of the machine could take place openly only after 1936. Until then Himmler was "merely" inspector of the Gestapa, under Göring, then Prussian Prime Minister. On February 10, 1936, by "Reich Law," the Gestapa was made a "Supreme Reich Agency." This made Himmler even nominally independent of Göring. He was now absolute master of the German police.

Himmler at once handed over the Security Police to his closest intimate, Reinhard Heydrich, SD chief and henceforth chief of the Gestapa as well. The Gestapo network was extended throughout Germany with the establishment of regional headquarters.

The Gestapa itself was given three main divisions:

Main Division I had jurisdiction over all regional headquarters, all Gestapo administration, all questions of personnel, and the files. It had no head of its own but was directed by the office of Heydrich's adjutant.

Main Division II comprised political affairs, with such subdivisions as illegal parties and organizations; associations and industrial groups; the church and reaction; freemasonry; sects; the Nazi party; homosexuality. It ordered arrests and made out the notorious Protective Custody Warrants. Its section chiefs reported directly to the chief of the Gestap*a*.

Main Division III dealt with treason and counterespionage. It had special desks for all the countries of Europe. Its longtime chief was Best, who was also Heydrich's deputy as chief of the Gestap*a*.

The Reich Criminal Police Office was under Nebe, a professional police official who became a high SS officer. Even under the Weimar Republic, when he had been with the Prussian State Police, Nebe had been a Nazi. He became Göring's confidential police expert, but later served Heydrich and Himmler. During the war he began working with the opposition. Among other things, the Reich Criminal Police Office applied the entire protective custody policy to actual or suspected criminals.

As early as March 1933, Göring had proclaimed: "Right is that which serves the German people." Under cover of this slogan he had "liberated" the Prussian Political Police from its "dependence" on the prosecutors' offices. Later Dr. Werner Best formally created the "legal" basis for this and similar acts. As chief of the Gestapo Legal Division, he became a member of the newly created Academy of German Law. There he proclaimed and jammed through a juridical variant of Göring's tenet: "Right is that which serves the State."

Once this principle had been accepted, the arbitrary exercise of the police power by those who had gained control of its machinery became "legal." The introduction of the so-called Protective Custody Warrants, likewise a proposal by Best, instantly accepted by Heydrich, put an end to all judicial review of arrests. It was tantamount to suspension of the right of habeas corpus. The way was now open to the liquidation of all opponents of the Nazi regime.

Under the Weimar Republic the German police had three partially overlapping branches. There was, first of all, the

Security Police, charged with the responsibility for maintaining order and security throughout the country. Next there was the Administrative Police, which embraced traffic, industry, public health and the like. Finally, there was the Criminal Police.

Himmler left only the Administrative Police to the Ministry of the Interior. Everything else was reorganized into the new Reich Main Security Office which replaced the SD Main Office in Berlin as the highest administrative organ of the SD. Henceforth three divisions of the Reich Main Security Office belonged exclusively to the SD:

Office III: Domestic Intelligence.

Office VI: Foreign Intelligence (to which the Military Counter-Intelligence Service was added in 1944).

Office VII: Files and Research.

Each of these offices had numerous sub-divisions and branches throughout Germany and abroad. There were extensive undercover organizations with telephone cables and call numbers of their own, and with dummy representatives known by harmless designations.

SD fieldmen only rarely knew each other's identity or their SD rating. They were divided into five classes:

V-men (*Vertrauensleute*), men who were trusted.

A-men, agents.

Z-men (*Zubringer*), informants.

H-men (*Helfershelfer*), secondary informants, as a rule men who acted from highly questionable motives.

U-men (*Unzuverlässige*), unreliables, who were altogether corrupt and had to be constantly watched.

Day by day, year after year, this far-flung intelligence network supplied a mass of individual reports from every sphere of life—the Party, the government, industry, high society, the private lives of ordinary citizens. Each report reached the central office, which kept one copy in its secret files, sending two copies to the chief of the SD administrative district concerned. One of these copies was kept in a file to which only this official and his deputy had access; the other in a place known to him alone.

The inner circle of the SD was known only to the higherups. Members of the broad outside organization seldom knew each other's identities. In the second half of 1934 and in early 1935 no less than 155 SS leaders were murdered by a secret group that called itself "Röhm's Avengers"—and so identified itself on slips of paper found pinned to each body. After that, the requirements for anonymity within the SD were sharply tightened. The number of members ran into the tens of thousands. Reliable estimates mention 100,000 to 120,000 up to the outbreak of the war, counting the whole army of agents, informers and stool pigeons. For the war period itself the figure is set at about twice that much.

They were everywhere—these indefatigable and fanatical mercenaries of the SS plot—in or near the top of every command and agency of any importance, whether public or private, tirelessly carrying out the orders of Heydrich, Kaltenbrunner, Himmler and Hitler.

All authoritative positions within the Reich Main Security Office were filled with SD men from the top ranks of the SS leadership. As the Third Reich expanded across Europe and as the German police machine became better organized and more dependable, most of these high officials took on big jobs abroad, positions involving the exercise of terror on a huge scale.

The evolutionary process within the Security Service and the Gestapo proceeded according to the same social and psychological scheme that prevailed with all the SS cadres. Not infrequently their chieftains selected for leading positions precisely those men who had already come into conflict with the law, or they deliberately involved them in such conflicts, to provide a "sound foundation" for loyalty in social degradation, to cut off any retreat.

The rank and file of the police machine consisted predominantly of men who had been unable to make headway in the ordinary police services, augmented by hordes of recruits who had been failures in civilian life and who generally lacked all technical and character training. Pay in all the lower grades, by the way, was so wretched that for this reason alone men of ability would always look for other and better opportunities. As for the network of stool pigeons and informers, it served as a catch-all for the scum collected from the aristocracy and the bourgeoisie, the working and white-collar classes. The fact that certain members of the Security Service, the Gestapo and auxiliary agencies showed intellectual traits does not rule out their essential cultural and political primitivism. For it was neither superior judgment nor critical reason that prevailed but conformity in conviction and loyalty in the performance of work. Even the most intellectual among them limited their intellects to the effective promotion of the SS super state and the execution of measures appropriate to that end.

In addition to the SD and the police, Himmler had command of the SS troops proper. The old SS squads that had protected Nazi rallies were nominally merged with the regular police. Actually they were considerably reinforced and turned into the so-called Special Duty SS (to which, during the war, were added foreign legionaries from many countries) and the SS Death-Head Units. In 1936 they numbered about 210,000 men, ninety per cent of them Special Duty Troops, later called *Waffen SS* (Armed SS). Toward the end of the war there were about 1,000,000 men, of whom some 25,000 were in the Death-Head Units, while about the same number consisted of foreign legionaries. The *Waffen SS* of some 940,000 was grouped into divisions and *Standarten*, each of the latter having the strength of a regiment, about 3,000 men. Together they formed an army with its own equipment and sometimes its own arsenals, a carefully calculated counterpoise to the *Wehrmacht* or regular German army.

The *Waffen SS* were Himmler's own special troops in the conquest of Europe, and they fulfilled this task to the best of their ability. They were shock troops now, rather than the "Defense Echelon" of the old days, and they were proud to be "the Führer's Elite." Hot on the heels of their victories always followed special SD liquidation units, called "Emergency Squads."

There was much naïve and boyish idealism in the ranks of the *Waffen SS*, coupled with a savage soldier of fortune spirit, all in the service of spreading the slave system of the SS super state. Himmler needed his quota of idealists, for some day, when the soldiers' task was done, he planned to retain the most suitable elements of the SS as a Nazi elite to maintain the new "Teutonic" oligarchy.

The SS Death-Head Units were trained from the start as a knuckle-duster brigade for domestic use. The first Death-Head *Standarte* was organized in 1933, from the old SS units that had been nominally merged with the Bavarian police. It was commanded by SS Colonel Eicke, a former German army officer and a veteran of the First World War, and was composed of men of particular savagery. It was trained from the start for concentration-camp duty. In 1934 the office of "Inspector of Concentration Camps" was created for Eicke. Himmler was unable at the time to afford him any material aid—money, uniforms, arms, or equipment of any kind. By his own efforts, with great energy, unscrupulousness and success, Eicke embarked upon the expansion of his single regiment into the later Death-Head Units.

All SS troops were controlled by the SS Main Office in Berlin, headed until the outbreak of the war by SS General Heismeyer. In 1939 this command was taken over by SS General Pohl and an SS Main Office of Budget and Buildings and an SS Main Office of Economic Affairs were added. In 1942 the two last named offices were combined into the SS Main Economic and Administrative Office, under Pohl. Among other things this office was responsible for the administration of the concentration camps.

The SS troops were recruited from every group of the socially disfranchised, mainly Nazi refugees from Austria and the Balkan countries, men who were professionals with club and gun, who had lost all social stability. Migrants, truck drivers, foresters, barbers, clerks, students and prison guards were among the callings represented in the enlisted ranks. Officers were drawn from veterans of the Baltic and other free corps,[1] the army and the police—men who had failed to make headway or who for some reasons had to give up their careers, mercenaries with something at least approximating military experience. They drilled and were drilled in the spirit of Frederick the Great. Their training camps were in remote locations, soon to be combined with the concentration camps taken over from the SA. But unrestrained begging, pilfering and extortion proved to be an inadequate material basis for maintaining these formations, and Eicke turned the concentration camps with their slave system into a source of financial support. Himmler helped out from funds of the General SS whenever it was feasible.

[1] Irregular formations that sprang up in Germany after the First World War to combat Communism and engage in extra-legal activities.—*Tr*.

These men were actually professional soldiers, or rather mercenaries, but that does not mean that they can be credited with the virtues sometimes attributed to the profession of arms. Those who blindly glorify the professional soldier as a type often seem to know little about true soldierly virtues, about the strict moral standards with which great soldiers always seek to counter the special moral hazards of their craft. I do not mean merely the vaunted virtue of comradeship. That is not enough—even in wartime.

From these higher standards the members of the *Waffen SS* cannot be viewed simply as prototypes of the soldier as such. A fanatical fighting spirit alone does not justify the soldier in a cultural sense. It is quite true that such SS outfits as the Hitler Youth Division consisted almost entirely of volunteers who were animated by a very real nationalist spirit of dedication. Certain SS regiments were formed, such as "Adolf Hitler's Own," "The Reich" and "Germania," all of them later expanded to division status, which were elite outfits in Himmler's sense. Hitler was proud of them, loved them. When it finally came to war, they became the spearheads in his assault tactics. But why should we regard any of these as any better than, say, the death-defying dervishes that followed the fanatical Mahdi? Merely because they felt themselves to be an elite?

The losses Himmler tried to compensate by the recruitment of SS foreign legionaries from all over Europe and by the impressment of German-speaking minorities in conquered territories. Here his office as Commissioner for the Strengthening of the German Racial Character stood him in good stead. Strengthening indeed! If anything, diluting.

It may have been at this time, incidentally, that Himmler took up the barbarous idea of clan liability, for the families of his legionaries who remained behind, especially in the Balkans, were often subjected to clandestine reprisals by the local population.

This foreign legion character, despite its Teutonic and European embroidery, together with the merciless character of the struggle, ultimately turned the SS into the desperate sworn fellowship it grew to be. In the long run it could be held in check only by the sharpest discipline and by personalities who excelled as leaders of a lost cause.

During the war the ranks of the Death-Head complements at the concentration camps were often replenished by members from this choice company who had either accumulated enough experience in the practice of cruelty, or who had had their fill of life at the front—in either case the worst elements.

In the course of the years Himmler did a great deal of shuffling and reorganizing within his numerous offices and sections, to adapt them to the needs of the moment and to keep his machine ready for instant action. He did not always succeed. In some fields an SS bureaucracy developed that failed to promote Himmler's aims. Toward the end Himmler himself can hardly have retained a clear grasp of all the ramifications of his far-flung organization, especially since the contending ambitions of his many underlings tended to impair the efficiency of the machine. In a sense Himmler himself was a bureaucrat who sought to control his super state by a carefully regulated system of masters and slaves. Around his own person he created the "Personal Staff of the Reichsführer SS." The functions of the top leadership were combined into the SS Operational Main Office, with numerous sub-divisions. Many functions and groups within the SS overlapped or actually ran counter to each other. But there can be little doubt that had Germany won the war Himmler would have succeeded in untangling the snarls and in creating a durable and efficient network of steel that would have held Germany and Europe in its firm grip. For Himmler was an excellent organizer and calculator, and only the headlong pace of Nazi expansion occasionally made things difficult for him.

His organization, the SS machine, permeated first the Nazi party, next Germany, and finally the whole of Europe; and gave the Hitler regime its true stamp. Hundreds of thousands of Germans never knew and do not know today the degree to which their work and their zeal, their virtues and their vices were put to the service of the SS super state.

It was a state made up of four groups. There were, first of all, those who were to rule with all the panoply of ancient Oriental satraps. There were those whose task was to fight and die for the system, under the guise of lofty ideals. A third group had the administrative service for its sphere, with carefully apportioned emoluments. Ordinary work was reserved for a fourth group—the broad masses of the German people, until they too were permitted to move up into the role of domesticated overlords of subjected enemy peoples. The last group consisted of the millions of resisters and "inferior races." For them there was death—swift death, or painful, lingering liquidation. Above the whole structure loomed Hitler, remote and beyond reach, the personification of the race myth some day to be actually worshiped.

Chapter Two

THE PURPOSE,
CHARACTER AND NUMBER OF
THE GERMAN CONCENTRATION CAMPS

The SS, as contemplated and created by Himmler, had a dual aspect. On the one hand it was to train the new ruling class, on the other eliminate all opposition. Like the Roman tyrants, Himmler was prepared to be the object of universal hatred—so long as he was also the object of universal fear. Love—well underlaid by fear—he expected only of his elite, the SS. His system of terror, unparalleled in the history of civilized nations, enveloped the whole land. The concentration camps were merely the extreme and most effective expression of this system which embraced in its toils every aspect of public and private life.

Himmler did not invent the concentration camps, though it was Heydrich who reorganized them along uniform lines. It was the SS that gave them their ultimate character as the most fiendish chapter in Germany's history. *Their main purpose was the elimination of every trace of actual or potential opposition to Nazi rule.* Segregation, debasement, humiliation, extermination—these were the effective forms of the terror. Any concept of justice was put aside. Better to put ten innocents behind barbed wire than to let one real enemy escape.

This policy, of course, resulted in the desired deterrent effect on the ninety per cent who were innocent. Opposition could be nipped in the bud, deprived of any chance to organize and spread.

The guiding spirits of the SD, Heydrich and Best in the lead, tackled and accomplished their task with truly German thoroughness. Their motives were not simply sadistic in character. They were in keeping with a certain universal German predilection—to justify the most abysmal barbarism by recourse to certain "idealistic" principles.

Heydrich was assassinated in Prague; but before he died, he lingered in fearful agony, his spinal cord severed. It is said that during this period he was tormented by his conscience, incessantly pleading for divine forgiveness for the unspeakable sufferings he had brought on hundreds of thousands. If this story is true, it fits into the picture perfectly. These members of the "master class" were embodiments of man's most primitive instincts, dressed up in an aura of heroism and nationalism. Guided by Teutonic concepts of power and virtue, they arrogated unto themselves the right to treat others exactly as they pleased. Every method was acceptable. Enemies had to be rendered innocuous. That meant they had to be exterminated—worked, beaten, flayed, garroted, shot, gassed to death. The choice of method was entirely subordinate to the main goal—total extirpation.

There were, of course, a number of subsidiary aims served by the institution of the concentration camps.

In the first place, they served as the training ground where the SS Death-Head Units were inured to brutality. To this end every base instinct was kindled and fanned to white heat in the concentration camps, by precept and practice. What Himmler needed, not only to keep the German people in check but to get the better of the rest of the world with its "inferior races," were experts in brutality, men no longer capable of any human stirrings, fanatical dervishes blindly marching behind their prophet's flag, while to the right and left their victims fell by the thousands.

Most of the young men scheduled for concentration-camp guard service and for the so-called concentration-camp station complements were first of all given basic training along the lines of extreme Prussian drill—until "the juice boiled in their tails," as the soldiers' jargon goes. Once they had learned at first hand what drillground discipline can mean, they were let loose on the prisoners to vent their fury twice over—once for their own rigorous training which already seemed to them the model of how men should live; and again for any trace of opposition to the Nazi regime. Those who distinguished themselves in this toughening-up process were quickly promoted. Those who showed softness, "sentimentality," or human sympathy were either kicked out or—if it was proved that they had made common cause with the prisoners in any way—stripped of their rank before their assembled fellows. Their heads were shorn, they were treated to twenty-five lashes and then they were themselves consigned to the company of the "sub-humans." This happened more than once, especially in the early years of the concentration camps. Most of the upper grades in the station complements owed their rapid advancement solely to their sadism. Before being entrusted with real responsibility, they had to complete a special course, always at Dachau, at Heydrich's specific order. In later years all the concentration-camp commandants were trained there too.

A second subsidiary purpose of the concentration camps, more mundane in character, was the collection and exploitation of SS labor slaves. So long as these slaves were permitted to live at all, they lived only to serve their masters. The degree and the methods of this unrestrained exploitation will be set forth further on in this book. It far transcended similar systems known from history. The ancients at least believed that slaves and beasts of burden had to be properly fed, but Germany's master class could afford simply to draft new slave contingents when the old ones had been used up or had grown too small. Here too the already dulled German conscience was put to sleep with moral pretexts. The program was masked as "labor discipline" for "loafers," as "productive work" for "harmful elements."

Finally, in another access of "idealism," Himmler and the SD used the concentration camps for large-scale scientific experimentation, supposedly for the benefit of mankind. Why should not creatures, doomed in any event, first be utilized for scientific knowledge? How often has not the desire been voiced that the harmful or healing effects of drugs be tested on large numbers of criminals? Here "criminals" were available by the tens of thousands. And working conditions were ideal. "Humanitarian sentimentality" was rigorously excluded. No jealous rival scientists could interfere. There was no problem about the consent of the subjects. What more could the SS physician, prototype of the medical overlord of the millennium, desire?

The satisfaction of the SS in its concentration camps grew steadily and the camps kept increasing in number, even before Nazism spread all over Europe. Together with other repressive measures, they fully accomplished their main mission. Resistance to the regime by disaffected elements grew feebler and feebler. Had the Gestapo, in its arrests, proceeded purely on the basis of opposition, the camps should have become deserted. But the subsidiary purposes—the deterrent effect on the population, the exploitation of slave labor, the maintenance of training and experimental facilities for the SS—came more and more to the fore in keeping the camps filled, until they experienced their greatest growth in the European war unleashed by Hitler and always contemplated and prepared for by the SS. In the end the camps grew to such monstrous proportions that the regime was no longer equal to the task it had set itself. The SS and all its camps drifted toward the abyss in a state of virtual paralysis.

The first concentration camps to be created in Germany were not of the type later to be developed by the SS. Some fifty of them were organized in 1933, mainly by the SA. Most of them were in the vicinity of Berlin, a smaller number in central Germany, especially Saxony and Thuringia—in places such as Lichtenburg, Sachsenburg, Hohenstein, Bad Sulza. There were also a few elsewhere in Germany.

At the very outset of Nazi rule the SA developed the habit of collecting its political enemies—chiefly Communists or people called Communists—in army barracks, abandoned factories, remote depots, ancient castles, where it gleefully proceeded to inflict all manner of tortures on its victims. Göring's own bully boys (known until 1934 as the Field Police and including some of the choicest fiends) installed their own agony plant in Berlin's General Pape Street. This Columbia House witnessed perhaps the ghastliest atrocities the human mind can picture.

More and more people were arrested in those tempestuous months when Nazism had its first fling. Relatives were unable to trace them. The courts, the police, and certain administrative agencies were flooded with inquiries and complaints. Occasionally there were outright protests even from nationalist sources. The SA soon grew to hate "reaction" as violently as it did the left, if not more so.

The chief of Göring's newly established Gestapo, Rudolf Diels, convinced his master that these excesses could in the long run only harm the prestige of the Nazi government. The regular prisons, moreover, were crowded to the bursting point. He proposed the establishment of regular camps, to be turned over to the Gestapo, the police and other law-enforcement agencies, to "normalize" the situation.

Göring was by no means averse to these excesses *per se*—unless they happened to enmesh some of his special pets—but he dreaded the growing power of the SA. He agreed to the proposal. Diels gradually took over virtually all the wildcat camps of the early period and by March 1934 had dissolved all but a few, excluding the Columbia House.

Outstanding among those that remained were the camps at Oranienburg and Dachau, where the SS had quartered its "protective custody" prisoners in a few barracks on abandoned factory or gravel-pit sites. Heydrich called them concentration camps from the very start. No sooner had he taken over the Berlin Gestapa as Himmler's deputy in March 1934, than he began to admit to these camps police prisoners he had singled out for "special treatment." After June 30, 1934, he began to organize both camps systematically, especially Dachau, which soon became a byword throughout Germany. When anyone was put in a concentration camp, the people said simply: "He's in Dachau," even if it happened to be another camp.

A small number of camps on the Oldenburg Heath (Papenburg, Esterwege and a few others) remained nominally outside the authority of the SS and under the control of the old law-enforcement agencies. All prisoners, nevertheless, stood in holy terror of these so-called *Emsland* camps. Only criminals under sentence were supposed to be sent there, but actually they held many political prisoners. Toward the end these camps numbered some forty thousand inmates. Their exemption from SS control had long since lost all practical significance, since all German law-enforcement agencies had become subordinate to Himmler.

Except for Dachau and the Emsland camps, the early concentration camps never exceeded a maximum of one thousand inmates each. Often they held only a few hundred, the smaller number all the more at the mercy of its tormentors. Accounts by the few surviving old "concentrationaries" agree that there was scarcely a form of perversion and sadism which the SA failed to practice. These, however, were always acts of individual bestiality. The system had not yet reached the stage of mass organization. That accomplishment remained for the SS.

From 1936 on, the Death-Head Units began to pick fixed headquarters, planned for permanence from the start. Camp, SS barracks, and SS housing projects were planned as a unit. In this way the three main camps of the SS came into being: Dachau near Munich, which was maintained and expanded; Buchenwald near Weimar, started in the summer of 1937; and Sachsenhausen near Berlin-Oranienburg. They were located in southern, central and northern Germany, respectively. The smaller camps were partly dissolved, their inmates transferred to the larger ones, partly attached to the latter as subsidiary details. Later the following camps were added: Gross-Rosen near Striegau in Silesia; Flossenbürg near Weiden in Bavaria's Upper Palatinate; Ravensbruck in Mecklenburg (for women); and after the occupation of Austria, Mauthausen near Linz.

All the German concentration camps were administered and controlled from Berlin. As early as the fall of 1934, Heydrich had created the office of Inspector of Concentration Camps, occupied by Eicke, chief of the Death-Head Units and now promoted to SS brigadier general. He functioned from Gestapo headquarters, 7 Prince Albrecht Street. In 1939 his office was incorporated into the SS Main Office for Economics, which in turn, in 1942, when Pohl was at the head, became the SS Main Economic and Administrative Office. The offices of this agency, meanwhile grown to monstrous proportions, were located in Oranienburg, adjoining the concentration camp. The Main Economic and Administrative Office autonomously controlled the entire administration and finances of the SS. All other matters—personnel, training, medical service, racial policy, etc.—were assigned to the SS Operational Main Office. In the end there was so much duplication and overlapping that even the SS itself could not find its way through the maze. Personal pull was the decisive factor in getting anything done.

The chief of the Main Economic and Administrative Office, SS Lieutenant-General Pohl, was universally feared as an inexorable disciplinarian. He organized his own Department D, which administered the concentration camps and published all central directives. Department D, in turn, grew so autonomous that it developed branches of its own, actually within the jurisdiction of the Operational Main Office. Thus it had a Chief Medical Officer for Concentration Camps. Not a finger could be lifted in the concentration camps without at least the general authority of Department D. Its first head was SS Lieutenant-Colonel Liebehenschel, later appointed commandant of the Auschwitz camp. His successor was SS Colonel Maurer.

The SS officers of Department D were generally a type distinct from the camp personnel. The business of the central office was to plan and calculate—though this too, of course, was a matter of life and death. But these gentlemen could afford to watch their manners. Their role was similar to that of an army general staff. *Their* tunics were never splattered by muck or blood. True, the chief bureaucrat of death, Pohl himself, bore the typical stamp of unrestrained brutality. He was a product of the German armed forces of the First World War, a former navy paymaster.

The Main Economic and Administrative Office designated three progressive classes of concentration camps. Class I (labor camps) represented the mildest form. Class II meant that living and working conditions were more rigorous. Class III stood for the "mills of death" which the prisoners seldom left alive. The Gestapo never fully achieved its goal—to place all criminals, homosexuals, Jews and political prisoners deemed especially dangerous in Class III camps. The regional Gestapo offices differed in their evaluation of cases. The camps themselves often refused to surrender prisoners whose work they had found useful. It was also held to be advisable to keep the prisoner categories in all the camps unsegregated, to deprive the political prisoners of any chance for entrenching themselves.

The central classification scheme never applied to any more than a general degree and altogether fails to convey a true picture. The actual situation in a given camp, whether infernal or merely barbaric, depended on many other circumstances. Dachau, for example, was always a Class I camp, which can only bring a grim smile to the lips of those who knew the camp. Buchenwald was assigned to Class I on April 29, 1944, but even when it was still Class II, it had long enjoyed better general conditions than Dachau. The only halfway tangible advantage that could arise from a more favorable classification was a somewhat better ration allotment. Even so it would be a fallacy to conclude that this meant a better diet for the individual inmate. All that can be said is that conditions invariably deteriorated even further whenever a camp was assigned to a lower class, and that the individual initially fared far worse if he was admitted to a lower-class camp. Few of the prisoners even knew that there was such a classification system. Certain camps were known to be "better," others "worse," quite apart from this scheme. The only exception was the outright labor camps, a large number of which were organized by the SS entirely separate from the concentration camps proper. There the prisoners enjoyed one supreme advantage. They knew that they would stay for only six to twelve weeks and would then be permitted to leave this hell. That knowledge alone made most of the torments bearable.

Of far greater practical importance than the classification scheme was the age of the individual camps. Whether before or during the war, the initial phase, when the camp was being built and organized, was always the worst. After the initial phase, misery at least consolidated itself. One knew, so to speak, what risks and dangers had to be taken into account. The factor of uncertainty remained relatively constant. Occasionally it was even possible actually to improve conditions in some narrow sphere or other. Newcomers could adapt themselves with less shock, and more of them survived the difficult period of adjustment.

By and large, however, it was true in all the camps that the first few months after the outbreak of the war—from September 1939 to about the spring of 1940—brought a steep decline. The food situation in those six months was disastrous. Malnutrition threatened to become famine. This situation recurred toward the end of the war, from the spring of 1944 to that of 1945, intensified by unimaginable over-crowding that brought another trail of epidemics, as in 1939–40. This sequence must be borne in mind when reading of general conditions in the camps in this book: far below the "normal" level in the initial camp phase; relatively stable in the ensuing years; near-disastrous in the first six months of the war; relative improvement during the war years, partly because of the increasing importance of manpower in war production; outright disintegration in the final four to eight months. This curve can be traced in all the concentration camps, no matter what their classification. Those in which conditions were generally low naturally suffered the greatest losses during the periods of decline.

For the reasons already mentioned, but also because it had to deal with new opponents in large numbers throughout Europe, the SS sharply increased the number of concentration camps during the war. Even before the war there had been a well-developed trend to support each base camp with a number of subsidiaries. Germany was systematically studded with these instruments of terror. By 1939 there seem to have been more than 100 camps of all kinds, though the large camps mentioned remained the most important. The spread of Nazi rule over Europe brought a veritable concentration-camp boom in its wake. Notorious new camps came into being, such as Auschwitz, Lublin, Maidanek, Riga, Stutthof near Danzig, Natzweiler in the Vosges mountains, Bergen-Belsen near Hanover, and a long series of smaller ones.

There are so far no reliable statistics as to the total number of persons the Nazi regime sent to the concentration camp. The rapid turnover makes even an approximation ex-traordinarily difficult. We are reduced to reasonable estimates. Beyond all doubt millions passed through the camps during the twelve years of Nazi rule. Counting the dead in Auschwitz (where alone they seem to have amounted to between 3,500,000 and 4,500,000) and similar camps, we readily arrive at a total figure between eight and ten million. The great base camps, such as Dachau, Buchenwald and

Sachsenhausen, seldom numbered more than 100,000 inmates each, including all their subsidiary camps. An indication is furnished by Himmler's directive to his Chief Medical Officer in early March 1945, according to which there were 600,000 inmates remaining in the camps of whom 120,000 were unfit for work. (Purpose of the directive, incidentally, was a belated effort to improve the health of the latter.) At this juncture the concentration camps at Lublin, Riga, Stutthof, Auschwitz, Gross-Rosen, Natzweiler and a few others had already been liberated by Allied troops or evacuated by the SS. An estimate of one million as the average number of prisoners in the concentration camps at any one time is therefore unlikely to be far off the mark.

Chapter Three

THE CATEGORIES OF
PRISONERS

Who belonged in a concentration camp, in the view of the Gestapo? Primarily four groups of people: political opponents; members of "inferior races"; criminals; and "shiftless elements" (called "asocial" by the Germans).

The Gestapo applied its qualifications most readily to the second group. This embraced chiefly the Jews and the Gypsies.

Originally the Nazis had intended to settle the Gypsies permanently. But efforts in this direction proved troublesome. Rural communities and police authorities no longer knew what to do with the "scum." In the old days the Gypsies were simply told to move on, but now Himmler had prohibited their freedom of movement. In order to get rid of them, it was decided simply to put them in the concentration camps. Effective it certainly was, for all but an insignificant remnant perished there.

The Jews were the target of Nazi bloodlust from the very outset. They were divided up among all the prisoner categories—political prisoners, criminals, shiftless elements, etc.—although they remained segregated in special barracks—which exposed them constantly to a heightened danger of annihilation—and usually had to be content with the most menial jobs. They were often the scapegoats for the cruel whims of the SS, which meant that the other inmates got off somewhat better. This led to particularly close co-operation between Jewish and non-Jewish political prisoners, expressed in countless acts of solidarity. This solidarity, as well as sheer luck, was the reason why a number of the Jews who were imprisoned in the early years managed to survive.

The Gestapo had definite ideas as to who was to be classified as a criminal. It distinguished first of all "prisoners in limited-term preventive custody" (*Befristete Vorbeugungshäftlinge*), who had served several sentences before. The initials of the German term (BV) also stand for "professional criminal," and that is the designation by which these prisoners were generally known. A second category was called "prisoners in security custody" (*Sicherungsverwahrte*), abbreviated to SV, also the initials of the German term for "arch criminal," which became the popular designation. The latter group consisted of convicts who were actually serving sentences.

Both categories were admitted to the concentration camps by the Reich Criminal Police Office and its branches. Nearly all the BV's and SV's were the dregs of society. In some camps they managed to secure a dominant position, temporarily or permanently, which they ruthlessly exploited against the other prisoners. There was an everlasting struggle for power between them and the political prisoners, sometimes open, sometimes underground. The outcome of such struggles varied widely. There were many SS officers who preferred to deal with the convicts, sometimes to the exclusion of all other categories, and who assigned them to all the important prisoner functions. The convicts also furnished the largest contingent of informers. Later on, when the German armed forces suffered from a serious manpower shortage after Stalingrad, the convicts won the distinction of being recruited into the SS units in large numbers. Of those that remained behind not very many left the camps alive.

Related to the convicts, though far more innocent in character, were the so-called shiftless elements. This was a blanket designation of the Gestapo for vagrants, touts, pickpockets, tinhorn gamblers, alcoholics, pimps, wifebeaters and the like. But in this group there were also men whose only offense was that they had shown up late for work once or twice, had stayed away from work or changed their job without authority, had spoken harshly to their Nazi servants, or had earned their living as gigolos. Hundreds of party-line foremen were in the habit of denouncing any worker whom they did not like as a "loafer"—which meant a term in a labor or concentration camp.

These shiftless elements were a very mixed group and had no marked effect on the character of the camp, through they brought with them many undesirable practices from their former lives. The other prisoners regarded them as shiftless and unreliable. Many failed to survive the grim struggle for existence. They furnished the largest quota of discharges and wartime recruitments into the German armed forces.

The political prisoners too were a motley crew. Beyond doubt the majority were members of the anti-Nazi parties and persons of like mind. But there was always a certain proportion of former Nazi party members guilty of some party infraction and veterans accused of anything from petty thievery to desertion. Returned or captured members of foreign legions were also classified as political prisoners, as were, on occasion, foreign-exchange violators, illegal radio listeners, grumblers and unfortunates who had become victims of denunciations to the Gestapo. The non-Germans who began to arrive after the outbreak of the war were almost all classified as political prisoners. Language difficulties and national differences created many painful problems, as did the inexperience of the foreigners in camp life. Obviously this diversity among the political prisoners was calculated to confuse the situation and sharpen mutual suspicion.

Opposition to the Nazi regime from moral and especially religious motives was regarded in the same light as political opposition. This involved principally clergymen of all the great denominations and members of the religious sect known as Jehovah's Witnesses.

The number of clergymen sent to the concentration camps may be put at between 4,000 and 5,500. Many of them were Poles. There were far more Catholics than Protestants, and the latter were almost all ministers of the Confessional

Church. All of them had a very difficult time of it, especially if they were known to be clergymen. They suffered not only at the hands of the SS but also from their fellow prisoners. Their situation improved only when they were all collected in Dachau in 1942. For some time they received certain privileges, supposedly granted on intervention by the Pope. High dignitaries of the church in Germany were never sent to a concentration camp. On one occasion a canon of the Olmütz cathedral chapter was selected as suffragan while he was at Buchenwald. He was immediately released by the SS. A different policy was followed with respect to French and Belgian prelates. Bishops, abbots and other ecclesiatics of these nationalities were imprisoned in German concentration camps without distinction.

The Jehovah's Witnesses sect had spread from the United States to Europe in the eighties, and after the First World War it won a considerable number of converts in Germany. The Nazis suppressed it as early as 1933, because its members refused to swear oaths and render military service, and in addition regarded all government as the devil's handiwork. The greatest wave of arrests of Witnesses began in the spring of 1936. The leaders at Magdeburg had already been locked up in the fall of 1934. In June 1937 the Reich Minister of Interior ordered all Jehovah's Witnesses handed over to the Gestapo, which sent them to the concentration camps. By the fall of that year their number at Buchenwald had risen to about 270. It reached a maximum of 450 a year later. Approximately the same number were in each of the other big camps, the women at Ravensbrück. Their families were scattered—men and women sent to different camps and the children taken away—a particular outrage, even from the Nazi point of view.

At times they had to endure great sufferings, but their patient faith in the end of the world made them loyal and willing workers, for the SS as well as for their fellow prisoners. Apart from a few skilled workers, nurses and calfactors (a kind of houseboy), they were at first assigned to the penal company. On September 6, 1938, the SS offered them the chance to abjure their principles in writing, especially their refusal to swear oaths and render military service, and thus to purchase their liberty. Only a very few failed to withstand this temptation. The others were henceforth subjected to savage pressure in order to break their spirit. On Easter Sunday of 1939 the Roll Call Officer at Buchenwald made another effort to persuade the Witnesses to acknowledge "State and Führer." The success was nil. On Whitsunday all the Jehovah's Witnesses again had to fall in on the roll-call area. A speech was delivered to them, and a fearful period of fatigue drill followed. For an hour and a quarter the wretched men had to roll about, hop, crawl and run, while the boots of the Block Leaders helped them along.

When the war broke out the Witnesses at Sachsenhausen concentration camp were invited to volunteer for military service. Each refusal was followed by the shooting of ten men from their ranks. After forty victims had been killed, the SS desisted. In Buchenwald this appeal to the Witnesses was made on September 6, 1939. First Officer-in-Charge Rödl told them: "You know that war has broken out and that the German nation is in danger. New laws are coming into force. If anyone of you refuses to fight against France or England, all of you must die!" Two SS companies with full equipment were drawn up by the gatehouse. Not a single Jehovah's Witness answered the officer's appeal to fight for Germany. There was a brief silence, and then came the sudden order: "Hands up! Empty your pockets!" The SS men began to assault them, robbing them of their last penny—a reprisal that seemed rather grotesque in view of what might have been expected. True, the Witnesses were assigned to the quarry and during this entire time were barred from hospital treatment.

On February 15, 1942, the Witnesses were assembled at the gatehouse, and the Roll Call Officer read off a regular indictment: "Twenty Jehovah's Witnesses are accused of rebellion for non-observance of camp regulations, bribery of the Senior Camp Inmate, and turning off radios during addresses by representatives of the Reich government." The consequence was not execution but "winter sport," conducted in powdery snow eight inches deep until the exhausted men steamed.

A similar incident took place in May 1944. Gestapo representatives came to Buchenwald and all Jehovah's Witnesses were thoroughly searched for anti-Nazi literature (in a concentration camp!) while assembled in the roll-call area. Their work areas were likewise turned inside out. The results, after days of waiting: nothing.

One cannot escape the impression that, psychologically speaking, the SS was never quite equal to the challenge offered them by Jehovah's Witnesses. They did not take the Witnesses altogether seriously, but rather had their cruel sport with them—a sort of cat-and-mouse game.

In addition to these main categories of prisoners, the SS made a number of other distinctions. Of these the homosexuals deserve special mention. This group had a very heterogeneous composition. It included individuals of real value, in addition to large numbers of criminals and especially blackmailers. This made the position of the group as a whole very precarious. Hostility toward them may have been partly rooted in the fact that homosexuality was at one time widespread in Prussian military circles, as well as among the SA and the SS, and was to be mercilessly outlawed and erased. The Gestapo readily had recourse to the charge of homosexuality, if it was unable to find any other pretext for proceeding against Catholic priests or irksome critics. The mere suspicion was sufficient. Homosexual practices were actually very widespread in the camps. The prisoners, however, ostracized only those whom the SS marked with the pink triangle.

The fate of the homosexuals in the concentration camps can only be described as ghastly. They were often segregated in special barracks and work details. Such segregation offered ample opportunity to unscrupulous elements in positions of power to engage in extortion and maltreatment. Until the fall of 1938 the homosexuals at Buchenwald were divided up among the barracks occupied by political prisoners, where they led a rather inconspicuous life. In October 1938, they were transferred to the penal company in a body and had to slave in the quarry. This consigned them to the lowest caste in camp during the most difficult years. In shipments to extermination camps, such as Nordhausen, Natzweiler and Gross-Rosen, they furnished the highest proportionate share, for the camp had an understandable tendency to slough off all elements considered least valuable or worthless. If anything could save them at all, it was to enter into sordid relationships within the camp, but this was as likely to endanger their lives as to save them. Theirs was an insoluble predicament and virtually all of them perished.

All prisoner categories in the concentration camps had to wear prescribed markings sewn to their clothing—a serial number and colored triangles, affixed to the left breast and the right trouser leg. At Auschwitz the serial number was tattooed on the left forearm of the prisoners. Red was the color denoting political prisoners. Second offenders, so-called recidivists, wore a stripe of the same color above the upper edge of the triangle. Criminals wore a green triangle, with a surprinted S for the SV category. Jehovah's Witnesses wore purple; "shiftless elements," black; homosexuals, pink. During certain periods, the Gypsies and the shiftless picked up in certain special campaigns wore a brown triangle.

Jews, in addition to the markings listed above, wore a yellow triangle under the classification triangle. The yellow triangle pointed up, the other down, forming the six-pointed Star of David. Jews and non-Jews who had violated the Nuremberg racial laws—so-called "race defilers"—wore a black border around or athwart the green or yellow triangle. Foreigners had a letter surprinted on their triangles—F for France, N for Netherlands, etc. Special political prisoners picked up at the outbreak of the war, for supposed unreliability, wore their serial number across the triangle, the others about an inch below the bottom point. Starting with the war, certain prisoners were admitted who had a K printed on their triangles. These were "war criminals" (*Kriegsverbrecher*) and they were always permanently assigned to the penal companies. Their offenses were often trifling. Occasionally a prisoner long in camp was likewise assigned to this K company. Only a very few of them survived. "Labor Disciplinary Prisoners" wore a white A on their black triangles, from the German word for labor, *Arbeit*. Most of them were in camp for only a few weeks. Members of the penal companies showed a black dot, the size of a silver dollar, between the point of the triangle and the serial number.

Prisoners suspected of plans for escaping had a red-and-white target sewn or painted on chest and back. The SS even devised a special marking for the feeble-minded—an armband with the German word *Blöd*. Sometimes these unfortunates also had to wear a sign around their necks: "I am a Moron!" This procedure was particularly provocative when the prisoner in question also wore the red triangle reserved for avowed opponents of the Nazi regime. The feeble-minded enjoyed the freedom of the camp and were the butt of the cruelest jokes. Eventually they all perished or were killed by injection.

The camps were a veritable circus, as far as colors, markings, and special designations are concerned. Occasionally prisoners were decked out in nearly all colors of the rainbow. There was one Jew, for example, who was a member of Jehovah's Witnesses, a "race defiler," a member of the penal company and also wore the escape targets!

It must be emphasized that the markings as such offered no assurance that the prisoners actually belonged to the designated classification. Time and again the greens, or criminals, included men with whom it was possible to work—who showed stanch loyalty, indeed—whereas many a red, or political prisoner, should of rights have worn the green triangle. Reclassifications did occasionally take place, with varying degrees of justification.

The distribution of the categories within a camp varied and shifted greatly. After the outbreak of the war, with its influx of tens of thousands of non-German anti-Nazis, red became the predominant color, but before that time there were camps known as red, and others known as green. Dachau, Buchenwald and Sachsenhausen were long dominated by political prisoners, the first two down to the end. Mauthausen, Flossenbürg, Gross-Rosen and Neuengamme were among the major camps to be predominantly green.

The Gestapo and the SS were always intent on having the categories well mixed within the individual camps. There was not a single camp with but one category. Two purposes were served by this policy. On the one hand the political prisoners, the most dangerous enemies of the Nazi regime, were to be degraded by being put on an equal footing with the scum of society. They were to be deprived of any sense of dignity, to be made to feel even lower than the criminals who, supposedly at least, accepted the basic premises of the Nazi State. On the other hand the intermingling of the prisoner categories was to serve the principle of "Divide and Rule." Conflicts were to be pointed up, every sense of solidarity undermined, so that a few could control the many. Control of each camp was in the hands of a very small group of picked Death-Head officers permanently assigned to the Commandant. They used different prisoner categories for their purposes in turn, playing one off against the other. In view of the motley character of the prisoners, the SS had no trouble in finding and planting its ever-present informers. Coupled with the merciless exercise of terror, these methods enabled a handful of men to keep even the hugest camps in check. They must also be taken into account in evaluating the accomplishments which the political prisoners were able to chalk up in the camps over the years.

I cannot conclude this chapter without mention of the children and minors who found their way into the concentration camps.

In the fulfilment of its imperialist aims, National Socialism preached the gospel of the large family, promoting this policy throughout Germany. At the same time it insisted that "Youth Must Educate Youth!" It snatched young people from the wholesome soil of religious devotion, of mutual trust in parents and teachers, of respect for their fellow men, only to expose them to racial fallacies and intoxication with power—and to a large extent to delinquency. Tens of thousands of German families were scattered to the winds. Hundreds of thousands of families of other nationalities were exterminated. And millions of minors were exposed to all the terrors of the times under such a regime. Not a few of them, with or without their parents, were carried off to the German concentration camps, where experiences extremely harmful to normal juvenile development left their imprint on them. Some fifteen per cent of the minors admitted to the concentration camps were less than twelve years old. Eighty-five per cent were between twelve and eighteen. During the final phase there were 877 minors at Buchenwald, the youngest a three-and-a-half-year-old Polish child whose file card actually listed him as a "partisan."

The first group of children arrived in Buchenwald in 1939, together with the Polish prisoners. The youngsters were quartered in a special building and in the beginning did not have to work. In the course of time a large proportion of them grew

abominably spoiled in camp—as did many of the youthful
Russians and Ukrainians admitted later on. Enough has been
published on the subject to show that sexual starvation among
men who are sequestered for years on end is a familiar
phenomenon. The brothel by no means satisfied this hunger.
Unprincipled prisoners, including many confined for political
reasons, created a cesspool of depravity, first by means of
homosexuality, and later on, when the boys had arrived, by
pederasty. The so-called "Doll Boys," unable to resist such
temptation as good food, sometimes forcibly seduced by im-
moral Senior Block Inmates and Prisoner Foremen, soon
played a vicious role everywhere. In Buchenwald this reached
its climax in 1943 under Senior Camp Inmate Wolff, a former
cavalry captain and German nationalist, who outrageously
misused his position. More and more he took the part of the
SS against his own comrades, until he was finally deposed by
the camp itself. By dint of such conditions the ranks of the
Polish youngsters who had come into camp in 1939 gave rise
to the most insolent ruffians and rowdies—regular hooligans
such as ravaged the Soviet Union in the terrible years from
1919 to 1923.

All the more praiseworthy was the example of those
prisoners who unselfishly helped the lads in camps whenever
they could, keeping them from slipping into the clutches of
the pederasts. A number of the juveniles had the advantage of
instruction under the supervision and direction of prisoners,
were assigned to appropriate light work, and were trained in
the spirit of true fellowship. Their stories show that they fully
grasped the sinister and terrible character of their fate, which
they had faced with perplexity and bafflement until they were
put on the right path under the care of older comrades.
Despite the Wild West atmosphere of the concentration camp,
not a few of them proved themselves, bringing much joy into
individual labor details. Even hardboiled prisoners were
deeply moved when the SS in the fall of 1944 suddenly singled
out and herded together all Jewish and Gypsy youngsters. The
screaming, sobbing children, frantically trying to get to their
fathers or protectors among the prisoners, were surrounded
by a wall of carbines and machine pistols and taken away to
be shipped to Auschwitz for gassing.

It would be a rewarding task for educators to trace the careers of the various types of youngsters described, to compare the behavior patterns of the few who escaped the concentration camps alive with those of their contemporaries who suffered no such ordeal.

Chapter Four

THE PHYSICAL SET-UP
OF THE CAMPS

As sites for concentration camps the SS invariably chose inaccessible areas, preferably forests and moors, not too far from the larger cities. This served a dual purpose. The camps were to remain isolated from the outside world, while the SS itself was to retain access to urban amenities. Again, the Nazis and their sympathizers were thus enabled to profit in supplying the camps, while the rest of the population was kept in a state of terror.

The prior existence of road and industrial facilities was not taken into account. SS industrial enterprises were generally self-sufficient, in any event. If there were indispensable plants already in existence at other locations, subsidiary labor squads were detailed from the camps. Traffic was fully motorized, and in case of need there was plenty of prisoner labor to build roads and even railroad lines. Not even the water supply played a dominant part in site-planning. Emergency water mains, adequate for the needs of the SS, were quickly installed—from far away, if necessary. As for the prisoners, they had to wait. More than almost anything else, the water shortage contributed to the wretched conditions under which the prisoners lived in many camps.

As a rule a site large enough to accommodate the SS and ten to twenty thousand prisoners was staked out. Only a small part of the area was allotted to the latter. First of all the quarters for the SS were built, while the prisoners lived in emergency shelters. Much later, when every need and whim of the overlords had been satisfied, construction of the camp proper was tackled.

Each concentration camp had three main areas: the headquarters area; the SS residential settlements; and the compound, surrounded by barbed wire.

The headquarters area included an administration building, barracks for the SS, fine residences with large gardens for the leading officials, and a whole series of show places, such as zoological gardens, hothouses, parks, riding academies and clubs—all carefully planned and beautifully landscaped. At some distance were essential installations ranging all the way from farms and truck gardens to armories and war plants.

Prime examples of SS parasitism at Buchenwald were a falconry court built as a tribute to Hermann Göring, and a riding hall for the wife of Commandant Koch. Construction of the falconry court was begun in 1938 and completed in 1940. The costs for materials alone ran to 135,000 marks. The area held the following buildings: the falcon house proper, in ancient Teutonic style, of massive and artfully carved oak; a hunting hall with hand-carved oak furniture, huge fireplaces and hunting trophies; a circular garden house; and the falconer's house, where later, when the sport of falconry could no longer be practiced, the former French Premier, Léon Blum, and other prominent persons were quartered. There was also a game preserve and a cage for wildcats. Fallow deer, roebucks, wild boar, a mouflon, foxes, pheasants and other animals were kept there. Outside the falconry court, in the so-called zoological garden, five monkeys and four bears were kept in cages. In the early years there was even a rhinoceros. Whenever one of the animals died, a "voluntary" collection was taken up among the Jews to provide a replacement. A wolf cost about 4,000 marks and a squirrel might cost the same amount. One of the satanic SS pastimes under the regime of Commandant Koch was to throw prisoners into the bears' cage to be torn limb from limb.

The animals enjoyed an excellent diet. As late as 1944,

when there was a serious food shortage in camp, the bears, monkeys and birds got a daily ration of meat abstracted from the prisoners' mess. The bears also received honey and jam, the monkeys mashed potatoes with milk, oat flakes, zwieback and white bread. The whole installation had to be carefully maintained by trained gardeners. The permanent falconry detail consisted of six to ten men. Göring, Reich Huntsman in Chief, never even set eyes on this park. But the SS had special pamphlets printed, advertising the attraction in Weimar and vicinity, and extracted an admission price of one mark a head.

The riding hall for Frau Koch was about 120 by 300 feet in size and at least 60 feet high. It held a tanbark ring and the walls were surfaced with mirrors. Construction took place at such a mad pace that some thirty prisoners died of accidents or exhaustion. Construction costs ran to about 250,000 marks. When the hall had been finished, Frau Koch used it several times a week for morning rides, each time for a quarter or half hour, the SS band being required to furnish music from a special platform. After the trial of her husband, Frau Koch was admitted to the police jail in Weimar and the riding hall was used as storage depot.

In the area outside the prisoner compound there were, at Sachsenhausen and Buchenwald, special barracks or small plain houses in which certain prominent personages were interned. These prisoners were kept from all contact with the others. The SS seems to have been anxious to counter rumors that these well-known figures were *in* concentration camps. In Sachsenhausen several years were spent in this fashion by the former Austrian Chancellor, Dr. Kurt von Schuschnigg, and his second wife who voluntarily shared his detention, as well as by several German general officers who had fallen into disfavor with Hitler.

In Buchenwald the isolation barracks for celebrities were hidden deep in the woods, opposite the SS officers' residences. It was protected by a solid ten-foot stockade and by a crew of twelve SS guards. In the final stage, just before the residents were evacuated to Bavaria on orders from Himmler, they numbered fifty-four, including the former leader of the German Social Democratic party, Rudolf Breitscheid, and his wife; the Italian Princess Mafalda of Hesse with her servant; Maria Ruhnar, a member of the Jehovah's Witnesses sect;

Fritz Thyssen, German industrialist and one of the chief financiers of the Nazi party in the early days—he had already been in custody for four and a half years, according to his own statement, first in a mental institution, then in Sachsenhausen; Röchling, another industrialist; six members of the family of Count von Stauffenberg[1]; General von Falkenhausen; five cabinet members of the Hungarian provisional government; the wife of the German ambassador von Hassel; Frau Goerdeler[2] with her children; the wife of General Lindemann, executed after July 20, 1944; at one time the former French Premier, Léon Blum; and the wives of several German labor leaders with their children.

Besides this building there was at Buchenwald the so-called Pine Grove, a group of several wooden barracks where 140 to 200 Rumanians of the Iron Guard were sheltered. Originally they had lived in an isolation block of the compound proper. In the Pine Grove they were kept busy as precision mechanics. After a number of them had been killed in the air raid on Buchenwald, they were transferred to Hohenlychen on orders from Himmler.

The SS residential settlements were generally placed around the outskirts of the headquarters area, two or three miles away, at most pleasant locations. They were, of course, constructed by prisoner labor. These handsome one- and two-family houses, each with its own garden, were occupied by lower ranking SS officers, not deemed important enough to live in the headquarters area, and by the permanently assigned SS noncoms.

At Buchenwald the south slope of the Ettersberg was somewhat less exposed to the weather than was the rest of the camp. There the prisoners had to build an asphalt road named Eicke Street. The residences of leading SS officers were built along this road. In the end ten luxurious villas equipped with every comfort stood there. These tasteful wooden houses had massive basements, garages of their own and wide terraces with a magnificent view of the Thuringian countryside. Long columns of prisoners dragged up the stone blocks for the terraces from the quarry.

---

[1] Count von Stauffenberg planted the bomb that almost killed Hitler on July 20, 1944.—*Tr.*

[2] Goerdeler was a leader in the plot of July 20, 1944.—*Tr.*

These homes were inhabited by the Commandant, the Officers-in-Charge, the Commander of Troops and certain other SS officers with their families and servants. Each house, in addition, had its prisoner orderlies, chiefly Jehovah's Witnesses of both sexes. Central hot-water and heating plants in the houses were likewise serviced by prisoners.

A sharp contrast to headquarters and homes was offered by the barbed-wire enclosure. The predominant impression was one of desolation. It was a bare area—a clearing when the site lay in the woods—surrounded by an electrically charged barbed wire fence many feet high. Every 250 feet there was a guard tower of wood or masonry, with a roofed-over platform from which a machine-gun was trained on the compound. The guard on it was relieved every three hours. Beyond barbed wire and towers the camp was surrounded by an area several yards wide called the "neutral zone," on which the machine-guns were zeroed in. Entrance to the camp was gained by a gatehouse, a narrow structure, generally of two stories extending a considerable distance from either side of the actual gateway, which was surmounted by another tower affording a view of the entire camp. In addition to a large clock, this tower carried the floodlights that illuminated the entire area at night. One wing of the gatehouse held the offices of the Officer-in-Charge on duty, the other, special camp prison cells. A public-address system connected the building to all important points in camp.

Inside the gate a large bare space extended into the compound. This was the so-called roll-call area. It was unrelieved by a single blade of grass, a quagmire in poor weather, a desert of dust when it was dry.

Here the "Little Camps" were established, either temporarily or permanently, in order not only to accommodate an excess of inmates when the camps grew over-crowded but to effect special liquidation programs. A section of the compound was marked off, once again surrounded with barbed wire, and filled with emergency barracks. Tent camps too were created for this purpose.

At Buchenwald, for example, a Little Camp stood on part of the roll-call area, between the gatehouse and the first row of barracks from October 1939, to the spring of 1940. Four tents and a board shack were surrounded by a high barbed-wire fence. Part of the fenced-in area served as a separate roll-call area, while another spot served as a dump for dead bodies. One corner held a cage of barbed wire, called the "Rose Garden." It consisted of nothing but barbed wire. It served as a receptacle for special victims, who were there starved to death, at 5°F. by day, and down to 22° below zero at night, watched by their comrades, who never knew when their turn might come. Not far away was the latrine. The Little Camp at the time had neither stoves nor straw pallets nor lockers nor blankets. The fate of its inmates will be described when the story of the Poles in Buchenwald is discussed.

In July 1943, 2,000 French prisoners came to Buchenwald from Compiègne. All the barracks were already overcrowded and the newcomers were placed in a fenced-in area beside the truck garden, below the last row of barracks. Two days later the SS provided five tents, each with a capacity of 200 men, and regarded the matter as closed. There were no cots, blankets, benches, no water for drinking or washing, not even the most necessary clothing, no mess gear, spoons, laundry, drugs, drainage, latrines—in short, not even the most primitive necessities of life. From the first day the entire camp was haunted by the specter of an epidemic. The prisoner administration tried feverishly to improve conditions in the tent camp. With material pilfered from SS depots, a water and sewerage line, latrines and a storeroom for bread were illegally constructed. Blankets, mess gear and spoons were scraped together. Dispensaries began to function, drainage ditches were dug, the roll-call area within the tent camp was paved, calcium chloride was frequently sprinkled throughout the area. Late in August the five tents were supplemented by a barracks constructed from salvaged lumber, and in the fall they were replaced by three barracks built to one side of the tents. The tents themselves were gradually torn down—the last one did not disappear until January 1945. The SS paid little further attention to the matter.

Construction of this new Little Camp had actually begun as early as 1942, when the influx of non-Germans into the concentration camps began to reach staggering proportions. Together with the buildings just mentioned it ultimately numbered seventeen barracks. There were 1,500 and even 2,000 men to a barracks, instead of the maximum capacity of 500. They lived in groups of six to ten in multidecked bunks arranged on both sides of a central aisle, without adequate light or air, each with one blanket—if he was lucky! The latrines were located outside. As the war continued, these barracks became the scene of unimaginable tragedies. The worst period began in the fall of 1944. Deaths in the Little Camp rose so sharply that at times there were up to 150 or 200 a day in it alone. Bodies simply lay about in the open, for the living, in order to make room, would sometimes simply toss them out of the barracks. The forces of order were almost powerless in the face of this mass dying. The Senior Block Inmates were faced by an impossible task, since hunger and deprivation unhinged many of the prisoners. There were incidents almost beyond comprehension. Nature's call was answered atop naked dead bodies. On one occasion a young Hungarian Jew asked permission of the Senior Block Inmate to extract his dying father's gold teeth, since otherwise they would be stolen by others. Savage struggles to the death took place over the pitiful daily ration, and the Barracks Orderlies could not break up the fights. The ravenous prisoners, fresh from death shipments, would tear out the light wires as soon as the food containers arrived, and a wild melee would ensue in which a few would get more than their share while most would get nothing. Mess gear was commonly used in place of the latrines, partly from feebleness that made it impossible to leave the barracks, partly from fear of the weather outside or of theft, partly because it was almost impossible to get out of the crowded bunks. Those on top often climbed to the roof, by removing boards and roofing, and fouled the rafters. The human mind is unequal to picture these awful scenes.

Behind the roll-call area came the one-story wooden and two-story masonry barracks. Each wooden barracks had two wings, the two-story masonry barracks four (one generally reserved for the "big shots," Senior Inmate, clerks, foremen, etc.). A wing consisted of a day room and sleeping quarters for one to two hundred prisoners. When a camp had been fully established, a washroom and open privy might be installed between each two wings. This was where the prisoners secretly smoked when they had the chance, smoking in the barracks being strictly forbidden. In the sleeping quarters, cots were arranged in tiers. They held straw pallets which until late 1941 were covered with checkered sheets in some camps. Each prisoner had one or two thin blankets. The day rooms held a number of tables and benches and the so-called lockers, plain wooden boxes divided into sections, where the prisoners kept their gear—mess kit, canteen cup and spoon.

In this same area were such camp installations as the mess, the laundry, the prisoner hospital consisting of an out-patients' clinic, a dental clinic, a so-called convalescent clinic, as well as regular wards. At Buchenwald a brothel was established in 1943, appropriately located between the prisoner hospital and Experimental Ward 46. It had to be completed in such haste that much more important additions to the hospital were postponed. Within the wired enclosure there was also a crematory. The permanent crematory at Buchenwald was completed in 1941 and consisted of a morgue, a postmortem room, two combustion chambers with an enormous smokestack, and living quarters for the personnel. It stood in a spacious court surrounded by a high wall. Certain other concentration camps had far larger plants, some of them with six to twelve furnaces—especially, of course, Auschwitz.

Though the SS area, naturally, had first-class paved roads and graveled garden paths, the camp streets, wide enough to permit prisoners to march eight abreast to the roll-call area, were almost always completely unimproved. The prisoners themselves would often have liked to pave their roads, but only in exceptional cases was this permitted, always at a very late date.

The words from Dante's Inferno might well have been inscribed on the gatehouse: "Abandon hope, all ye who enter here!" The actual inscription at Dachau read "Labor Means Liberty!" and at Buchenwald "Right or Wrong—My Country!" The bitter mockery of these words cannot be conveyed by a dry description of the physical set-up of a finished concentration camp. The actuality of its growth and development must be borne home. Let the story of the initial phase of Buchenwald serve as an example.

Buchenwald is located on the wooded Ettersberg, five miles from Weimar. On July 19, 1937, there arrived at this spot a so-called advance squad of 149 convict inmates from the

Sachsenburg concentration camp, under heavy SS guard. The next day another 70 greens, or criminals, arrived. On July 27 came the first political prisoners, including seven Jehovah's Witnesses. Only three days later 600 prisoners from the Lichtenburg concentration camp were added. By August 6, barely three weeks after the first arrival, when scarcely any shelter was available, some 1,400 prisoners were on hand—greens, reds, purples.

Here is what they found: the SS had accepted as a gift from an aristocratic estate some 370 acres of hardwood and pine forest. It was an area utterly unsuited to human habitation, with a harsh climate subject to sudden changes. The location itself was symbolic. Weimar has long been regarded as the cultural heart of Germany, the one-time seat of the German classicists whose works lent the highest expression to the German mind. And here was Buchenwald, a piece of wilderness where the new German spirit was to unfold. This contrast and juxtaposition of sentimentally cherished culture and unrestrained brutality was all too characteristic.

The work of clearing the forest was begun that summer on the fog-shrouded peak of the Ettersberg. It was a trackless region of tumbled trees and jumbled roots. An oak tree known throughout the countryside as the "Goethe Oak," after the great German poet who had given Weimar its reputation, was respectfully spared by the SS and designated as the center of the camp!

Wooden barracks were built in rows of five and surrounded with ordinary barbed wire. The last row, outside the wire, was occupied by the SS guard complement headed by three SS officers: SS Colonel Koch as camp commandant; SS Major Rödl as First Officer-in-Charge—he wore Hitler's Order of the Blood, denoting participation in the 1923 Beerhall *Putsch*; and SS Captain Weissenborn as Second Officer-in-Charge. Koch had begun his notorious career as an SS sergeant in the so-called moor camps, as had Weissenborn, a one-time prison guard with a predilection for convicts—with whom he had a good deal in common. He is best characterized by the slogan the SS itself used to chalk up on walls: "God in his wrath created Captain Weissenborn." Rödl had come with the group from Sachsenburg.

The large number of labor details in existence even then

reveals the high pressure with which work proceeded. There were two quarry details, a logging detail, a lumberyard detail, two excavation details, a grading detail for the neutral zone, a barracks construction detail, a road-building detail, a drainage detail, a water works detail, a powerline detail, a materials dump detail, an unloading detail, five transport details, a construction office detail, a number of shop details, a number of skilled construction workers' details—masons, carpenters, tile-setters, plumbers, electricians, roofers, painters—SS and prisoners' mess details, SS and prisoners' KP details, a domestic service detail (calfactors). The work day usually lasted fourteen hours, Sundays included, from six o'clock in the morning to eight or nine at night. Work on the water mains regularly continued to ten and eleven o'clock under floodlights, and sometimes to two and three o'clock in the morning. The lunch period was one hour, most of it going for two roll calls. There were four roll calls a day, the first in the morning before moving out, two on moving in and out again at noon, the fourth after work at night. There was practically no time for eating or for personal hygiene—these things were not considered important by the SS. From July 15, 1937, to February 28, 1938, the daily ration allowance per prisoner amounted to the equivalent of about twenty cents! Virtually every Sunday, rations were withheld altogether as a disciplinary measure—a practice kept up by the SS deep into the war. Sanitary conditions beggared description. The chief cause of suffering was the water shortage. For a full year the SS was content to use an improvised system, barely sufficient for its own needs. The prisoners had to do with crude water pipes running between barracks. Holes had been drilled into these pipes. The water trickled out drop by drop and had to be collected. The sewerage system was no better. At first there were nothing but open latrine pits twenty-five feet long, twelve feet deep and twelve feet wide. Poles accommodating twelve to fifteen men were set up along the sides. One of the favorite games of the SS, engaged in for many years, was to harass and bully the prisoners even during the performance of this elemental human need. Those unable to get away quickly enough when the SS put in an unexpected appearance received a beating and were flung into the cesspool. In Buchenwald ten prisoners suffocated in excrement in this fashion in October

1937 alone. Whenever an SS man appeared near a latrine, the prisoners instantly took flight—in what condition may be imagined. In the barracks the prisoners had to use old tin jam buckets. At night these were, of course, full to overflowing within a few hours. Not until 1939 was work on a real sewerage system begun.

During the initial phase, each work detail moved out with its own SS guard detachment. The SS men posted themselves around the work area and engaged in acts of terrorism at their pleasure. There was a great shortage of tools, and deliberately senseless rules made the work even more difficult. Thus the tough hardwood tree roots had to be dug out by hand, while the loose pine stumps were blasted out. Beatings and cruelties of all kinds were administered as a matter of course. The shooting down of prisoners on the slightest pretext of an attempt to escape was rewarded by bonuses in the form of extra pay, furloughs and rapid promotion.

The initial phase of construction ended with the completion of the electrically charged wire enclosure. At Buchenwald the barbed-wire fence was something over two miles long, enclosing about one hundred acres, of which the roll-call area accounted for not quite four acres. The entire area within the guard line, including the work areas outside the fence, amounted to about three-quarters of a square mile.

Chapter Five

THE ORGANIZATION
OF THE CAMPS

The SS station complement at each camp was broken down into three sections—Section I: Headquarters; Section II: Headquarters Staff; Section III: Camp Administration. In addition there were the actual SS troops that furnished the guard details.

At the head of the camp was the Commandant with his immediate staff. He did not necessarily hold high rank. Smaller camps were even commanded by SS non-coms. In the larger ones the Commandant was at least a captain, generally a major or lieutenant-colonel in the SS. He had complete authority over the camp, within the limits of the directives issued by the SS Main Economic and Administrative Office, to which he was responsible. His adjutant put his orders into effect and took care of all communication with higher and lower echelons.

The Administrative Officer was subordinate to the Commandant and was responsible for all matters of camp administration. His was an office of great importance, and much depended on his favor. In the larger camps he had a large noncommissioned staff.

Direct command power over the prisoners as such was wielded by the Officer-in-Charge (*Lagerführer*), of whom up to three were authorized. They rotated in duty every twenty-four hours. It was they who instituted all measures deemed necessary by the SS. Nominally they were responsible to the Commandant. Actually they were absolute overlords of the prisoners.

The most important connecting links between the Officers-in-Charge and the camp itself were the Roll Call Officers, through whose offices all prisoner affairs passed. There were generally two of them, likewise rotating in duty day by day.

Subordinate to the Roll Call Officers were the Block Leaders. Aside from a few exceptions, soon removed as unsuitable, these men were hardened bullies and brutes and they were in charge of the individual prisoner barracks. In rank they ranged from SS corporal to technical sergeant. The fact that they were responsible to their superiors did not mean that they were under any restraint. On the contrary, they were constantly encouraged to proceed against the prisoners as severely as possible. They lived outside the compound but were likely to show up in a barracks at any hour of the day or night, often remaining among the prisoners, alone or in groups, for hours at a time. In their presence the prisoners scarcely dared breathe.

No camp but had fiends among these Block Leaders, the memory of whom is forever graven in the minds of thousands of inmates. Almost invariably they became better known by some nickname than by their real names. It was from the ranks of the Block Leaders that Master Sergeant Sommer, the "Hangman of Buchenwald," who for years was in charge of the camp prison, rose to heights of infamy. He was fond of wearing black gloves. Whenever he entered the camp a wave of fear preceded him.

On an equal footing with the Block Leaders were the Detail Leaders, who were in charge of the labor details. They too had the power of life and death over the prisoners.

Organization and direction of all camp labor was in the hands of the Labor Service Officer, over whom was placed, later in the war, a Manpower Utilization Officer. Any prisoner reported by Block or Detail Leaders, or attracting attention for the most trifling reasons, could be transferred by the Labor Service Officer to working conditions that might well cost the prisoner his health, if not his life. The Labor Service and Manpower Utilization Officers also made up the shipments scheduled for the construction of new camps or other outside labor details. These shipments were the object of particular dread.

The Gestapo was represented in camp by a Political Department, which was to some extent independent of camp headquarters. In fact, there was frequent friction between the two, growing mainly from the desire of the camp authorities for complete autonomy. They were loath to tolerate the slightest interference with their prerogatives, lest the huge profits arising from the ever-present corruption were uncovered, endangered, or shared. All admissions and discharges, as well as all communications with the Gestapo, were channeled through the Political Department.

Interrogations by the Political Department constituted an extreme form of mental torment, for everything having to do with the Gestapo was shrouded in terror deepened by mystery. Prisoners often disappeared without a trace after having been summoned to the Political Department. Such a summons was quite likely to induce a heart attack in a prisoner, when suddenly announced over the public-address system.

Before the war the SS Death-Head Units stationed at a given camp frequently provided Block and Detail Leaders as well as guard details. The latter were organized in special guard battalions. After 1939 Block and Detail Leaders became part of the permanent station complement. The troops, now called *Waffen SS*, were entirely independent, merely furnishing guards for the towers and labor details. At times, especially during the war, these troops increased in number to two regiments per camp, some six thousand men. Barracks for them were built by the prisoners. Originally the guard battalions consisted only of Germans, but in the course of time many foreign nationals were recruited, especially Croats and Ukrainians. Generally speaking, these foreigners fired their weapons only when ordered to do so. Their attitude toward the prisoners was not outspokenly hostile. As the SS grew more and more demoralized, its foreign hirelings began to commit many infractions on behalf of the prisoners, and grew to be frequent subjects of SS courts-martial.

Many of the guard battalions had special dog platoons, consisting of bloodhounds and police dogs trained to attack men in striped clothing. They were used outside the guard line—on railroad-building details and the like—and did a great deal of mischief. They were also used for tracking prisoners attempting to escape and as a means of "punishment."

The attitude of the guards was largely determined by the character of the Commander of Troops. SS First Lieutenant Reimer, for example, became battalion commander at Buchenwald in 1943. He was a teacher's son from the Sudetenland, the German-speaking part of Czechoslovakia. Even as a sergeant he had attracted attention by his brutality toward prisoners, and his servility had brought him rapid promotion. One of his first acts at Buchenwald was to instruct the guards to shoot when prisoners approached within five paces of the guardline. Heretofore the prisoner actually had to cross the line. In the ensuing inquest he had to be found shot in the back, his head in the direction of flight.

Among the prisoners there was an official and extensive system of self-government with the Senior Camp Inmate, appointed by the SS, at its head. At first there was only one of these in each camp, but as the camps grew larger there were up to three. In the course of time the prisoners in many camps succeeded in placing their own nominees in these offices. The Senior Camp Inmate was the responsible representative of the prisoners before the SS. It was to him that the SS turned whenever it had any general directives to issue. His job was crucial and dangerous, and to take it on required courage and character. The wrong man in this spot meant untold harm to the camp. In the beginning, especially, the SS was anxious to appoint as Senior Camp Inmates men who were its creatures and could be used against the prisoners. The first one of this type in Buchenwald was Hubert Richter, once a member of a notorious Berlin Nazi Storm-Troop Unit. He was the unscrupulous instrument of the SS and himself a man of incredible brutality. He was relieved in 1937 for covering up an escape attempt by two convicts, and was sentenced to be whipped. He went to the camp prison, and about half a year after his release again became Senior Camp Inmate, this time for the blacks ("asocials") who had meanwhile arrived. These he tyrannized in unspeakable ways. In the spring of 1939 he was once more sent to the camp prison, in connection with a case of SS graft. There he died a dreadful death at the hands of the SS. His successor was a convict, Paul Henning, in no essential way distinguished from Richter.

The first political prisoner to become Senior Camp Inmate was Paul Mohr of Wiesbaden. He tried to stem the criminal tide, but he himself was too closely linked to the criminal elements to be able to proceed with sufficient vigor. He too was killed by the SS in the course of a graft scandal. With a single unfortunate exception, the office of Senior Camp Inmate from that time on remained a prerogative of the political prisoners at Buchenwald, much in contrast to many other camps.

Corresponding on the prisoner side to the Roll Call Office was the Orderly Room. In some camps it was at times supervised by an SS man, in other camps never. Its entire personnel was made up of prisoners. It took care of all internal camp administration—files, assignment to barracks, preparation for roll call, ration distribution, etc. It was an institution of great importance to a camp, and for the most part its achievements were constructive. It is no exaggeration to say that in the course of the years the Orderly Room preserved the health and lives of literally thousands of inmates, maneuvering many into positions where they could do effective work on behalf of their fellows.

All contact between prisoners and Labor Service or Manpower Utilization Officers passed through the Labor Records Office, which maintained classified card indexes for the entire camp and did the necessary bookkeeping for work done. Its importance grew enormously in the course of time, when the Manpower Utilization Office was no longer capable of making up lists for outside labor details. Here was another citadel of prisoner power in the camp, exerted both for good and evil. Hundreds of valuable inmates were saved only by the intervention of the Labor Records Office, either by being secretly scratched from death shipments, or by being smuggled into outside labor details when their life was in danger in camp. Sordid intrigue, on the other hand, resulted in many others being transferred to details, inside the camp and out, where they were inevitably exposed to grave danger or death. It was a thankless and difficult job that faced this office. On occasion it had but two hours' time to make up prisoner shipments running into the thousands. Many a prisoner clerk performed prodigies on behalf of his fellows.

Each barracks had its own Senior Block Inmate, nominated by the Senior Camp Inmate and confirmed by camp headquarters. He was responsible to the Block Leader for everything that happened within his domain. For each barracks wing the Senior Block Inmate picked as his assistants two or three Barracks Orderlies, who had to be confirmed by the Senior Camp Inmate. They were responsible for maintaining order and distributing rations. Under the prevailing circumstances this was a necessary and, on the whole, a useful institution.

There were certain prisoners of low character, of course, who shamefully misused this authority. It is true that they were often under considerable pressure from the SS. Many of them, regardless of the color they wore and even in the Jewish barracks, were unable to withstand the temptation to brutality and corruption. Those who know human nature will readily appreciate the effects of herding hundreds of terrorized men of every description together for many years. But in some camps the constructive forces among the prisoners did in time succeed in ameliorating a few of the worst abuses.

The situation was similar with respect to the so-called Capos or Prisoner Foremen, placed in charge of labor details and responsible to the Detail Leader, who had them appointed by the Labor Service Officer. The Prisoner Foremen organized the work of their details, without actually working themselves. They were aided by Assistant Prisoner Foremen. Only when absolutely necessary did the SS appoint skilled workers to these posts. What they were after, especially in the early years, were burly fellows, chiefly convicts, former Storm Troopers or Foreign Legionaries—men who knew how to wield a club, though the SS often enough let them feel the end of it themselves.

In sharp contrast to the horde of brutes who functioned as Prisoner Foremen, a few old-time inmates stand out as shining examples of integrity, humanity and personal courage. I regard it as my duty to mention at this point the Buchenwald prisoners Robert Siewert of Chemnitz and Baptist Feilen of Aachen. Both were Communists. (Siewert became Deputy Minister President of Saxony in 1946, Feilen Chief of Property Control in Thuringia.)

Feilen, a leading member of the camp underground, was foreman of the laundry. He was equally popular among German and foreign inmates on account of his imperturbable fairness. Siewert was foreman of several details through the years and had the courage to come to grips with SS Detail Leaders, something he did each time at the risk of his life.

Sometime in 1939 Siewert happened on SS Sergeant Abraham, who was fond of bullying the prisoners in the latrine and had hundreds of lives on his conscience. Abraham had driven four Jews into a deep waterhole and was preventing them with his club from climbing out. Siewert ran up with several other inmates and was able to rescue three of the Jews, the SS man, curiously enough, beating a retreat—probably because he had had his fill.

Siewert had the audacity to report the sergeant to the Roll Call Officer, barely escaping a beating himself. In time the Roll Call Officers seem to have grown accustomed to the reports of this singular Prisoner Foreman. They received them, at any rate, even though they took no further notice.

Siewert would not give in. In 1943 the Gustloff Works, an armament plant, was built at Buchenwald. During its construction Detail Leader Schmidt was particularly fond of maltreating Russians, Poles and Jews. Early in the morning he was in the habit of assaulting them like a maniac with club, spade, or pick. One of his chief victims was a certain Schreiber. Schmidt severely abused Schreiber almost every day, making him strip to the skin, climb a tree and call down: "I am a filthy Jewish swine!" Often the man was too weak to scramble up the tree fast enough, whereupon Schmidt beat him until he got up.

Siewert, Prisoner Foreman of the detail, asked to see the Commandant—something that was occasionally possible in the case of SS Colonel Pister—and made a full report of the circumstances. The Commandant questioned the accuracy of the report, but promised to put an end to Sergeant Schmidt's mistreatments. This intervention did no immediate good, for the Detail Leader went right on with his savagery. Siewert's courage, however, succeeded in gaining him a certain respect among the SS men. They grew vaguely apprehensive of his "tattle-taling," which usually involved a good deal of bother for them. Late in October 1944 the Gestapo removed Siewert from the camp. He was kept in solitary confinement and severely mistreated. He was not returned to Buchenwald until April 4, 1945. The next morning he was to be executed, together with forty-five others, including the author—all of them men considered politically dangerous to a special degree. For reasons to be set forth further on, the execution never took place.

It must not be thought that it was possible to oppose the SS as a general thing. Such opposition would have been interpreted as mutiny, and would have resulted in a general blood bath. Siewert was an exceptional case. The fact that the SS failed to eliminate him as a "troublemaker" borders on a psychological miracle. To a more limited degree, however, every concentration camp had its examples of upright prisoner functionaries.

Senior Camp and Block Inmates and Prisoner Foremen wore a distinguishing black armband with white lettering on their left arms.

In the course of the years, the political prisoners, especially at Buchenwald, contrived to restrict the SS more and more to purely disciplinary powers, whereas matters of actual camp administration began to slip into the hands of the prisoners. This development made necessary some kind of prisoner police force, nominally an organ of the SS, though actually serving the prisoners' own purposes. By the time this Camp Police was actually organized (June 1942), the danger of its being exploited by the SS against the prisoners had grown relatively small. Authority to organize the Camp Police was literally "put over" on the SS, although it was obtained only after considerable maneuvering. To some extent the Camp Police had had a forerunner in the institution of so-called Overseers, who in some camps had become mere hoodlums for the SS. They were now absorbed into the Camp Police and effectively held in check.

For a long time—until 1944 when they were internationalized—the Camp Police remained the prerogative of the German inmates. It was only with them that the SS could readily communicate. The SS, of course, wanted to use the Camp Police to run the camps as it saw fit, and when there were enough unscrupulous characters available, it succeeded to some degree.

The jobs of the Camp Police were to maintain order and discipline, to guard food depots and other supplies coveted by the prisoners—ultimately this ended the roving SS patrols at night—and to take over newcomers. These were thankless and difficult assignments. They were rarely accomplished without strong-arm methods—in some camps more so than in others. The difference may by gauged by the fact that prisoners transferred to Buchenwald always went through an initial stage of terror when they found themselves received by prisoner police, until they learned to appreciate their treatment. There were members of the Camp Police, of course, who can only be described as frustrated SS men. But the advantages of the institution were obvious. Thousands of prisoners would have fared infinitely worse—on admission, during shipments and disciplinary actions, and finally in the liberation phase—had not this prisoner cadre provided an impeccable camouflage of discipline toward the SS. In Buchenwald at least the assets of the Camp Police were far greater than its initial liabilities.

Chapter Six

ADMISSION TO THE CAMPS
AND DURATION OF IMPRISONMENT

Only an infinitesimal number of prisoners had any idea of what awaited them when they were admitted to a concentration camp for the first time, though most of them were filled with grave forebodings. Many had heard about the atrocities in the camps and had already been mistreated by the Gestapo. They were prepared for the worst. But their expectations were at best vague and were invariably exceeded by reality.

Prisoners were usually arrested at home, preferably at night, and placed in a police jail. There they might be kept for days, weeks and sometimes months, in an isolation cell or with as many as twenty or thirty fellow sufferers. Treatment at the hands of the police was indifferent, depending on the whim of the officers, traditionally sworn to fealty to any regime that happened to be in power. Few prisoners had the good fortune to deal with amiable or even helpful guards. From the concentration-camp viewpoint, police treatment was quite tolerable. From a broadly humanitarian viewpoint, the behavior of many German policemen toward political prisoners, especially in the early years of the Nazi regime, was beyond belief.

After a certain time, at any hour of the day or night, whenever the Gestapo official in question pleased, the prisoner was brought up for interrogation. Those who were lucky were not beaten at all, or not immediately. As a rule there was at least mental torment. Jews never got off without mistreatment.

On another day the cell door opened. The constable offered a slip of red paper for signature. This was the Protective Custody Warrant, listing vital statistics and a vague general reason for detention: "Placed in protective custody for suspicion of treasonable activities"; or simply, "Because of the danger that he may exploit his liberty against the interests of the National Socialist State and its institutions." There were a number of other variations.

There followed more days of waiting—sometimes weeks—until off went the prisoner to the concentration camp. Shipment was always in convoys—dozens, hundreds, even thousands, including many who had never even seen a red slip!

The trip might take twelve hours or twelve days and longer. It might lead through half a dozen jails with stop-overs of several days. It was always an ordeal, even when the police escort did not happen to consist of bullies. Hunger and thirst, overcrowding, lack of sleep, heat and cold—these were the minimum hazards. Most larger shipments were nothing but a series of brutalities. As many as 150 prisoners were herded into a single cattle or freight car. When the doors were opened again, as many as thirty bodies might topple out, crushed or suffocated en route. When passenger cars were used, the prisoners had to sit for any length of time up to thirty-six hours staring into the lights—the windows were screened—six to eight men to a compartment, continuously covered by guns. When streets or squares had to be traversed to and from jails, the prisoners were shackled like felons and marched under armed guard. The final railhead was reached in a state of exhaustion.

From the railroad station the prisoners might be taken to the concentration camps in the familiar "Black Marias," or herded into trucks. Or they could be marched on foot, in long straggling columns. This latter method was especially bad, since many of the arrivals had bags which they had to lug along in double time, with blows raining down on them. If they fell, they were beaten into insensibility or simply shot down. Those who carried no luggage had to march the final distance to the camp with hands raised above their heads. Millions of men made this march, often over roads built by their fellow sufferers.

The arrival in camp was followed by "welcoming ceremonies." A horde of loitering SS noncoms would greedily hurl itself at the fresh game. There was another barrage of blows and kicks, reinforced by stones and cold-water hoses. Men were thrown to the ground by hair or beard. Those who wore ties were choked. Next, hours had to be spent waiting outside the Political Department, arms laced behind the head in the so-called "Saxon Salute," often in a deep knee-bend. This took place regardless of heat or cold or rain, without food or water, without a chance to go to the toilet. All the while any SS man might vent his spleen on the exhausted men.

On one occasion a prisoner named Heribert Froboess was admitted to the Sachsenburg concentration camp. Froboess was arrested as a supposed member of the Franciscan Order and treated as such throughout his camp sojourn, though he did not happen to be a monk at all. He was standing in the "Saxon Salute" after his arrival, when a certain SS Sergeant Kampe, to the great glee of the assembled SS, urinated over him from head to foot. SS Major Rödl, wearer of the Order of the Blood, nearly split his sides with laughter. Kampe later advanced to the rank of captain and came to be a much-feared man in more camps than one.

When larger shipments arrived late at night, or when the waiting period extended beyond the end of the working day, the arrivals were placed in the camp prison overnight. Groups of ten to twelve men were herded into cells four by six feet in size, kicks and blows serving to get the doors closed. The windows were tightly closed and screened. The radiators, which could not be shut off inside the cells, were turned on full blast. Within half an hour the oxygen in the cells had become all but used up, and within an hour or two most of the men had fainted—it was physically impossible for them to fall to the floor of course. The doors were opened only after morning roll call was over, and the admission formalities were resumed, with the prisoners in worse condition than ever.

The first step, accompanied by the usual quota of blows and kicks, was the recording of personal data by the Political Department. This department had to keep careful records of every camp inmate, every death, every discharge, every transfer. An accurate record on admission was therefore essential. A personal record form was filled out for each prisoner, listing his physical description, military and police record, classification and the agency that admitted him. The prisoner had to certify the accuracy of his statements with his signature. False statements were subject to severe penalties.

Essential data from the personal record form were transferred to a file card, and a photograph of the prisoner was attached to both documents. Other documents were attached to the personal record form—Protective Custody Warrant, a transcript of the Gestapo interrogation, etc. Together these formed the prisoner's personnel file. Later, copies of birth and marriage certificates were obtained from the prisoners' home communities, as a check on the accuracy of their statements. In this way the camp administration got a clear picture of the background of each prisoner. The assembled personnel file was submitted to the Commandant and then filed alphabetically in safes in the Political Department, where it was available at any time. The prisoner himself never saw his file. For all he knew, it might be completely forged.

The file cards were included in a separate file, from which each prisoner's name, number and other data could be instantly established.

In the early years especially, the SS noncoms took advantage of this first examination to indulge in the wildest excesses. A favorite method was to ask the prisoner the reason for his admission to the camp—something many did not know—and to deal out penalties for the reply. Many prisoners were simply put down for twenty-five lashes to be administered the following day as a matter of principle. Jews scarcely ever got off with less than five or ten lashes, simply for being Jews.

The tone that prevailed at these ceremonies is almost beyond description. Here is one typical example. The scene was a crowded room, with six SS clerks shouting at the same time and pecking away at their typewriters. A prisoner stood smartly at attention before one of the clerks, who had reached the line in the personal record form marked "Parents." "What was the name of the whore that shat you into the world?" the sergeant asked. The wretched prisoner, unfamiliar with the choice jargon of racialism, did not grasp what was meant. After much invective and a few slaps, it developed that the prisoner was one of six children, whose mother had been decorated by Hitler with the Golden Order of Parenthood!

Processing by the Political Department was followed by admission to the camp proper, through the gate surmounted by the inscription already cited. Its iron grating carried another legend—"To Each His Own!" The prisoners now had to stand facing the wall of the camp prison, again giving the "Saxon Salute," with periods of knee-bend. This might last for two hours, or five, or ten. SS noncoms who happened by were allowed to treat the arrivals as ready game. It might please them to chase the men—some of them still carrying their bags—around the roll-call area to the point of utter exhaustion; or they might be forced to roll around in the mud in their civilian clothes.

Next, there was a so-called "indoctrination lecture," delivered by the Officer-in-Charge, the Roll Call Officer, or one of the staff members of the Political Department. This was to provide the prisoners with their first basic orientation. It was limited to threatening the death penalty twenty or thirty times, for an endless series of offenses. I cannot recall a single permissible act that was mentioned. During the time that a gallows stood in the Buchenwald roll-call area, this indoctrination lecture appropriately took place at its foot.

The next stopping place, to be reached in double time, was the bathhouse. The men had to strip, and during this process the first part of their property began to disappear. They passed under the hands of barbers who applied the clippers—of far from excellent quality—front and back, top and bottom. There followed a shower. In some camps the bath was preceded by a disinfectant dip. The freshly and crudely shorn men had to jump into a vat of antiseptic solution which grew fearfully dirty in the course of time and severely burned the scored skin. By way of "control," the men had to squat down before the SS noncoms, backside forward and legs spread out. This was a source of particular glee to perverts among the SS, especially when celebrities were involved. The prisoners were then conducted to the Clothing Room, by a circuitous route of camp streets and roll-call area, often traversed stark naked, even in winter. This procedure claimed hundreds of victims, either immediately or because of resultant pneumonia.

Without respect to his size, weight, or peculiarities, the newcomer next had his striped "duds" flung at him in the Clothing Room. They consisted of shirt, jacket, trousers, underpants, cap, possibly a pair of socks, and a pair of shoes. Civilian connotations of these terms, however, fail altogether to convey a picture of the apparel issued in the camps. A few prisoners might be lucky, if new supplies had recently arrived. Most of them received rags and tatters, sketchily patched, their only asset being that they were freshly laundered. Only in the course of time, by trading and "finagling," were most men able to improve their outfits.

Hundreds of thousands of pieces of underwear were shipped in from Auschwitz, property of the murder victims. They ranged from infants' wear to lingerie and men's shirts. A good half of this had to be discarded, however, since the pieces were full of gunshot holes and blood stains. The rest consisted largely of nightshirts and priests' surplices, in which many prisoners went about.

The situation was particularly bad with regard to footwear. Many prisoners who were issued wooden shoes could scarcely walk after a few days. The so-called "Dutch Clogs" were worst of all. Those unused to them, especially if they lacked socks or winding rags, could not even walk, let alone run in them. They caused countless foot injuries and abscesses, and when manpower had become essential during the war, the SS was compelled to permit prisoners to have shoes sent from home.

The next station in the prisoners' martyrdom was the Personal Property Room. Here, remaining personal effects were sorted, recorded and placed in a bag, where they were kept for the duration of the stay in camp. Money had to be surrendered, likewise all valuables, such as watches, wedding rings, and the like. Trade in stolen property was rife in all camps during the initial phase. Opportunity for theft existed at all of these way stations, and it was exploited not only by the SS, but shamefully enough by many fellow prisoners as well. In every camp the malevolence of the prisoners in this respect stood in direct proportion to the power wielded by the convicts. Conversely there were prisoners who did everything within their power to help newcomers, to improve their chances and soften the impact of this first ordeal by valuable whispered advice.

The end of the admission formalities removed the prisoners for the time being from the clutches of the SS which few prisoners survived without some damage to their personality. Many kept their bearings only by a kind of split personality. They surrendered their bodies resistlessly to the terror, while their inner being withdrew and held aloof.

Normally the prisoner passed through the prisoner Orderly Room the same day, having his data again recorded in a file. He was then assigned to a barracks. The following day there was a medical examination, and another large form was filled out for the medical file of the prisoner hospital.

In the barracks a wealth of new and confusing impressions overwhelmed the prisoners. Making up beds was a particular source of SS chicanery. Shapeless and matted straw pallets had to be made as even as a board, the pattern of the sheets parallel to the edges, head bolsters set up at right angles—all the hoary tricks of Prussian drill, reinforced by new SS goads. The tiniest wrinkle in a bed could visit the most drastic penalties on the entire barracks. Many prisoners had no experience in making up a bed, or were careless and indifferent about the art. The Barracks Orderlies—one for each wing, with two or three unofficial hangers-on—therefore developed a harsh and inexorable discipline that greatly contributed to the general atmosphere of indignity in camp.

There was a perpetual struggle for authority to keep the few wretched possessions acquired in the course of time by the prisoners in their lockers. Often enough they were simply thrown out and confiscated during inspection. There was no other place where a prisoner could keep anything.

Newcomers often brought infection into a camp, and some camps therefore established special quarantine barracks, where new prisoners were confined for seven to twenty-one days, before being assigned to an ordinary barracks. Nowhere could this institution be maintained for any length of time.

The influx during the war years grew too great, as did the everlasting transfer shipments between camps.

After about 1941 the "standard atrocities" described in this book were to a large extent slowed down in the base camps. The admission of newcomers took place under tolerable conditions. Bath-house, delousing dip and the various processing rooms functioned fairly well. Apart from the "official" imposition of corporal punishment, there was in general far less beating and kicking. The camps were still way stations of human degradation, but they lost those shameless and exquisite torments that had long characterized them. In addition to a Senior Block Inmate, Deputy Seniors from the various nationality groups were appointed for each building. The Block Officers paid little attention to what went on. Many of the older Detail Officers were transferred, while others were somewhat tamed. These latter developments did much to curtail the terror that had once haunted the old "consolidated camps."

These changes must be emphasized, in the interests of truth. They do not by any means imply that the concentration camps were transformed into rest homes! Far from it. The stories of what happened to various special groups of prisoners prove that to the hilt. What it does mean is that the daily onslaught of terror which exceeded all human capacity in the early years tended to dwindle more and more in some of the camps. What remained was the "standard" hardship affecting the daily lives of from twelve to thirty-five thousand men herded together in an area of less than half a square mile. These conditions remained inhuman enough, even when they were not intensified by all manner of deviltry.

Newcomers, unaware of any changes and developments, were as horrified over conditions in the camps as ever. And certainly there can be no question of amelioration in the many newer concentration camps, subsidiary camps and outside labor details. Even in some of the base camps the change came only very slowly, at an uneven rate in various fields, and often accompanied by grave setbacks. Thus the decline in cruelty directed toward individuals had a frequent counterpart in growing mass liquidations.

Death was always much more likely to end a concentration-camp term than the Gestapo. Most prisoners entered the camps under the illusion, carefully fostered by the Gestapo or the police, that their imprisonment would be limited to between three and six months, according to good behavior. There could have been no greater fallacy. On one occasion, in 1936, even Himmler publicly declared that thousands of political prisoners would be kept behind barbed wire for life.

Once a man was arrested, his chances of escaping the clutches of the Gestapo, with or without a sojourn in a concentration camp, were largely a matter of either caprice or bribery. I myself was present in Gestapo offices when officials laughed at the countless teletype petitions that always "get lost." I also have personal knowledge of instances in which bribes were paid to effect a release. In one case the sum involved was 6,000 marks. The Gestapo official had originally demanded 10,000 marks, but an attorney had beaten down the price. In another case the amount was 250,000 marks in pounds sterling—the victim was a Jew who finally managed to emigrate. In a third case there was a 50,000-mark "contribution to the Party" and a 20,000-mark "fee."

On rare occasions, just for fun, the officials might dig up a dusty file and apply for the release of its subject. The opposite was the general rule. Files were left unattended until they crumbled into dust. What did one prisoner more or less matter?

The families of many prisoners kept wandering from pillar to post in their efforts to effect the release of a husband or son, a wife or daughter. Most Gestapo officials were quite generous with promises. During the early months of my own detention, my wife on one occasion actually had my house keys smuggled into my cell, so that I might gain admission if I were released at night and no one were home. She had been definitely promised that it would be only a matter of days before I would be free. During a period that ultimately ran to eighty-five months she learned to have no faith in Gestapo promises. One of the most outrageous cases that has come to my attention is that of an Austrian general, whose wife was ill of heart disease. A Gestapo official had instructed her to be at the gate of the police jail at four o'clock in the afternoon, at which time her husband would be released. By three o'clock a patrol wagon with a dozen prisoners, including the general, was on its way to the station where the Dachau train was waiting!

Theoretically applications for release and releases themselves took place in the following fashion:

Every three or six months—and sometimes as a result of special intercessions—the regional Gestapo offices, if they were so disposed, requested reports on the behavior of individual inmates in the concentration camps. These reports in themselves constituted a nasty chapter. The prisoner who was subject to such an inquiry was summoned for "questioning" by one of the Officers-in-Charge, if that worthy happened to be in the proper mood. The summons was issued for the next day by way of the prisoner Orderly Room, and the reactions aroused by the announcement during roll call of "Prisoners under orders to the gatehouse!" can be imagined.

Questioning, of course, involved hours of standing and waiting and was generally limited to three questions: "How long have you been in camp?" "What is your labor detail?" "Have you had any camp penalties?" Whatever the answers, the results were almost invariably abuse, blows and a transfer to a less desirable detail. As for the actual report forwarded by headquarters to the Gestapo, it was likely to be wholly arbitrary. Whether the prisoner had been "questioned" or not, the Gestapo was nearly always told that he was recalcitrant, incorrigible and altogether unsuitable for release. As a result he would often be implored and reproached by members of his family, especially his mother. Divorces too were common, the prisoner having no chance whatever to deal with the real situation in his letters. All this tended to make his situation infinitely worse.

The Gestapo could order the release of a prisoner without any such report on his conduct. The Political Department of a concentration camp would simply receive a teletype message and the case would be settled. Nor did the Gestapo have to be guided by the reports from the camps. There were cases in which highly unfavorable reports were transmitted, yet the prisoners in question were released within a few weeks. Ordinarily the regional Gestapo office having jurisdiction over the prisoner would file an application for release with Berlin headquarters, with or without a report from the concentration camp on his conduct. The decision then lay with the Berlin department head, who usually consulted three other agencies to see if they had any objections: the Reich Main Security Office, Department DII of the SS Main Economic and Administrative Office, and camp headquarters. It is not surprising that this system had few loopholes through which a prisoner could escape.

There was a much better chance under certain discharge programs meant to serve propaganda purposes. Herr Streicher, *Gauleiter* (Provincial Governor) of Franconia and publisher of the *Stürmer*, was in the habit every Christmas of effecting the release of a couple of dozen Communists from Dachau. These he then ceremoniously dined and wined in Nuremberg, as "repentant racial comrades." The Nazi need for nauseating sentimentality and lying propaganda utilized allegedly converted Communists as a kind of Christmas tree decoration for the brown confraternity. I do not know whether any of these prisoners later relapsed and were again arrested, though I think it is entirely possible and in some cases even probable. The most extensive of these mass discharges took place on the occasion of Hitler's fiftieth birthday in 1939, when some twenty-three hundred Buchenwald prisoners, mainly so-called "asocials," were sent home.

Every prisoner slated for release had to pass through the Political Department when his old civilian clothes had been returned to him. There he was given a discharge certificate listing his personal data. He was told to what Gestapo office to report at home. If he was without means, he was given a slip entitling him to a ticket home at the nearest railroad station. Before his actual release he had to sign a declaration fixing nine conditions for his future conduct. Among them were: complete silence on every aspect of camp life; no communication with former fellow prisoners; and the duty to denounce any violators. His own violation of any of the nine conditions made him liable to serious penalties. This constant threat, together with the generally imposed obligation to report regularly to the Gestapo or the police, as well as the vivid memory of what they had undergone, combined to break the spirit of most of the men when they resumed civilian life—at least in a political sense. Only a very small number of the political prisoners who were released ever returned to their old activities. Such work was even more difficult for them than for others, for they were under constant observation as "men who had been in a concentration camp" and were regarded with fear and suspicion by the people who surrounded them.

Only on very rare occasions did the Gestapo seek informers and confidential agents among the political prisoners, and curiously enough not every prisoner who rejected such recruitment was then "finished off" by the SS in camp. Prisoners who received such an offer were in a very bad way. It took great strength of character not only to risk possible death but to forfeit any further chance of being released. A few hoped that once they were at liberty they would succeed in deceiving the Gestapo until the war ended and the Nazi regime collapsed. I know of two cases at Buchenwald in which the men were returned to the camp after six and eight months because of "lack of evidence that they had changed their convictions." Apparently the Gestapo had such poor experiences with this expedient that it was used, fortunately, only very rarely.

During the final war years some tens of thousands of German concentration-camp prisoners were released apparently because they were requisitioned by the armed forces. The majority of political prisoners rejected this road to freedom; but it was not in their power to prevent compulsory army drafting. If camp headquarters approved the army request —which was by no means always the case—the prisoners were not even given leave to visit their families whom many of them had not seen for years. They had to report directly from the concentration camp, where they had worn prison stripes, to the appointed army installation, where they were instantly "honored" with the uniform. Quite a few prisoners staked all their hopes on this chance to escape the concentration-camp hell. Some thought they might be able to engage in anti-Nazi activities in the armed forces—in contrast to the concentration camps where they were generally no more than passive victims of the terror. These hopes were quickly dispelled; for most of the former concentration-camp inmates were put into army penal battalions.

On occasion, prisoners were granted leave. True, this happened in only an infinitesimally small number of cases. The reasons might be serious illness, deaths or urgent business affairs. The latter, from which the grantor of leave might reap a profit, were likely to rank much higher than the death of a mother or father. But the mere enumeration of reasons for release conveys a false impression, for the granting of leave actually depended on the good fortune of having excellent connections either with camp headquarters or with a Gestapo official.

It was with good reason that old concentrationaries heaped scorn on every newcomer who believed he would be there for "only a short while." "The first fifteen years are the hardest," they used to say. "Then a man gets used to it."

Chapter Seven

DAILY ROUTINE

The camp was awakened by whistles, in the summer between four and five o'clock, in the winter between six and seven o'clock. Half an hour was allotted to washing, dressing, breakfasting and bed-making, sometimes an impossible job within that period.

A number of camps insisted on morning calisthenics, performed winter and summer at break-neck pace for half an hour before the regular rising time. They consisted mostly of everlasting push-ups in the snow and muck. Because of numerous fatal cases of pneumonia, this practice never persisted for very long.

Breakfast consisted of a piece of bread from the ration issued for the day and a pint of thin soup or so-called "coffee," without either milk or sugar. The bread ration was issued at different times to different barracks. Those who had got it at night and had immediately eaten it up had no bread for breakfast.

Next came morning roll call. On a signal the prisoners from each barracks fell in on the camp street and marched eight abreast to the roll-call area. Thousands of zebra-striped figures of misery, marching under the glare of the floodlights in the haze of dawn, column after column—no one who has even witnessed it is likely to forget the sight.

Each barracks had its own assigned place in the roll-call area. The entire strength of the camp was counted, and this roll call usually took an hour, until it was light enough to start work. Morning roll call was not as important as its evening counterpart, still to be discussed, for little change was likely to take place overnight—deaths during the night were reported ahead of time from the prisoner hospital. After roll call came a thunderous command from the Roll Call Officer over the public-address system, addressed to the army of shorn men: "Caps off!" and "Caps on!" This was the morning salute for the Officer-in-Charge. If it was not executed smartly enough, it had to be repeated again and again, to the accompaniment of such comment as this: "You god-damned ass-holes, if you're too lazy to ventilate your filthy pates, I'll make you practice till the juice boils in your tails, you sons of bitches!"

Now came the dreaded call: "Prisoners under orders to the gatehouse!" It affected all those who had received a slip from the Orderly Room the night before. In Buchenwald six numbered signs were mounted at the wall of the left wing of the gatehouse. There the prisoners had to await the nameless terror about to engulf them. When they had painfully come to learn which number meant a summons before the Political Department, and which indicated more harmless matters—records, signatures, notarizations, etc—the assignment of the numbers would be suddenly changed. The prisoners often had to wait for hours, haunted by uncertainty. If their families had only known the fear they could engender by routine inquiries and business matters! It was impossible to evade such a summons, and the waiting prisoners were at the mercy of the SS men who always loitered near the gatehouse.

Often prisoners so summoned were not given notice the night before at all. Their numbers were simply called out at the end of morning roll call and they were ordered to report to such-and-such a sign. I can state from personal experience that such an unexpected announcement of one's number was like a stab in the heart, regardless of what was involved.

The next command was "Labor details—fall in!" There was a wild milling about, as the prisoners moved to their assigned assembly points with all possible speed. The camp band, in the winter-time scarcely able to move its fingers, played merry tunes as the columns moved out five abreast. At the gatehouse caps had to be snatched off again, hands placed at the trouser seams. The details then marched off in double time, the prisoners compelled to sing.

Work continued until late afternoon, with half an hour for lunch, out in the open. For a long time the prisoners were not permitted to carry bread with them. Under an alternate plan, the details marched back into camp at noon, for half an hour or three-quarters, to bolt down their lunch. This hot meal, the only one all day, generally consisted of a single dish—a quart of soup or broth, often very thin and devoid of nourishment. The work schedule differed from camp to camp, but by and large it followed the schemes here described.

In the winter work ended around five o'clock, in the summer, around eight—between March and November the time was periodically shifted by half-hour intervals. At the conclusion of the work day the prisoners were marched back to camp, past the band, again ordered to play sprightly tunes. Then came evening roll call.

In every camp this head count was the terror of the prisoners. After a hard day's work, when ordinary men look forward to well-deserved rest, they had to stand in ranks for hours on end, regardless of rain or storm or icy cold, until the SS had tallied its slaves and established that none had escaped during the day. The preliminary work for these roll calls often had to be done by prisoner clerks, since few SS men were capable of making an accurate tabulation. The prisoners always endeavored to avoid the slightest error, especially in counting the numerous inmates on "permanent detail," whose work brooked no interruption and who therefore never appeared in line, though they were, of course, counted. Any slip, even though not a man was missing, was likely to result in hours of checking and delay, depriving the exhausted prisoners of the last shreds of leisure. So long as the number of prisoners to be accounted for did not exceed 5,000 to 7,000, any absence was quickly noted. It was a different matter when the number swelled to 20,000, to say nothing of 50,000. A great many non-German inmates looked on this roll call as just another form of Prussian drill, to be evaded whenever possible. On many occasions a shirker would simply sleep away roll call in some hiding place, while tens of thousands of his fellows stood in stupor and agony until the culprit was found. (His would be an unenviable lot—no one took pity on him!) If a single prisoner was absent, hundreds of names and numbers from various barracks had to be called out—Polish names, Russian names, French names that could be pronounced only with the aid of interpreters. The SS men would lose their tempers, bellow, and let their fists and boots fly. Few roll calls took less than an hour and a half.

Whenever a prisoner actually escaped, the whole camp was kept on its feet until he was recaptured, often a matter of many hours. Guards were kept posted around the entire camp area during roll call, to insure that no prisoner could lurk about the headquarters area. The search within this guard line was the job of the Senior Block Inmates, the Barracks Orderlies, the Prisoner Foremen and the Camp Police. Successful escapes drew such savage punishment upon the entire camp, especially in the early years, that the political prisoners renounced even the attempt until the final months. Then a few escapes, undertaken with the approval of the underground leadership, proved necessary in order to establish contact with the approaching Allies.

During evening roll call on December 14, 1938, two convicts turned up missing at Buchenwald. The temperature was 5° above zero and the prisoners were thinly clad—but they had to stand in the roll-call area for nineteen hours. Twenty-five had frozen to death by morning; by noon the number had risen to more than seventy.

During the fall of 1939 there was another occasion when the entire camp was kept standing for eighteen hours on end, because two convicts had hidden in the pigsty. Oh, it is easy enough to write about now—standing like that, after a full day's work, throughout the night and until next noon, without food! The cold death figures can be set down—but not the permanent damage suffered by hundreds who later perished of the after effects. What a relief when the war in the air forced even the SS to black out, when the floodlights could no longer be turned on! From that time onward, roll call simply had to be called off after a certain period, whether there were any absences or not. In the complete blackout the SS would have lost control of the camp, would have had good reason for fear in its own ranks.

From time to time the Block Leaders were ordered to "frisk" the inmates during roll call. Pockets had to be emptied and the contents were examined by the SS, a process during which as a rule much money and tobacco simply disappeared. One Sunday in February (!) 1938, the prisoners were compelled to stand stripped to the skin for three hours on such an occasion. The wife of Commandant Koch, in company with the wives of four other SS officers, came to the wire fence to gloat at the sight of the naked figures.

Roll call was a time for many special tortures. Often, following the head count, the command would be heard, "All Jews, remain behind"—to sing over and over again deep into the night the vile jingles known as the "Jew song":

> For years we wreaked deceit upon the nation,
> No fraud too great for us, no scheme too dark,
> All that we did was cheat and lie and swindle,
> Whether with dollar or with pound or mark.

It ended with the following verses:

> But now at last the Germans know our nature
> And barbed wire hides us safely out of sight.
> Traducers of the people, we were fearful
> To face the truth that felled us overnight.
>
> And now, with mournful crooked Jewish noses,
> We find that hate and discord were in vain.
> An end to thievery, to food aplenty.
> Too late, we say, again and yet again.

This choice product of Nazi culture was the work of one of the "asocials" who sought to insinuate himself into the favor of the SS. Rodl, a man who could hardly be described as very discriminating, had the Jews sing it twice and then even he had enough. He forbade it. It was Officers-in-Charge Florstedt and Plaul, vicious anti-Semites, who restored it to Nazi honors. An especially popular procedure for entertaining visitors to the camps was to have the Jews line up in the roll-call area to the left of the tower and sing the vile tune.

Everyone had to appear for roll call, whether alive or dead, whether shaken by fever or beaten to a bloody pulp. The only exceptions were inmates on permanent detail, and those in the prisoner hospital. The bodies of men who had died during the day, either in the barracks or at work, had to be dragged to the roll-call area. During particularly virulent sieges, there were always dozens of dying and dead laid in neat "rank and file" beyond the block formations, to answer the final roll call. For the SS exacted order and discipline down to the last breath. Not until after roll call could the dying be taken to the hospital, the dead to the morgue.

Once evening roll call was over, with the commands of "Caps off!" and "Caps on!" there usually followed another command: "Left face!"—and the public punishments, yet to be discussed in a separate chapter, were meted out. Or one of the Officers-in-Charge might call for a song. It might be raining or storming. The prisoners might scarcely be able to keep to their feet. All the more reason for exacting a song, as much as possible at odds with the situation—once, three times, five times in succession—"I saw a little bird flying," or "Something stirs in the forest." Most of the camps had songs of their own, written and composed by prisoners, on command. Some of these have become widely known, notably "The Peat-Bog Soldiers" and "The Buchenwald Song."

It might have been thought that once the final "Fall out!" had sounded the day's torments were over and the prisoners could sit down to eat and rest at leisure. But often they returned to the barracks, only to be confronted by the results of the inspections conducted during the day by the Block Leaders—lockers overturned, their contents scattered in every direction. The search for one's mess kit often led to savage clashes among the prisoners, driven beyond the limits of human endurance.

When the prisoners worked through the day, the main meal was issued at night. Of course it was cold by the time a protracted roll call was completed. The remaining ration, when issued at night, consisted of bread, a dab of margarine, and a bit of sausage or possibly a spoonful of cottage cheese.

At any moment during "dinner" the Barracks Orderly might suddenly sing out: "Attention! B-wing of Barrack X reporting! One hundred and thirty-five prisoners at mess!" Some SS sergeant had conceived the notion to pay a visit. Not yet through the door, he would bellow: "Get under the tables, you swine!" Benches would be overturned, mess gear clatter to the floor. Still, there were always a few left over who, try as they might, could not find room under the tables and became the particular whipping boys. There were many variations on this tune. A Block Leader might simply order a barracks cleared during the meal, having the prisoners execute some senseless command, such as standing on their heads in the snow. To execute a headstand is not the easiest thing, even for a youngster. But even the aged and decrepit had to do it as a matter of course, just as they might have to double-time endlessly around the barracks. Any hesitation drew kicks and beatings. Even when nothing whatever happened in the barracks after roll call, the prisoners were obsessed by the fear that lightning might strike at any moment.

If roll call had been concluded with reasonable dispatch, work had to be continued for several hours deep into the night by certain prisoner groups. The rest might stroll about the camp streets, in front of the barracks, in the washrooms or toilets—unless they preferred to retire immediately. When taps sounded—between eight and ten o'clock, according to season—everyone except those on detail had to be indoors, half an hour later in bed.

Prisoners were permitted to wear only their shirts while sleeping, even in the deep of winter, when the barracks grew bitter cold and the damp stone walls often coated with ice at the windows and corners. Block Leaders frequently conducted night inspections, ordering all the inmates in a barracks to line up beside the beds or even outdoors, in order to catch those who might be wearing an additional garment. Whoever was found in socks or underwear could expect merciless punishment. On occasion an entire barracks was chased around the block for as much as an hour, barefoot and dressed only in shirts.

These nocturnal invasions did not occur regularly. They came from time to time, at irregular intervals, unexpectedly, generally when the Block Leaders were drunk. But they *could* happen at any moment. The threat was ever-present. Mercifully, the prisoners were far too exhausted to brood on the danger. For a few short hours each night sleep spread its balm over the misery. Only the aged, the fretful, the sick, the sleepless, lay awake in a torment of worry, awaiting the ordeal of another day.

Chapter Eight

WORKING CONDITIONS

It was forced labor that marked the day in the concentration camp. Its stamp was deeply imprinted on camp life.

The very assignment of workers was accomplished in characteristic fashion. The morning after their first roll call, newcomers had to report to the Labor Service Officer. There would be the usual dressing-down and bullying, and then came the command: "Skilled workers, front and center!" Those who knew the ropes invariably stepped forward, even though they knew virtually nothing about a skilled trade. But not many had the courage and presence of mind to pretend to be craftsmen, to depend on their nerve and resourcefulness in overcoming the problems that would inevitably arise.

Skilled workers were assigned to the various shops, a preliminary form of life insurance. All the others, regardless of strength, experience, and aptitude, were assigned to whatever labor details happened to be shorthanded, usually the quarry and excavation details, involving toil and punishment of the most excruciating character. Intellectuals and white-collar workers, especially if they wore glasses, were inevitably launched on the path of doom, a ghastly mockery of the "survival of the fittest."

Reassignment to another detail was a very difficult thing. Getting a better job within a detail depended entirely on the Prisoner Foreman and his assistants. Usually they could be bribed. But to leave a detail and join another required complex connections. The standard procedure in such cases was that the SS Detail Leader of the new detail filed a specific requisition with the Labor Service Officer. The Detail Leader of the old detail signed a release, and the Labor Records Office effected the actual transfer. If all this was done without the knowledge and co-operation of the Prisoner Foreman, the prisoner involved was lost, for such a procedure was interpreted as "collaboration with the SS." In actual practice a transfer could be effected only by devious means. The Detail Clerks had to alter their records—which could be done only when the Prisoner Foreman was in on the plot—and then friendly prisoners in the Labor Records Office had to substitute a new file card. Hundreds of inexperienced prisoners tried time and again simply to absent themselves from their assigned details and join others. It was impossible—they were caught at once. There was the strictest check on names and serial numbers. An attempted switch brought swift retribution even from the prisoners; for an entire detail might suffer severe disciplinary measures if it attracted attention in any way.

Who, then, was able to secure such a reassignment? It is a fact that there were few long-time concentration-camp inmates who did not in the course of time rise to more favorable, if not comfortable, working conditions. Those who failed in this endeavor simply perished. A common work slave of the SS could not long endure, as will be seen. It took money to improve one's lot, or some other inducement for corruption, or influential friends—among the greens, if they happened to be in power, or among the reds. In the latter case, Communists were at an immediate advantage. Whenever political prisoners were in a position of dominance, it was the Communist party that was in the lead. It was difficult for other political prisoners to rise.

Occasionally the SS asked for volunteers for certain better labor details. To respond to such a call involved serious risks, for the improvement might be wholly illusory; and a volunteer might "attract attention," invite rejection and even mistreatment. Personnel files were likely to be consulted by the Political Department on such occasions, and the whole incident might end in disaster.

Every concentration camp without exception had its own penal companies or special labor details in which prisoners were treated with intensified harshness. They were isolated in a special building, which they could not leave even during their sparse leisure time. The penal companies generally slaved in the quarries, usually much longer hours than other details and including Sundays. Their lunch period was curtailed so that many of them hardly had time to eat, provided rations were not withdrawn altogether, which happened often. They were used for the hardest and most menial labor, and were not permitted to receive money. They could not write letters at all, or at best one letter every three months. They were often compelled to do fatigue drill. For them life was literally hell on earth.

Many of the prisoners helped members of the penal company whenever they could, otherwise none would have ever survived the treatment. What made life in the penal companies even more unbearable was their motley composition. They consisted of prisoners of every color designation— Jehovah's Witnesses, homosexuals, convicts with special records. Newcomers were often assigned to them, as were prisoners whose files carried special instructions, whether from the Gestapo or from camp headquarters. Some were assigned permanently, others for only six to twelve weeks. It was all a matter of whim. Political prisoners were not the dominant group in the penal companies, a fact which merely emphasized their lack of cohesion.

Early in 1944 the penal companies were officially dissolved on orders from Berlin. It is a matter of some doubt whether the order was actually carried out in all the camps.

Some of the work in camp was useful but some of it was utterly senseless, intended only as a form of torture, a diversion engaged in by the SS "for fun." The Jews, especially, often had to build walls, only to tear them down the next day, rebuild them again, and so on. Often much of the labor was unnecessary or poorly planned and had to be done over two or three times. Whole buildings had to be reconstructed, since their foundations sometimes collapsed, for lack of proper planning.

In all the labor details, the concern of the prisoners was primarily directed toward two things: shelter and fire. This meant a great rush on certain desirable details during the winter season. Huge premiums were paid to corrupt Prisoner Foremen for jobs near a fire, even out in the open.

A basic distinction must be made, in this and in other respects, between details inside the compound and those outside, in the headquarters area but still within the guard line.

Generally speaking, the interior camp details were the softest. Among the most important were: the details for mess, supply depot, laundry, bath-house, personal property room, clothing and equipment room, shoe-repair shop, tailor shop, sock-darning shop, carpenter shop, machine shop, a series of other shops, lunberyard, pigsty, prisoner hospital, prisoner orderly room, labor records office, prisoner post office, library, and the details for maintenance and for gardening. Certain of these details, such as sock-darning and the lumberyard, were mainly pre-empted by handicapped prisoners. Counting the numerous Barracks Orderlies and the skilled workers in the "German Armament Works" (an SS enterprise, centrally directed from Berlin, with branches in every camp), up to two-fifths of the working prisoners were often busy on interior camp details.

At times, especially before Christmas and special SS holidays, whole sections of the shops, and details were given over to the private interests of the SS officers. As much as half the work time of the prisoners in Armament Works was taken up with "boondoggling"—illegal work for private purposes. Choice lumber, copper and bronze, gold, silver, wrought iron and many scarce raw materials were in this way constantly diverted to the use of SS officers on a large scale. The prisoners actually had no choice but to be party to these practices. Such graft was, in fact, deliberately promoted since it contributed both to the further corruption of the SS and the sabotage of war production.

The output consisted of luxury goods of every description, some of them of high artistic value. There were whole living-room suites, inlaid furniture, precious individual pieces, metalware, busts and figurines, never paid for except with a few occasional cigarettes. These articles found their way not only into the SS quarters but into the homes of friends and acquaintances throughout the land and even beyond its borders. Especially gifted prisoners were sometimes farmed out to Berlin or to other camps and headquarters for weeks at a time, to help meet the demand for luxury goods among the SS.

In 1941 the potters were transferred to the German Earth and Stone Works in Berlstadt near Buchenwald while the porcelain painters went to the SS china plant at Allach in Bavaria, which was under the jurisdiction of Dachau. In the sculpture shops worked architects, sculptors in stone and wood, carvers, masons, gold- and silversmiths, painters, potters, draftsmen. They provided artistic interiors for the homes of the SS officers. They produced the countless gifts exchanged among the clique. On the occasion of the 1939 "Yule Festival," Himmler was presented with a green marble desk set valued at 15,000 to 20,000 marks and made in the Buchenwald sculpture shop. Prisoners created the splendid facade of the camp, behind which misery festered. Materials and tools available to these shops were of the highest quality. The "Viking Ships" they were compelled to produce became an article much in demand in SS circles.

The photographic departments, in the camps, originally organized to take identification pictures of the prisoners, served in the main to develop and print amateur shots taken by the SS officers and to prepare magnificent photo albums for their families and friends. Assignment to this department carried certain risks for a prisoner, for headquarters were always in a panic lest any photographic evidence of atrocities be smuggled to the outside world. On one occasion in 1939 this actually happened at Buchenwald. The foreman, Alfred Opitz of Leipzig, a political prisoner, was thrown into the camp prison, where Sommer strangled him after inflicting ghastly tortures.

Of the painters in their custody the SS officers demanded pictures of every kind. Payment consisted of a handful of cigarettes—or nothing at all—though the "collectors" often resold the paintings to their friends at fancy prices. At least two dozen valuable canvases, mostly portraits, from the brush of the Dutch painter Harry Pieck, were in the hands of

Buchenwald SS officers. The painter at least had the advantage of not losing his life in some quarry or excavation detail. Instead, he was able to practice his art, even though but as a slave of these upstarts. The connections he thus made again saved his life when he was to be assigned to a "Never-Never Shipment" on orders from Berlin.

The print shops and binderies in the camps prepared all manner of luxury books, greeting cards, artistic tablets and inscriptions, and the illustrated magazine, *The Pelican*, for the social evenings organized by the SS. The high standards of workmanship maintained in these shops were well known. Whenever an SS officer would forward a beautifully bound report to Berlin, there was the invariable comment from other SS members who had no access to such services: "Typical concentration-camp work!"

Many of the new lords and masters, of obscure origin themselves, aspired to long family trees and magnificent escutcheons. They organized special "Genealogy Details." At Buchenwald this detail consisted mainly of former Czech officials who, together with special SS registries, were given the job of manufacturing tables of ancestors and family chronicles. All the heraldic devices of Himmler's elite guard units were designed by prisoners and then entered in the official heraldic rolls by the Family Office at Berlin. SS Major Max Schobert, appointed Second Officer-in-Charge in 1940, had a six-foot family tree painted, which he then dedicated to his native city, where it was exhibited in the museum. The genealogy details often faced almost insurmountable difficulties, since the antecedents of many members of this Teutonic elite were lost in the broad expanses of the Slavic east, because of numerous illegitimate progenitors.

The small fry emulated the big shots. For years, on orders from SS Technical Sergeant Henschel, we made well-tailored civilian suits and non-regulation uniforms of stolen material at the prisoner tailor shop, for the Detail Leaders in the machine shop, the mess, the gardening detail, all without payment of any kind. One of Henschel's "customers" paid him in vegetables. (For a full summer I was among the prisoners who had to shell the peas and cut the beans, so that Henschel could can them. It was just as well, for I certainly knew little about tailoring!) Another customer provided the cans, while still another did the actual canning. While I was there, at least one thousand cans were produced on official time for this one SS man alone.

Henschel posted prisoners to give warning of surprise visits by unwanted SS officers, i.e., those who were not in on the deal. When the warning was sounded, a whole column of prisoners loaded down with the suits and cloth bales quickly retired to the cellar with its many nooks and crannies where the contraband was hidden. The cellar, incidentally, also held a clandestine rabbit farm operated by the Detail Leader with his accomplices from the excavation and carpenter detail. It was truly the cave of Ali Baba—run by slave labor.

SS officers and noncoms usually regarded all useful articles in the shops or details under their control as a form of private property, even though illicit. But if demand could not be met from SS-owned installations, private industry and shops were called on. Few firms had the courage to refuse a request from a leading SS officer. The Hereditary Prince of Waldeck-Pyrmont, an SS lieutenant-general who headed the Fulda-Werra region and was stationed at Cassel, simply sent his own prisoner purchasing agent into town to buy whatever he needed. When goods could not be obtained through ordinary channels despite every effort, the Prince was never at a loss. In 1941 he needed pipes and wiring. He simply ordered details from the Buchenwald subsidiary camp at Cassel to dismantle the necessary materials from the houses of citizens who had been bombed out.

A well-known German refrigerator manufacturer (Linde) received an urgent high-priority order for an installation by way of the Institute of Hygiene of the *Waffen SS*, Division of Typhus and Virus Research (Building 50 at Buchenwald). This was to enable the Prince to store the deer he shot. The military priority certificate listed as the purpose of the installation: "Production of serum for combat troops"!

Not all the interior camp details boasted tolerable working conditions. There were important exceptions—the gardening detail, the cobblestone detail for the camp streets, the latrine detail. And members of other details, such as the prisoner hospital, bore a crushing responsibility.

Next to the quarries, the SS gardening details were the most feared work assignments. At Buchenwald they were in charge of SS First Lieutenant Dumböck, a native of Salzburg, who with his own hands killed àt least forty prisoners and was particularly tenacious in persecuting his own fellow countrymen in camp. Many a prisoner hanged himself from the trellises amid the ornamental plants. One morning before roll-call assembly, walking for a moment along the garden fence behind my barracks, I myself saw a Gypsy dangling in the tall flowers. He had committed suicide during the night. A dead cigarette was still stuck in the swarthy face, now pale.

It is almost impossible to grasp what concentration-camp "gardening" meant, unless one has witnessed it. It had almost nothing in common with the kind of work known throughout the civilized world as an agreeable and even invigorating pastime. The gardening detail involved labor in a wide, flat area, under constant control, exposed to every weather. It meant transporting stones or soil, by twos, using a carrying-rack, at a pace and in quantities quite capable of "doing in" even strong men. Conditions in this detail scarcely improved at any time, either at Dachau and Buchenwald, or anywhere else.

On May 1, 1943, a job of manure-carrying was scheduled at Buchenwald—in place of a May Day celebration. Those prisoners who collapsed under the loads were attacked by dogs accompanying the drunken SS sergeants. Two Russians, Sergei Ncolaev of Voronesh and Fedya Fedorkim of Stalingrad, were struggling with a rack at quick time. Fedya, utterly exhausted, stumbled and fell. The rack with its noisome contents turned over, spattering SS Corporal Fritz Schulz. The corporal instantly shot the fallen Russian to death. The other Russian was attacked by the dogs and dragged to the ground. In an insane rage, the SS man trampled the prisoner with his hobnailed boots. What was left was torn apart by the dogs.

In the immediate vicinity another bloody scene was enacted. Vladislav Schezmit, a Pole, was a member of a stone-carrying detail, lugging loads at a run from the garden to the sewerage plant. An SS guard ordered the Pole to lift a stone slab of considerable size. The man was simply unable to do so. He could not even budge the slab, let alone lift it. "Get going!" roared the guard, aiming a brick at the Pole, who collapsed in a welter of blood. "Pick up the slab, you Polish dog! Pick it up!" Several SS men brought around the unconscious man by pouring a bucket of water over him. They dragged him up, propped him against a tree, and executed him for "sabotage" by using him as a target and slowly shooting him to death. Six men were killed outright that day. Another three died during the night of beatings and dog bites.

The latrine detail was no less notorious, quite apart from the revolting character of the work. SS and prisoners had both appropriately dubbed it the "4711 Detail," after the famous brand of Eau de Cologne. This detail was a prerogative of the Jews. At Dachau it long included Dukes Max and Ernst Hohenberg, sons of the erstwhile Austrian heir apparent, Franz Ferdinand, from his marriage to Countess Chotek.

The stone-splitting detail at Buchenwald included at times, among others, the sixty-year-old former Austrian Minister of Justice, Dr. Winterstein, and the Austrian State Youth Leader, Baron Duval. In rain and snow, heat and cold, these prisoners had to squat in rows on bricks, "making little ones out of big ones." They were naturally at the mercy of every passing SS man.

Nearly all the outside labor details operated under similar conditions. It is hard to say what aspect affected the prisoners most deeply—the beatings inflicted by the Detail Leaders, the methods used by many Prisoner Foremen, or the nature of the slave work itself. The very start of the workday brought a tragic farce—the struggle for tools. Tools were at a premium, and many of them were of poor quality. A prisoner who came off second best in this struggle was exposed to the constant danger of "attracting attention," of being reported as a loafer. Even so, this was but the least of the problems for those in the excavation and transportation details or, even worse, in the quarry detail. Only a factual report of incidents that actually occurred can convey the almost incredible reality.

Here is an incident that took place in the excavation and construction detail at Buchenwald in the spring of 1944. A group of Jews and Poles was attacking the stony soil, under the personal supervision of the SS Detail Leader. Even for vigorous men the work would have meant extreme exertion.

To these emaciated and starved wrecks it was almost impossible. Fear alone drove them to try their utmost efforts. The fear was more than justified.

The Detail Leader spied two Jews whose strength was ebbing. He ordered a Pole by the name of Strzaska to *bury* the two men, who were scarcely able to keep to their feet. The Pole froze in his tracks—and refused! The sergeant took a pick handle, belabored the Pole and forced him to lie down in one of the ditches in place of the two Jews. Next he forced the Jews to cover the Pole with soil. They complied, in terror of their lives, and in the hope of escaping the ghastly fate themselves.

When only the head of the Pole was still uncovered, the SS man called a halt and had the man dug out again. The two Jews now had to lie down in the ditch, while Strzaska was ordered to cover them up. Slowly the ditch was filled with soil. When the work was done, the Detail Leader personally trampled down the soil over his two victims.

Meanwhile the rest of the prisoners kept on working at a mad pace, without a let-up, fearful only that they too might attract the attention of the brute. Five minutes later, two of them were called aside and ordered to dig up the two men who had been buried. The spades flew—perhaps it was still possible to save the comrades. In the dreadful haste, a spade cut open the face of one of the Jews—but he was already dead. The other still gave feeble signs of life. The SS man ordered both to be taken to the crematory.

It would not be correct to say that such scenes took place constantly. Had that been the case, there would not have been a single survivor of the concentration camps. But the significant fact is that they *could* take place at any moment. The stone carriers on these details—mainly Jews, Russians, and Poles—were often compelled to run the gauntlet, staggering under their heavy loads. The most notorious of the SS punchers were always ready for such a "pastime." Of 181 Poles who arrived at Buchenwald on October 15, 1939, more than half perished in this way within ten days. From time to time the situation in these details became a living hell for the Jews. Forced to "wash their faces" in thorny thickets, they naturally felt a sense of relief when they were employed in the senseless tasks already mentioned, such as building walls and tearing them down again.

Another example—the transportation detail. Fifteen to twenty men, harnessed to a heavily laden wagon, in place of horses, whipped on at double time. An SS officer on a motorcycle in the lead, to set the pace. The men, in addition, compelled to sing! SS officers Plaul and Kampe, while still noncoms at the Sachsenburg camp, had coined the term "Singing Horses" for this procedure, to the enthusiasm of their fellows. The work lasted from morning until dark, interrupted only by a half-hour lunch period and the evening roll call. The trips were often broken by "calisthenics"—up, down, up, down! Snow, sand, and gravel often had to be loaded with bare hands. Of course there was the inevitable quota of blows and kicks.

An old concentration-camp graduate is assailed by a curious feeling when citing such incidents. In camp they were scarcely noticed—they happened every day. It took an altogether different category of events to attract real attention—the events in the quarries, for example. In all camps these quarries were veritable death traps. Some of the camps, like Mauthausen, consisted of almost nothing but quarries, apart from interior camp details. Work in the quarries was always hard, especially dragging the lorries uphill—if any one aspect can be singled out at all. Every night saw its procession of dead and injured, trundled into camp on wheelbarrows and stretchers—oftentimes there were two or three dozen. The mistreatment was indescribable—stonings, beatings, "accidents," deliberate hurlings into the pit, shootings, and every imaginable form of torture. Thousands fell victim. A favorite method of disposing of death candidates was to have them *push* empty (or even loaded) lorries up the steep slope. Even two men were altogether unequal to such a task. Inevitably they were crushed under the backsliding weight and the blows of their tormentors.

The penal companies, especially, were assigned to the quarries, as were certain selected victims. These pits were the hunting preserves of notorious SS sergeants and Prisoner Foremen. On May 1, 1943—a date already mentioned—the SS men at Buchenwald bet each other six cigarettes or two glasses of beer apiece as to who could kill a prisoner in a given group by throwing stones from above. When their throwing marksmanship grew poor, they lost patience and simply started shooting. The result of this "pastime" was seventeen dead and wounded. "Shot while attempting to escape," as the official reports read. In every camp the number of such mass murders was legion.

At the Buchenwald quarry Master Sergeant Hinkelmann was inexhaustible in devising new tortures. He forced older men to climb trees, which he then had shaken—to his satanic glee—until the poor wretches fell off and broke their necks or were mortally injured, to die miserably in the hospital. Most of the quarry foremen were no better, and sometimes they were worse. Vogel, a homosexual sadist, sought sexual gratification in mistreating his fellow prisoners. It was to him that Roll Call Officers Kent, Petrick and Stribbel handed over for "liquidation" at least fifty political prisoners who seemed dangerous to them.

A Dr. Gerdes, a high government official, had in civilian life been engaged to marry a daughter of the Austrian President, Miklas—reason for him to draw odium in camp as "Miklas' son-in-law." Vogel demanded three hundred marks of Gerdes. Gerdes was unable to raise the money quickly enough, whereupon the foreman, with his assistant Wittvogel, ordered the "black dog" (a reference to the prisoner's clerical affiliations) to be driven into the guard line—which was promptly done.

During 1942 the quarry was in charge of a Prisoner Foreman named Müller who became the tool of Second Officer-in-Charge Gust. Gust visited Müller almost every day, bringing him cigarettes and stolen packages and ordering him to do away with certain prisoners. Power completely corrupted Müller. A man without character, he developed into a terrifying sadist. Later on he and several others volunteered for a Buchenwald outside labor detail in the Rhineland, where he was strung up by his own comrades.

In the course of the summer of 1943, the number of prisoners "shot while attempting to escape" rose alarmingly, and as a sort of camouflage a number of prisoners were appointed auxiliary guards, ostensibly to dissuade their comrades from running into the guard line. The guards were relieved at nine o'clock in the morning. It was agreed that one prisoner would be provided before nine, and one after. There was a fixed agreement between Müller and the SS guards. In return for smoking and chewing tobacco, he furnished the desired victims. The guards agreed among themselves who was to do the shooting and thus earn bonus and furlough. Day after day at least one prisoner was driven into the guard line, sometimes two. Müller thus insured his tobacco supplies during a period when tobacco was very scarce.

Müller's softening-up methods varied. Sometimes he would torment his victim to such an extreme that the man would voluntarily run into the muzzles of the guns. Or he would dispatch a prisoner across the line to gather kindling wood. Or he would personally escort a prisoner on the verge of exhaustion, telling him that he could lie down and take a nap beyond the line, and asking the guard to let the man pass. After a few paces the guard would simply shoot down the prisoner. A commission consisting of the adjutant or his deputy, the Camp Medical Officer, and a third SS officer would then establish that "another prisoner tried to take it on the lam."

On one occasion such a commission was still conducting its inquest, when another prisoner approached and stood hesitantly behind a bush. One of the SS men asked him what he wanted. The prisoner replied that he desired to be shot. "Wait a moment!" said the SS man. The commission mounted its motor-cycles and rode off a little distance. The prisoner was shot, the commission returned and straightway established another "attempted escape"!

Such was labor in the concentration camps. . . .

Not everywhere and at all times. The headquarters details, for example, were better off than any of the other outside details. Often they worked but a few feet away from the scenes of these fiendish crimes, yet their life was paradise compared to that of their comrades. They enjoyed many advantages. In particular, they were able to relieve the SS of treasured articles. Some of them exploited this solely for their own benefit, while others smuggled into camp as much as they could, to help their fellows. This entailed grave risks, and many a prisoner was whipped in reprisal and relieved.

Whenever the distances that the outside labor details had to traverse to their work grew too great, or when special conditions in SS plants, mines and shops called for it, such details were invested with a limited degree of independence. They had to build their own subsidiary camps, though remaining within the organization of the base camp. When such camps grew in size and when circumstances within the total framework of the SS Main Economic and Administrative Office allowed it, such subsidiary camps were completely separated from the base camps, becoming in turn bases for subsidiaries of their own. This trend increased especially during the war, when the SS began to farm out tens of thousands of its concentration-camp labor slaves to German industry for the construction and operation of plants. In the end, Buchenwald construction brigades were dispatched as far as the Channel Islands, while thousands of Buchenwald prisoners slaved in plants and on fortifications on the Rhine. In the north, Buchenwald subsidiaries extended as far as Magdeburg; in the east, to beyond Leipzig.

Most of the new installations were called for in the so-called "Closed Areas" of the SS. These areas were often of considerable size—many dozens of square miles. "Closed Area B," for example, lay in the vicinity of Nordhausen, some fifty miles north of Buchenwald. In this area alone, counting all foreign workers and German civilians, some 150,000 men were engaged in the construction of underground plants for the Junkers Works at Dessau and several other German industries. Conditions in these closed areas can be described only as utterly inhuman. Outside the Harz area, they were most numerous in Bavaria, Saxony and Bohemia. They were in charge of SS Major-General Kammler, who was stationed in Berlin, from where he ranged the country like a wild man. The great base camps were called upon for ever new contingents of slave laborers. Toward the end Sachsenhausen had several dozen subsidiary camps, Dachau around fifty, Auschwitz almost forty, Buchenwald more than seventy (fifty for men, more than twenty for women). The SS economy had an extraordinary appetite for expansion, and its ties with German industry were very close. Nor did the ties between the concentration camps and German industry spring solely from the SS drive for power. Industrialists, suffering from the manpower shortage, scorned no method of keeping ahead of their competitors. The crucial element to achieve this was an adequate labor pool, and the SS received many applications, all arguing that in this way alone could the "patriotic duty" of maximum contribution to the war effort be fulfilled.

All manpower utilization involving concentration-camp prisoners in outside details was directed by the SS Main Economic and Administrative Office. Whenever a private or public agency sought prisoner help, it had to apply to Oranienburg. If the application was approved in principle, the Manpower Utilization Officer of the nearest concentration camp—sometimes, if the resources of one camp were inadequate, a whole group of camps—was ordered to check the situation on the spot, the results to be reported to Oranienburg.

These investigations were not always conducted by experts. In Buchenwald, for example, the leader of the SS band platoon, Captain Schenk, occasionally pinch-hit in this capacity. The SS Main Office would approve or disapprove applications on the basis of these reports. When specialists were requested, plant engineers might actually come into camp to select suitable skilled workers. The firms were required to pay a daily wage of four marks for an unskilled worker, six to eight marks for a skilled worker. This was payable to the camp that farmed out the worker.

If a firm was unable to provide the requested prisoners with shelter, a so-called advance squad was dispatched from the base camp, in order to build barracks. When these were completed the subsidiary camp would be filled up with the authorized quota of prisoners.

The prisoners were selected by the Labor Records Office of the base camp on orders from the Manpower Utilization Officer. In theory good physical health was a fundamental prerequisite, though in practice this condition was a mere farce. It sometimes happened that the Camp Medical Officers examined as many as 1,100 prisoners in two hours—in other words, at the rate of almost ten per minute—exempting only a couple of dozen as unfit for travel, though hundreds suffered from chronic malnutrition at the very least.

In certain cases the Political Department or other camp agencies ordered prisoners shipped to subsidiary camps of particularly bad reputation by way of penalty. Certain details were composed solely of Jews, others of convicts or "shiftless elements." Prisoner functionaries for the subsidiary camps —Senior Camp and Block Inmates, mess and clerical personnel, etc.—were nominated by the Senior Camp Inmate of the base camp and approved or disapproved by headquarters or by the Manpower Utilization Officer.

Every SS officer in charge of an outside detail had to give a daily accounting of hours worked. These reports were filed with the Labor Records Office and served as the basis for the monthly bills which the SS rendered the firms in order to collect payment for the slave labor of the prisoners. In the case of private industry, the money had to be paid into an SS bank account. With government agencies a clearing arrangement was in force. At Buchenwald total SS revenue for prisoner labor farmed out ran between a million and a million and a half marks a month. It goes without saying that the prisoners never saw a single penny of this money.

Living and working conditions in the outside details and subsidiary camps were usually indescribably bad, the food wretched. The workers often had no chance to change their clothes for four or six weeks on end. There was not even a change of underwear. Disease wrought havoc among the slaves. Only in rare cases was there any alleviation. (Here too much depended on the particular spot assigned to an individual, and whether he belonged to the tiny elite of "big shots.") It is not necessary to think of these installations as penal details. In such places as the tile yards and clay pits of the SS-owned "German Earth and Stone Works" one did not have to be beaten down by Prisoner Foremen. The labor itself was sufficient to finish off anyone in short order. The pottery works attached to these plants produced all manner of earthenware—utilitarian and luxury—for the SS.

The ordinary outside details and subsidiary camps were murderous enough. At Ohrdruf near Weimar, one of Hitler's numerous headquarters, with subterranean command posts, conference rooms, etc., had to be constructed, among other things. Some 10,000 prisoners, working in three shifts at a speed-up rate under the goading of the SS, of the Technical Emergency Auxiliary and of civilian supervisors, had to drive galleries into a mountainside. The very approach to the site represented a sizable distance. Yet footgear and clothing were issued in only inadequate quantity. During five months in 1944 the prisoners were given but one bath and disinfestation, and this only because typhoid had broken out in a neighboring camp. Of 1,000 men forming a single Buchenwald shipment to Ohrdruf at this time, but 200 escaped with their lives; of 1,500 from Flossenbürg, men already in a wretched physical state, only a fraction survived.

When the distance to the work sites had grown to six miles and more, making it necessary to transport the prisoners in buses, the gasoline shortage induced the SS to create two new subsidiary camps, one at Crawinkel, the other a tent camp. There general conditions were even more unfavorable, food being extremely short. The prisoner hospital at Ohrdruf, to which numerous casualties were returned, lacked almost every facility—medical aid, drugs, even fuel. From time to time "Invalid Shipments" were dispatched to Bergen-Belsen.

The dead were generally shipped to the base camp for cremation. Twice a week they arrived at Buchenwald from Ohrdruf. Of the 15,000 prisoners who, during two months in the fall of 1943, had been shipped to the subsidiary camp "Dora" near Nordhausen (which after October 1944 became the SS base camp for a so-called "Operation B"), at times at least 100 bodies were received at Buchenwald every other day. The bodies were filthy, louse-infested, neglected. Their weight was seldom as much as ninety pounds. They were intertwined into knots that could hardly be separated. From December 1943 to May 1944, mortality at "Dora" never fell below 1,500 a month—often it was much higher. The autopsies almost without exception showed a degree of credibility indicating that the men would have succumbed even to a cold.

The cost in lives that had to be paid to achieve a given job held little interest for the SS—none whatever when a record was at stake that might bring decorations, promotions or other advantages. An outstanding instance of this kind was Himmler's order issued March 18, 1943, to run a rail line from Weimar to Buchenwald, as a traffic artery for the Gustloff Works, which had settled on the outskirts of the camp with thirteen huge sheds. Himmler ordered that the trial trip over this line must at all costs take place within three months, on June 21, 1943.

On with the prisoners! The soil consisted of clay with a

strong admixture of rock and there was a difference in elevation of almost a thousand feet. Everyone realized that in so short a time even an emergency track could hardly be laid. The construction chief, SS Second Lieutenant Bertram, pointed out this impossibility. Berlin's reply was to replace Bertram with a notorious slave driver and bully, SS First Lieutenant Alfred Sorge, a man with an evil reputation from Sachsenhausen that went back years. Sorge brought along two of his chief strong-arm men, SS Master Sergeants Baumann and Sohn. The project got under way.

In a day and a night shift of twelve hours each, with an unceasing rain of blows and the assistance of the dog platoon, with no surcease on Sundays and holidays, the work proceeded at a murderous pace heretofore unknown. Accidents soon exceeded a dozen a day. It did not matter. The main thing was that the line had to be finished by the night of June 20. And the trial trip actually took place on June 21, in the presence of SS Major-General Kammler and a host of Nazi big-wigs. There was a hail of promotions and decorations. The SS staff and the civilians employed on the line celebrated with beer and *Schnaps* and also got a cash bonus. The prisoners had a "good" day of their own. They were at last allowed to take a bath.

The deadline had been met. But actually the line was like the villages of Potemkin—it ran for a single day. No sooner had the trial locomotive passed when foundations began to sag. Actual completion of the line took another six months. It is unfortunate that there is not surviving record of the profits made by Nazi business houses of Weimar on this SS railway project. The bids which they were supposed to submit were actually received nine months after the work had started, precisely when it was finished!

Like everything the SS did, its "War Manpower Utilization Program" was staged with a great show of organization. Plants were constructed everywhere, machinery was assembled from all over Europe, managers and officers raced about, there were orders and deadlines, the slave host was whipped up—and relatively little or nothing emerged at the other end, except the dead and the maimed.

The growth of outside details and subsidiary camps brought

much motion, back and forth, to the masses of prisoners. Liaison was established between camps and many prisoners had a chance to communicate with the outside world. All this did much to deprive the SS, by and by, of rigid control over the whole structure. As a result, while the situation seriously deteriorated almost everywhere, there were occasional ameliorations, achieved because the directives of the guiding security service spirits were no longer capable of execution.

Insofar as the SS with its limited forces was able to do so, labor was rigidly supervised. But of course the Detail Leaders and even the Prisoner Foremen could not be everywhere at once—though in the quarries they were able to occupy points of vantage that enabled them to exercise constant control. Excavation details often embraced more than a thousand men, distributed over several construction sites at distances of as much as a mile or two apart. As a result the universal policy among the prisoners was to reduce work and output to the absolute minimum as soon as there was no supervision. The main thing was to "work with the eyes." There was an effective warning system that went into instant effect as soon as one of the slave drivers put in an appearance.

In the peat-bog details of the moor camps it was possible to set a fixed output quota, but in most of the camps the nature of the work made that impossible and output remained at an irreducible minimum. In the construction, excavation, drainage and water-main details, entire columns stood stock-still when there was no supervision, only to fall to at a mad pace as soon as the warning sounded.

An infinite expenditure of resourcefulness, pull and corruption went into the everlasting quest for a soft spot where work might be shirked "by the numbers." Under the pressure of necessity hundreds devised the most incredible stratagems to achieve their goal, many of them literally never lifting a finger until they happened to "attract attention"—unless it was to fry some stolen potatoes over a secret fire, while only a few hundred paces away their comrades were driven to the brink of utter exhaustion.

The SS system of slavery was a liberal education in how to shirk work. A rational labor system, using incentives and humane treatment, might well have achieved two or three times the actual output, with one-fifth of the labor force. But of course the SS did not really care about output. It was out for blood.

If the struggle for tools started the workday, the struggle for stones ended it. Every member of an outside detail had to lug a stone with him back into the compound. The required quota was five bricks or a rock weighing at least ten pounds. In the final minutes before knocking off work it was necessary, at considerable risk, to be on the lookout for a suitable stone, one that looked large and heavy enough, that was free of sharp edges and clean enough not to ruin one's clothing. Loaded down in this fashion the slave columns marched back to camp at the onset of darkness, carrying their casualties with them, to face the endless ordeal of roll call.

Chapter Nine

DISCIPLINE

Concentration-camp labor, as has been plainly shown, was in no sense the fulfillment of the normal human urge for activity. It had no educational—to say nothing of recreational—value. It was subordinate to the main purpose of the concentration camp—punishment. But punishment was by no means limited to labor.

Himmler had ordered large signs posted everywhere in the concentration camps. They read: "There is a road to freedom. Its milestones are: obedience, hard work, honesty, sobriety, cleanliness, devotion, order, discipline and patriotism." The milestones on the prisoners' road—which led to the crematory—were: whipping post, prison cell, rope, gun, club, hunger, cold and torture of every kind.

There were certain acts, of course, against which the SS, from its viewpoint, had to proceed drastically—such as political propaganda, listening to foreign broadcasts, unauthorized contact with the outside world, efforts to kindle disaffection in its own ranks, sabotage, anti-Fascist meetings, political activity of any kind in camp, the smuggling in and out of letters, and actual escape attempts. The punishment of these offenses was savage to an unimaginable degree. In the spring of 1938 a Gypsy tried to escape. Commandant Koch had him placed in a wooden box, one side covered by chicken wire. The box was only large enough to permit the prisoner to crouch. Koch then had large nails driven through the boards, piercing the victim's flesh at the slightest movement. The Gypsy was exhibited to the whole camp in this cage. He was kept in the roll-call area for two days and three nights, without food. His dreadful screams had long since lost any semblance of humanity. On the morning of the third day he was finally relieved of his sufferings by an injection of poison.

Usually recaptured prisoners had a sign placed round their neck reading: "I am back!" Then, already beaten to a pulp, they had to stand for hours on a stone mound or under the gallows, in heat or rain, until they received twenty-five or fifty lashes, were thrown in the dungeon for further torture, or were hanged before the assembled camp.

The most terrible penalties were reserved for "sabotage." Actual sabotage the SS men were usually far too stupid to discover. But their interpretation of this offense may be judged from the following example: Portland cement was shipped in big paper bags, which were stacked at the construction sites. Anyone caught with even the smallest scrap of this paper—worn under the thin prison garb to ward off the cold or used to protect clothing while carrying stones—was instantly reported, if he was not treated to a beating on the spot.

Apart from these more or less reasonable pretexts for discipline, the SS seized on the most trifling offenses as occasions for punishment: keeping hands in pockets in cold weather; turning up the coat collar in rain or wind; missing buttons; the tiniest tear or speck of dirt on the clothing; unshined shoes, though the mud be ankle-deep—for years there was a special after-hours inspection for this purpose; shoes that were too well shined—indicating that the wearer was shirking work; failure to salute, including so-called "sloppy posture"; entering barracks during working hours, even though but to use the toilet; latrine absences that were considered too long—at times it was altogether prohibited to step out before ten o'clock on labor details (remember the thin morning coffee!); straightening up even once while working in a stooped position; eating during work; smoking in barracks or during working hours; picking up cigarette butts—which cost many an "asocial" his life; clandestine food foraging and cooking; and every form of unauthorized procurement. The nightmare of the "roll call" has already been discussed. The slightest deviation in dressing ranks and files, or arranging the prisoners in the order of size, or any swaying, coughing, sneezing—any of these might provoke a savage outburst from the SS. No enumeration of such offenses used by the SS as pretexts for punishment can be even approximately complete. Denunciations for "loafing"—liberally interpreted—were common, not only on the part of malicious sergeants and foremen, but by civilian employees in the armament works as well. Serial numbers were often confused, and in place of a prisoner who could scarcely be considered guilty, one who was altogether innocent might be punished. There was no possible defense—that would have meant questioning the veracity of an SS man. On one occasion a newcomer was assigned the serial number of a prisoner who had just been released and who had been reported for some offense. The new man promptly drew twenty-five lashes.

Besides the abuses incident to supposedly faulty bed-making, other barracks regulations furnished the SS with an inexhaustible source of pretexts for punishments of every kind. Some Block Leaders would mount the tables and pass their fingers over the ceiling beams in search of dust, or inspect the inside of the stoves for trash, until the Barracks Orderlies proceeded to wire them shut in the summertime.

If there were no real thefts in camp to be punished, the SS would invent them. Theft was usually motivated by hunger, and brought swift retribution from the prisoners themselves. A bread thief, for example, was lost the moment he was caught. The camp simply could not tolerate him, even if he had acted from hunger. No one had any more than the barest necessities, and theft only made the situation worse. Many a theft, however, was motivated not by hunger, but by a desire to get bread to trade for tobacco.

Prisoners who mistreated their fellows or even tortured them to death were, characteristically enough, never punished by the SS. Prisoner justice had to catch up with them. This was often very difficult and took much time, since the SS had its eyes on these creatures and protected them. Many prisoners who were unfamiliar with the inner workings of the camp, were baffled that such killers were "allowed" on the loose.

Even experienced concentrationaries sometimes marvel that it was at all possible to survive this jungle of penalties. There were occasions when there seemed to be no way out. In Buchenwald, for example, the SS officers were finally forbidden to procure firewood for their homes from the camp. In contravention of this prohibition, the Prisoner Foreman concerned had supplied a basket of logs to the wife of a Camp Medical Officer—a man on whose whims hundreds of prisoners were directly dependent, to say nothing of the rest of the camp. Unfortunately there was a feud between the doctor's wife and Frau Koch, the wife of the Commandant. Frau Koch reported the matter to her husband, who had twenty-five lashes administered to the foreman. The next day Frau Koch herself sent for a sack of firewood. The foreman refused the request, citing his express orders and the punishment he had just suffered. Koch at once had him whipped again, for refusing to obey an "order by the commandant's wife."

The lash as an instrument of punishment was covered by a general directive from the SS Main Economic and Administrative Office. This punishment was administered on a special wooden rack, to which the delinquent was strapped on his stomach, head down and legs drawn forward, exposing the buttocks. This *Bock* was a familiar device in all camps. From five to twenty-five lashes were dealt out, with cane or horse whip, to be repeated up to four times at intervals of two weeks. On April 4, 1942, Himmler personally ordained an "intensified" version of this punishment, to be administered to both male and female prisoners, on the naked buttocks.

Theoretically camp headquarters had to apply for confirmation from Berlin when corporal punishment was to be adminstered, and the camp physician had to certify that the prisoner was in good health. Down to the end, however, the procedure widely practiced in many camps was that the prisoner went to the whipping rack immediately, while on receipt of confirmation from Berlin the punishment was repeated, this time "officially." Submission to Berlin depended on the "gravity" of the offense in the first place. In "minor" offenses, headquarters simply went ahead and imposed the punishment on its own.

SS sergeants were detailed to administer the whippings, unless they volunteered with a show of enthusiasm. If one of them showed any trace of sympathy or lack of vigor, an "expert" would take over. "Expertness" consisted chiefly in unerring kidney blows. The camp physician had to witness the estrapade. Only a very few cases have become known in which they intervened on behalf of the prisoners. On the other hand, it did happen that they painted the torn buttocks with iodine! After receiving the whipping, the delinquent usually had to execute from 50 to 150 knee bends—to "strengthen the muscles."

At times prisoners were forced to adminster the whippings to their fellows. There were those who lacked the courage to face the consequences of a refusal, and others who did not seem to mind lending themselves to the occasion. Political prisoners usually refused outright or administered the whippings in such a way as to displease the SS. They were then either subjected to the same punishment themselves, or "softened up" in other ways.

Whippings usually took place before the assembled prisoners in the roll-call area. The rack was carried in by four prisoners, lifted up high like a throne. It was placed on a big stone mound up which the delinquents had to clamber one by one. Names, offenses, and extent of punishment were announced over the public-address system in the coarsest way. Hundreds who underwent this ordeal never uttered a sound. Others made the area echo with their screams and moans. When the screaming began to irk the officers, they would order the band to strike up a march. On one occasion at Buchenwald, SS Major Rödl actually stationed an opera singer by the rack and had him accompany the performance with operatic arias.

Often, of course, the SS officers administered whippings merely as a form of private pastime. When they suddenly assaulted prisoners in this fashion it was impossible to take the precautions that were otherwise often employed—extra-heavy underwear, or some protective layer next to the body. Anyone caught trying such an expedient was beaten on the naked buttocks. To the credit of the prisoners working in the hospital it must be said that they did everything within their power to heal and restore the victims who were often left in a very bad state.

Dreaded even worse than whipping was the punishment that involved being trussed up against a tree. Like all other penalties, it was imposed in entirely arbitrary fashion. It was executed in the following way: the hands were tightly tied on the back and then the body was hoisted up by them and suspended some six feet high from a tree or post, the feet hanging free and the entire weight resting on the twisted shoulder joints. The result was extremely painful shoulder dislocations. The victims screamed and moaned frightfully. Often they received beatings on face, feet or sexual organs to boot. The helpless sufferers cried for water, for their wives and children, for a bullet to end their torment. Those who lost consciousness were revived by being drenched with cold water. This punishment lasted from half an hour to four hours. Those who survived it almost invariably sustained permanent injuries.

Fatigue drill, imposed on entire details or barracks at a time, was another form of punishment that exacted a heavy toll. It often lasted for hours, on the uneven roll-call area, studded with holes and gullies—a vicious combination of sadistic Prussian drill with customary concentration-camp brutality. The prisoners came to call it "Geography," for it afforded them ample occasion to study the terrain at close hand. Not only individual barracks or groups of barracks, but the entire camp had to engage in such drill on countless occasions, for the most trifling reasons. Block Leaders who reported their charges to headquarters were often told: "Go ahead and impose your own discipline"—a blank check for sadism. Up! Down! Double time! Duck walk! Roll!—alone, by twos, all together, up the area and down. All this to a barrage of abuse from the sergeants, who were particularly fond of walking over the prone men with their heavy boots. They loved to pick on the weak. Prisoners who could not stand the pace, who staggered or fell, were in imminent danger of death. There were months when scarcely a day went by that some noncom did not harry an entire detail—they were too slow, the stones they carried were too small, they carried too little lumber. Fatigue drill would be ordered on the spot.

Standing in the roll-call areas was one of the worst forms of punishment, as has already been mentioned—and the SS seasoned the monotony with "diversions" of many kinds. The punishment might be imposed on the entire camp as in the rare case of a successful escape, or on individual barracks or details. For years the penal company had to endure it every Sunday afternoon.

The penalty of being forced to stand was frequently combined by the SS with fatigue labor—always after working hours, of course. On Sunday afternoons, twenty minutes after mess time, there was a regular call: "Prisoners on fatigue labor to the gatehouse!" These prisoners were first put through a spell of standing and then had to carry stones, sand, soil, or manure until nightfall—always in double time. The supervising SS men were furious at having their Sundays spoiled and abused the prisoners with club and whip to the point where it was impossible for them to walk three steps in normal fashion, let alone to take a break. It was the noncoms who sometimes had to rest, from the sheer effort of beating.

The death penalty in the concentration camps took many forms. When it was not officially imposed—by the firing squad, the garrote, the gallows, or the poison syringe—the SS always camouflaged it as "shot while attempting to escape." The post-mortem reports showed that it was apparently the weak who hatched all the escape plots, not the strong and vigorous.

In the spring of 1941, Buchenwald witnessed the unique incident of a prisoner daring to protest against such SS methods. Sergeant Abraham of the garage detail had thrown a certain Hamber into a water hole. Hamber had been a well-known Vienna film producer. He was a Jew—reason enough for Abraham to trample him viciously underfoot until he died miserably. Hamber's surviving brother went to the First Officer-in-Charge and reported the murder. The entire detail was thereupon summoned to the gatehouse, "to tell the truth." No one dared say that he had seen anything. Names were taken down and the men sent back to their barracks.

"I know," said the brother of the murdered man, "that I shall die for having made this report. But perhaps these

criminals will restrain themselves a little in future, if they run
the risk of being reported. In that case I shall not have died in
vain.''

Toward nine o'clock that night Hamber was again called to
the gatehouse. To the surprise of everyone, he returned within
half an hour. He had been questioned by Commandant Koch,
the adjutant, the Officers-in-Charge, the Camp Medical Officer, the Roll Call Officer. Koch had told him: "We want
you to tell the full truth. I give you my word of honor that
nothing will happen to you." Hamber repeated his story. Half
an hour before midnight he was again called and this time he
did not return. Four days later he was taken dead from the
camp prison.

The testimony of the other witnesses, to the effect that they
had not seen anything, availed them nothing in saving their
lives. Hamber's deed, courageous as it was, swept them all to
their death. Within three days, five of them were called to the
gatehouse. Within a week none was left alive. A few days later
it was the turn of the next five. Within three weeks the Jewish
portion of the detail—twenty-nine in all—had been exterminated by way of "punishment." Curiously enough a
single man was left alive, Löwitus, a shoemaker in his forties,
who had the good fortune to receive his discharge papers
before his name was called. He was a citizen of a Balkan state
and had been in possession of complete emigration papers
when he was arrested. Such inconsistencies happened to the
SS on several occasions. They are explained only by the fact
that the various sections were poorly co-ordinated and over-
all control of the machinery was deficient.

Apart from the directive covering corporal punishment,
there were no standards applying to the extent of the punishment the SS could impose. Even when the whole camp was
penalized—indeed, especially in such cases—it was a matter
of whim and arbitrary judgment. Ration withdrawal, for
example, whether for certain sections of the camp or the camp
as a whole, could last twenty-four hours, or it could continue
for three or four days.

Chapter Ten

FOOD

Statistics are always capable of more than one interpretation. They can merely offer clues to the realities of the situation. This applies with full force to such figures as are available on the subject of the food situation in the German concentration camps. They must be evaluated critically. Three thousand calories a day does not mean the same thing to a manual worker as to an intellectual, to a woman as to a man, to a growing youngster as to an old man. There are differences too between indoor work and work in the open, between work in good and in poor weather. These differences become more marked when the daily caloric intake is reducecd to eighteen hundred. Men suffering from chronic malnutrition are not restored to full health by a diet that might suffice undcr normal conditions.

Another difference must be taken into account—the difference between the figures recorded on paper and the food actually issued. Concentration camps never got in full even the small ration allotment authorized for them. The SS skimmed off the cream. Prisoners detailed to the supply rooms and messes had a well-organized system of pilferage.

Barracks Orderlies retained plenty for themselves and their immediate friends. The run-of-the-mill concentration-camp inmate got only what was left.

Nor it is a matter of indifference how a given quantity of food is prepared and served. "Slop," unseasoned and unappetizing, does not have the same nutritive value as the same food, when palatably cooked, for digestive reaction is not the same.

To these factors must be added the general wretchedness that pervaded the camps, especially the everlasting nervous strain, and the difficulty in supplementing the diet by any outside means. Only when all these factors are considered does the table applying to Class II camps given below offer any valid data.

Up to the start of the war a blanket allowance was made for the purchase of food for the concentration camps. From July 15, 1937, to February 28, 1938, fifty-five pfennigs per head per day was authorized. This was the equivalent of less than seven dollars a month! Even with large-scale purchasing, the quality of the resulting diet can be readily imagined. Even the SS administrative authorities found the allowance too low. From April 1 to 16 it was tentatively increased by ten pfennigs. This proved too much for the SS Main Economic and Administrative Office and on April 17, 1938, the amount was reduced to sixty pfennigs, where it remained until the war broke out.

Starting in August 1939, the most important foods were rationed throughout Germany. The diet grew generally worse. Fixed money allowances were out of the question, and the SS did as it pleased in the camps. Not until August 1, 1940, were standardized ration tables introduced, which remained in force thereafter. Their fluctuations during various periods are shown in the table:

WEEKLY RATIONS IN GERMAN CLASS II
CONCENTRATION CAMPS

	Aug. 1, 40 to May 14, 42		May 15, 42 to Apr. 27, 44		Apr. 28, 44 to Feb. 28, 45		Mar. 1, 45	
	lb.	oz.	lb.	oz.	lb.	oz.	lb.	oz.
Meat and processed meat.....		14.1[1]		9.9[2]		7		8.7
Fat.......................		7		6		6.4		2.9
Including margarine.......		5.2		4.5				
Lard, etc..............		1.8		1.5				

WEEKLY RATIONS IN GERMAN CLASS II
CONCENTRATION CAMPS

	Aug. 1, 40 to May 14, 42		May 15, 42 to Apr. 27, 44		Apr. 28, 44 to Feb. 28, 45		Mar. 1, 45	
Cottage cheese..............		3.5		3.5		3.5		1.4
Or skimmed-milk cheese....		1.6		1.6				
Bread.......................	6		5	6	5	12	3	14
Sugar......................		2.8		2.8		2.8		
Marmalade.................		3.5		3.5		3.5		8.5
Cereals....................		5.1		5.1		8.8[3]		
Flour or flour mixture........		7.9		4.4		4.4		
Skimmed milk..............						(½ pt. daily)		(½ pt. daily)
Coffee substitute [4].........		2.7		2.2		2.2		1.1
Potatoes...................	7	12	11		6	3	7	12
Fresh vegetables (turnips, etc.).........	6	3	5	12	8	13		13.2
Supplementary Diet for Heavy Manual Workers								
Meat and processed meat.....		14.1[5]		9.9		9.9		13.3
Fat........................		3.5		3.5		3.5		1.9
Bread.....................	3		3[6]		3		2	7

[1] Low-grade beef or horse meat, reduced to 11.2 oz. on Oct. 1, 1941, and to 9.9 oz. on Jan. 1, 1942.

[2] Reduced to 7 oz. on May 31, 1942, in return for additions of 2.6 oz. bread and half an ounce of fat.

[3] With an additional 6 oz. legumes.

[4] When "German Tea" was issued, it was at the rate of a little more than one-tenth of an ounce per day, in place of one-third of an ounce of coffee substitute.

[5] Low-grade beef or horse meat, reduced to 11.2 oz. on Oct. 1, 1941, and to 9.9 oz. on Jan. 1, 1942.

[6] Or less.

Prisoners transferred from one camp to another were issued a daily travel ration of a little more than a pound of bread, not quite two ounces of sausage, and about two ounces of margarine.

The nutritive value of this diet fluctuated greatly for more reasons than those already pointed out. The meat served in camp was of inferior quality. In the early years—as long as Germany still had access to the high seas—a good deal of it was whale meat, later low-grade beef and horsemeat. In the camp messes it was thoroughly boiled, the rich soup skimmed off, and the meat shreds dumped into the food for the prisoners, which thus contained but a fraction of the original nutritive value. The black army bread issued in the camps, unless it happened to be moldy, was often better than that available to the German people in many regions. Sugar, so essential to the diet, almost invariably disappeared. The main sweetening—if any at all—was saccharine and other German synthetics. During the final phase of the camps, there was virtually no jam. The skimmed milk listed in the table was reserved for a few favored details. From the aspect of nutrition, the coffee substitute could have been readily dispensed with—its taste was indescribable, as was its color. It might just as well have been issued as "tea" or "German Acorn Cocoa." The prisoners infinitely preferred so-called "German Tea," especially since it was sweetened. Unfortunately it was issued only rarely. Potatoes were generally rotten and almost always served unpeeled. The prisoners seldom had the time to peel them properly, because of the frightful rush at mess, and when they did, the valuable nutriments under the skin of course found their way into the garbage cans. On the average, I believe that scarcely ever was more than two-thirds of the potato quantity given in the table actually issued—for long periods certainly much less. The item described as "Fresh vegetables" is no more than a statistical abstraction, and can only bring a wry smile to the lips of a survivor. "Fresh vegetables" were either "German pineapples"—turnips, inadequately cooked and as tough as wood—or turnip greens and discarded cabbage leaves and stalks.

The supplementary ration for heavy manual workers was a most welcome boon, if one was lucky enough to draw it, especially because it included blood sausage of relatively good quality. The so-called liver sausage was often inedible and stank. It is improbable that it ever contained liver, since usually ground fish bones were found in it. Unfortunately only a small number of prisoners ever drew the supplementary ration, toward the end of the war virtually none at all.

A special diet was established for patients in the prisoner hospital. It was much in demand as a supplementary ration, and large quantities of it always went to the "big shots" among the prisoners—Senior Block Inmates, Prisoner Foremen, and other powerful gentry. There were such favored persons in every camp, enjoying hospital diet year after year, in addition to their other privileges. It was generally a matter of "pull" with the hospital mess, staffed entirely with the camp's ruling class; or it was a matter of barter. In return for hospital food, the foremen of the tailor shop, the shoe-repair shop, the clothing room, the supply rooms, would provide whatever was wanted. By dint of bribery of several SS Camp Medical Officers, even eggs were provided for the hospital—though the patients rarely saw them, let alone ate them. In Buchenwald alone, from 1939 to 1941, some forty thousand eggs, disappeared on the "black market." It would be unfair, however, to fail to mention that hospital food helped to "finance" many useful things that benefited all the prisoners.

If one substitutes actuality for paper statistics in judging concentration-camp food, the following situation emerges: The great majority of the prisoners were in a state of malnutrition and exhaustion. Newcomers usually lost up to 50 pounds in weight in the first two or three months. Many weighed less than 110 pounds. There was a marked shortage of vitamins, which greatly contributed to the spread of disease and epidemics. The clearest evidence supporting these statements is furnished by the post-mortem reports. Autopsies were not performed on every prisoner who died, but the available reports can be regarded as fairly representative. Ninety post mortems at Buchenwald, from February 13, to April 30, 1940, showed the following results:

	No. of cases	%
Poor or very poor state of nutrition........	63	70
Moderate or adequate state of nutrition....	14	15.5
Good state of nutrition...................	13	14.5

From May 31, to September 1, 1940, seventy-five post mortems showed the following results:

	No. of cases	%
Poor or very poor state of nutrition.....	44	59
Moderate or adequate state of nutrition....	15	20
Good state of nutrition...................	16	21

It should be borne in mind that in these post-mortem reports the SS Medical Officers approximated the truth only in cases of specified disease involving an impaired state of nutrition. In other cases even completely emaciated bodies were marked "good state of nutrition."

A revealing light on the frightful food situation in the German concentration camps is thrown by the following excerpt from a letter of March 17, 1945, that passed between the Chief Medical Officer for concentration camps and Dr. Schiedlausky of Buchenwald. We read:

> *The field office of the Todt Organization[1] reports that post mortems [of prisoners in an outside labor detail from Buchenwald] reveal a state of chronic starvation. They are unable to account for this, since the prisoners received supplementary rations for heavy manual workers. Their letter hints at the possibility of irregularities in the issuing of rations. To check on this I discussed the situation with the officer concerned here, SS Major Barnewald. He states that the Todt Organization itself has taken over the feeding of the prisoners, so that in the unlikely event of any irregularities, they cannot be placed at our door. We stated as much in a letter of March 10, 1945, addressed to the Chief Medical Field Officer of the Todt Organization, requesting him to institute an investigation of his own.*

Any investigation that may have resulted doubtless consisted of nothing more than another exchange of letters—if indeed it took place at all at that late date—March 1945. Besides, there was, of course, honor among thieves. "In the unlikely event of any irregularities" indeed! Those who know about Barnewald and Schiedlausky can only smile bitterly.

The insistent need for supplementing the subnormal official diet in some way or other enabled the SS to engage in a profitable sideline—the prisoner canteen. Until about 1943 the canteens were centrally supplied from camp headquarters at Dachau. Before the war they offered a considerable variety of stock for sale, even cake and fine canned goods. But for most of the inmates this had very little meaning, even if they had the requisite money. For them the good things were always "out of stock"—the greedy and corrupt foremen with their connections and crooked barracks purchasing agents took care of that.

After the war broke out canteen stock grew scantier and

---

[1] The Todt Organization was the nation-wide Nazi construction organization.—*Tr.*

scantier, until apart from occasional smokes there was only so-called "Viking Salad," a vari-colored synthetic of doubtful description, apparently based on potatoes and ground fish bones.

Tie-in sales were strictly prohibited throughout Germany, but they flourished in the concentration-camp canteens. Tobacco was always at a premium, and usually cigarettes, pipe tobacco and cigarette paper were sold only in combination with a pair of suspenders or a two-pound can of unsalable mussels, spoiled herrings, red beets, or the inevitable Viking Salad. The greatest Buchenwald expert in this field was Master Sergeant Michael, a nephew of Commandant Koch. He coined the slogan: "To each his own, and most of it to me!"

On one occasion he organized a collection among the prisoners, to finance a bulk-purchasing expedition to the Netherlands. The collection netted fifteen thousand marks and Michael took off, traveling by first-class sleeper and spending two weeks in high living. He returned when he had almost been given up for lost. For every six or ten marks he distributed a few paper-wrapped cigars and low-grade cigarettes, a bar of chocolate and a can of condensed milk for every three men.

Michael was finally tripped up in another affair. Alcohol was strictly barred in camp, but on one occasion, in 1942, he smuggled 750 gallons of apple wine into the canteen, where it was cut to more than 2,000 gallons. It had been purchased for thirty-five pfennig a quart, but was sold at one mark and twenty pfennig. For this exploit he was reported by envious SS colleagues.

Canteen-purchasing was the prerogative of special Barracks Purchasing Agents. We need not waste many words on the ambiguity of this function. In 1942 a special canteen building was opened in Buchenwald—a similar one had long existed in Dachau. Few of the prisoners ever saw its inside.

To the credit of the Prisoner Canteen Office, it must be said that it succeeded in assembling considerable quantities of food through clandestine channels. This was on occasion made available to the individual details in the form of nourishing soups served on the side. These issues were made to all, regardless of the prisoners' means. From 1944 on, at the initiative of the Buchenwald canteen foreman, light beer was sold fairly regularly.

When the food situation in the camps grew steadily worse in 1944, Red Cross mass shipments to certain nationality groups ensued, especially to the French, the Danes, and the Norwegians. The SS profited vastly by such aid from abroad.

Understandably, despite the ever-present threat of beatings and the justifiable vigilance of the prisoners, who were fearful of the spread of disease, there were hundreds who time and again tried to ransack the garbage pails in search of edible offal, who gathered and boiled bones. Among the Ukrainians there were even cases of cannibalism, or rather necrophagy!

And outside the barbed-wire compound the pet dogs that most of the SS officers kept were fed on meat, milk, cereal, potatoes, eggs and claret; so fine a diet, indeed, that many a starving prisoner took advantage of every chance to work in the dog mess, hoping to garner some of the animals' food.

Though originally the SS mess had three sections—enlisted men, headquarters staff, officers—the officers managed to have their own private cuisines at home. Excellent sources of supply to maintain their parasitic life of plenty were the sheep folds, poultry farms, angora rabbit hutches, truck gardens and farms located in the immediate vicinity of the camp. When the basement of the Commandant's house at Buchenwald underwent repair, thirty whole hams were unearthed, together with more than fifty smoked sausages, hundreds of jars of fruit preserves and some six hundred bottles of choice French vintages. And such supplies sometimes proved a good source of income. On one occasion two hundred glass jars with preserved duck, belonging to Commandant Koch, sprang open. Afraid that the meat would spoil, Koch sold these preserves, a mere fraction of his stock, to the prisoners at two marks a portion.

There were sharp differences among the various official categories of SS food. The reservists who were located next door to the Officers' Club, had to be satisfied with the official one-dish meals, unless they maintained very good connections. But the Officers' Club itself was a lavish restaurant in which regular SS officers were daily served the most ample food—poultry, steaks of heroic size, genuine coffee, choice wines, branded liqueurs from abroad. The required meat and fat were procured by black-market purchasing and slaughtering on a large scale. For this purpose the Buchenwald pigsty detail always maintained between three and five hundred so-called "headquarters hogs" and another five hundred geese, ducks and chickens. This stock was fed from concentration-camp "scraps."

The SS officers by no means scorned the prisoner depots as a source of supply. Jan Robert, who was masseur to their lordships whenever they were in need of ministration, had as one of his clients Master Sergeant Hans Schmidt, the adjutant, who was friendly with Dr. Hoven. At Hoven's orders, Robert daily supplied Schmidt with eggs, butter and milk from the hospital mess. The adjutant was also eager for soap, jewelry and food from Red Cross packages. Often it took all of Robert's cunning to evade such demands.

Schmidt headed the SS canteen—a nest of corruption beyond compare. It had a record of years of fraud and embezzlement. SS Major-General Eicke had personally organized the central canteen administration for all the concentration camps and Death-Head Units, the agency that governed central purchasing and selling. The Buchenwald SS canteen was part of this set-up. It had long been headed by a close confidant of SS Colonel Koch, a convict named Meiners, with a record of eighteen convictions for theft and fraud. He was a concentration-camp inmate, but had trusty status, wore civilian clothes and was not required to have his hair shorn. He had built the canteen into a private profiteering outfit for the "sworn fellowship" for which he traveled freely about the countryside making monthly purchases running up to 120,000 marks, collected from the prisoners.

Master Sergeant Schmidt, to say the very least, was Meiners' equal in his capacity to "cheat and lie and swindle, whether with dollar or with pound or with mark." This man was really a pathological case. One of his hobbies was to urinate in champagne glasses. This sinister figure had "connections" all over Germany, with every SS headquarters, and his diversion of canteen supplies intended for the troops was on a systematic scale. Tobacco and wine were strictly rationed for the enlisted men, for example—a bottle of wine for every six men. But for the SS officers, champagne flowed in streams.

Frau Koch, who had once been a stenographer in a cigarette factory, occasionally bathed in Madeira wine, which was poured into her tub. Once, when the Commandant, for his own purposes, confiscated several truckloads of lemons intended for SS members, doling out only a little of the fruit to the higher officers, a rumor arose among the enlisted men that Frau Koch was having herself massaged with lemon juice by her prisoner masseur who had to "treat" her every day. It did not happen to be true, but it shows the degree of demoralization carried into their own ranks by the corruption among the SS officers. Hundreds of thousands of cigarettes were made available to them for their private use by the canteen staff.

A special chapter was the social evenings of the SS which started at Buchenwald with a magnificent open-air celebration in 1938, subsequently taking place about once a month for the headquarters staff. They were eating and drinking sprees that almost invariably ended in wild orgies. Every table setting was flanked by six or eight wine glasses. During the war the required drinks were regularly procured in France and the Netherlands by SS Master Sergeant Rieger, at the time in charge of the motor pool. The man actually in charge was SS Master Sergeant Michael, already repeatedly mentioned. When Prince Waldeck or some other high SS officer paid a visit, there might be as many as six "breakfasts" throughout the day. Among the profiteers from this revelry were the businessmen of Weimar.

Chapter Eleven

MONEY AND MAIL

For their life of luxury the SS naturally needed vast sums of money—in the early years at any rate. Among the most profitable means of procuring such sums was overcharging in the Prisoner Canteen—Viking Salad at two marks sixty pfennig a pound, about ten times the actual value—and withholding rations from the prisoners. In the course of time the first method alone probably produced a revenue of 2,000,000 marks in Buchenwald, to say nothing of numerous "gifts" for SS officers. For this purpose Commandant Koch kept a special "black account," into which Meiners, according to a single cashbook that has been preserved, paid 52,000 marks. According to Koch's own statement, the unrecorded sums were many times this amount.

Frau Koch on one occasion received a diamond ring valued at 8,000 marks. For Adjutant Hackmann, Meiners bought a new car from the "profits" of the Prisoner Canteen. Indeed, Meiners even contributed the money for the construction of a villa on Lake Eder near the watering resort of Wildungen, but this was stopped when Prince Waldeck objected. Among other things, Koch purchased a motorboat on the lake from the money handed over by Meiners. The mark-ups, ranging from 100 to 300 per cent, also served to cover the deficits of the Officers' Club. SS Master Sergeant Schmidt personally managed to embezzle about 65,000 marks in the almost impenetrable financial maze.

The second financial source—the withholding of rations from the prisoners—brought in 6,000 to 10,000 marks on each occasion, and as we have seen, it happened regularly.

There were in addition a number of frauds, forays, extortions, "penalties," "voluntary contributions," that further swelled the always quickly emptying SS till. The pretexts for obtaining additional revenue were often of the shabbiest kind. The "Singing Horses" were said to have broken a whiffletree; footprints of prisoners were supposed to have been found on a freshly cemented walk in front of an officer's home; flowers had been stolen in the gardening detail. Damages: two to four hundred marks, to be made up within half an hour. In the winter of 1939 a stove burned out in Building 42 at Buchenwald. Rödl ordered each of the forty-odd barracks to pay fifty marks for the repair of the stove. At the same time he let it be known through the Senior Camp Inmate that any building collecting no more than fifty marks could expect fatigue drill the next Sunday. Most of the barracks thereupon collected amounts up to one hundred marks.

During the reprisals that followed in the wake of the Vom Rath assassination in 1938, SS Master Sergeant Bayer, Detail Leader in the Prisoner Supply Room, sold the Jews' mess kits, canteen cups and spoons at three to ten marks apiece, simply pocketing the money. Five hundred marks were demanded for the disinfection of one of the Jewish barracks. On Bayer's orders the job was done while the prisoners had to remain in bed. The disinfectant used was Super-Tox, and it was used in a concentration that can be described only as deliberate torture.

Generally speaking, the armament plants were another profitable source for financing the parasitic life of the SS. At Buchenwald alone, revenue from farming out prisoners for labor ran between one-and-a-half and two million marks a month in 1944. Many SS officers, furthermore, held management jobs in the plants that drew large orders from the Ordnance Department and thus reaped even further profits. SS Colonel Pister, to cite but one example, was not merely Commandant of Buchenwald. He was also General Manager of the German Armament Works, with a salary and profit-sharing interest, as well as of the German Earth and Stone Works and of the Gustloff Works.

In the course of time the total lack of control over SS affairs led to something like outright banditry. In 1942 three SS officers of the Institute of Hygiene of the *Waffen SS*, headed by SS Major Ding-Schuler, went to Paris to purchase instruments for the Technical Health Office in Berlin. They were provided with 30,000 marks in French francs. In Paris they ordered special equipment that cost far more, at the same time wantonly spending on night life the money that they had.

The equipment was delivered to Germany, but the French firms never received payment. For two years one of them tried to penetrate the jungle of SS organization from Paris to Berlin, in order to obtain the 225,000 francs that were due. Despite rebuff after rebuff it refused to desist, going as far as the Reich Main Security Office. The entire long-drawn-out correspondence passed through my hands. Dr. Ding-Schuler openly admitted that he and his cronies had spent the money in the black market in Paris during the three weeks of their visit. Nothing had been left for the purchase of equipment. At the same time, through one of his friends in Paris, Major Günther Fritze who was assigned to the office of SS Lieutenant-General Oberg, Ding-Schuler advised the owner of the French firm that he would land in a concentration camp if he had the audacity to assert his claim any further. This restored peace. Evidently the French firm decided to write off the amount to the account of the *"Roi de Prusse."*

In order to supply the SS with funds in the various ways described, the prisoners themselves, of course, had to have money. Inmates who brought large sums with them into camp in the first place were likely to arouse the rapacity of the convicts as well as of the SS. So to patronize the canteen, prisoners were permitted to have money sent from home. Remittances were limited to thirty marks per prisoner per month. About one in every three inmates was actually in a position to receive money from his family. The others lived on this one-third—which helps to explain the corruption that was rampant among the prisoners.

Payments were made into credit accounts which the prisoners maintained with the Prisoner Finance Office. Withdrawals were at monthly or semi-monthly intervals, often entirely at the whim of the SS and attended by every form of chicanery. Prisoners had to stand in line for hours, especially before the major holidays, such as Christmas, when it took two or three days of waiting in the cold to draw money. The prisoners might be commanded to throw themselves down in the muck, lie prone for half an hour at a time, or turn the line front end backward, so that the men in the front rows who had been standing for four or five hours were the last. Until the prisoners managed to gain control of the institution themselves, the procedure was conducted with such haste that countless bills and coins were lost in the shuffle.

In the fall of 1943 the SS introduced special scrip money in the camps. It was valid only in the camps and was distributed in the form of bonuses for special effort. If the purpose was to get more work out of the prisoners, it failed dismally. In the end headquarters simply distributed the coupons among the details every week, in small amounts and at utterly capricious ratios. There might be sixteen marks for sixty-five men—there was no rhyme nor reason. The use of ordinary currency was stopped altogether. The reason for this generosity was, of course, that in every large concentration camp it fed several million marks into the coffers of the SS.

The most improbable tricks were employed by well-to-do inmates in order to obtain more money from home than was authorized. Not infrequently the SS got its rake-off.

Packages from home were not permitted until 1941, apart from a few scattered, farcical exceptions at Christmas time. After 1941, a prisoner could theoretically receive as much as he could eat in one day—the rest was confiscated by the SS. The life led by the parcel robbers may be imagined. They took what they pleased, especially the articles in greatest demand, such as tobacco, chocolate, bacon and tea. Many an SS man employed in package inspection shipped home his booty by the crate-load.

The solicitude of the families of the prisoners was touching. They sent whatever they could, often enough food they could ill spare from their frugal rations. Substantial quantities of food were received from rural sections and certain planned collections, especially for the Czechs from Bohemia and Moravia. In the end, the impossibility of maintaining rigid package inspection did much to help some of the camps to endure to the end. The shipments, however, also resulted in harsh conflict, feuds and bitter enmity along nationality lines, since they were never large enough for general distribution.

In the course of time money and news began to trickle into camp regularly through this unauthorized channel. In the summer of 1944 all incoming packages were suddenly seized and in Buchenwald alone more than five hundred illegal letters were found. They were submitted to the Political Department for scrutiny—many of them were in foreign languages, especially Czech. The camp was threatened with a major disaster, averted only by an air attack which burned to the ground the building where the letters were stored.

Only once, in the winter of 1939-40, was permission granted to have warm clothing shipped in, and of this much soon disappeared. Late in 1941 the SS professed to believe that as the result of parcel-post shipments the camps were adequately supplied with warm underwear. It therefore graciously condescended to extend to the ostracized camps Hitler's appeal for woolens for the German army in the east. This invitation was transmitted to the barracks by the Senior Block Inmates in approximately the following way: "We must contribute voluntarily to this collection. Those who do will receive a favorable entry in their files. Those who don't will go to the whipping post. Suit yourselves!"

There were some twelve thousand prisoners in Buchenwald at the time, and they got together an impressive pile, commended in the local Nazi press as a "contribution from SS headquarters, Buchenwald." Jehovah's Witnesses and the Dutch Barracks, however, firmly and unanimously declined to contribute. The SS took no action against the Dutch, but the Witnesses were punished by having to stand in the cold roll-call area on New Year's Day, by fatigue drill and labor deep into the night. This was the verdict of the Roll Call Officers: "You arch criminals, you heavenly sons of bitches, you'll slave tonight until dark at four degrees below! Take off your underwear at once!" This was done. In addition, when the Witnesses moved back into camp that night, they had to turn in their leather shoes for the cumbersome wooden clogs. They were also removed from all the preferred details, but this had to be rescinded a few days later, when it was found that they were indispensable.

From 1942 on, Red Cross packages began to arrive in the camps in increasing numbers. They were addressed only to non-Germans whose names and identification numbers were known to the Red Cross organizations of their homelands or to the International Red Cross at Geneva. Occasionally Germans, Poles and Austrians received such shipments. Packages frequently arrived for addressees who had died, and sometimes these were distributed among certain details—the SS, of course, keeping the lion's share. Since receipt of the packages was supposed to be acknowledged on special printed cards, the prisoners in question always added their barracks and serial numbers, with the result that some of them seem to have been included in the Geneva lists.

When the International Red Cross asked for an accounting, it developed that in Buchenwald alone at least seven carloads—probably twenty-one to twenty-three thousand packages—were unaccounted for. In April 1945, when the front drew near, it was amusing to watch the SS officers frantically clear their offices of telltale empty Red Cross cartons.

Understandably, these packages with their wonderful contents at first caused sharp conflicts to develop among the prisoners. A wave of gratitude swept through the camp when the French comrades agreed to surrender a substantial portion of their share to the other barracks. But for weeks actual distribution remained something of a scandal. For example, the Frenchmen in the Little Camp were particularly badly off. Yet they received but one package for every ten men, while the prisoners entrusted with the distribution, with the aid of certain Frenchmen, reserved whole stacks for themselves and their "big shot" friends.

In contrast to parcel post, letter mail between the prisoners and their next of kin was always permitted in principle, though severely restricted. Messages could be written twice a month, in most camps a letter and a postcard in turn, each with a prescribed number of lines. The messages could discuss only family affairs. Not a word was permitted about the camp or the conditions in it. The space allotted to the prisoner's message on both cards and letters was further curtailed by a long printed excerpt from the so-called Camp Regulations—no prisoners had ever seen a full copy of them. It stated that the prisoner could buy everything in camp and therefore could receive money. The amount was not specified. As already pointed out, no more than thirty marks a month was paid out to a prisoner. Families were led to believe that they could send as much money as they liked. The surplus stuck to the fingers of the SS.

The mails were closed to Jehovah's Witnesses until after 1939, when they were permitted to write one letter of twenty-five words a month to their families. Jews were often not permitted to write letters for months at a time. Members of the penal company could write only once every three months. From time to time, on some pretext or other, mail privileges for the entire camp were suspended.

Prisoners frequently got only cut-up clippings of their incoming letter, or even an empty envelope, the result of SS censorship. This was a particular trial. Yet such letters as did get through sometimes brought disaster.

One of the prisoners, Johann Stürzer, was deeply concerned about his aged mother and his sister who now had to farm his seven acres of vineyard without him. He was a thirty-two-year-old wine grower, a member of a Christian-German gymnastic club from Lower Austria, who stood accused of having interfered with a radio broadcast on April 8, 1938, when Hitler exhorted the Austrian people to approve the *Anschluss* by one hundred per cent participation in the plebiscite two days later. Sent to Dachau and Buchenwald, he spent two years in the penal company where he contracted a severe case of lumbago. Two of us often had to support him on either side and drag him to the roll-call area.

One day he got a reproachful letter from his family who had been advised that he would have long since been released, except for his poor conduct. They appealed to him to be a "good boy," not to grieve his poor mother, to "obey his superiors" and so on. All the arguments were recited in the tone of a loyal, well-meaning, simple-minded old mother who had fallen for the lies of the Gestapo.

The situation profoundly affected Stürzer and he slunk about in a state of extreme depression. The Senior Block Inmate, who disliked him, reported that he had gone insane. Stürzer was taken to the hospital, where he was given a fatal injection as "feeble-minded." Four men had to hold down the poor fellow so that the poison could be squirted into his veins.

Telegrams, special-delivery letters, and the like, could bring serious consequences for the addressee. On Christmas Day, 1939, a Viennese friend of mine was called to the gatehouse, he did not know why. For two full days he had to stand motionless, with not a scrap of food throughout the day until at last he was handed a telegram announcing the death of his father.

On another occasion Roll Call Officer Hackmann told a prisoner that his brother had died. The prisoner asked which brother—he had several. The Roll Call Officer said: "Take your pick!" Kubitz, a Buchenwald Block Leader, sometimes came into Barracks 36 with a stack of mail for the inmates. He would read off the names and then slip the whole stack into the stove, saying, "Now you know you've had mail, you swine!"

Mail censorship was entirely at the whim of the SS men detailed to it. Some of them were only semi-literate. Only in the rarest cases were outgoing letters and cards that fell afoul of censorship returned to the prisoners, so that they never knew whether their painstakingly composed and compressed messages had reached their families. This meant weeks of anxiety; worse still, prisoners were haunted by doubt as to the fate of their families. They lost faith in the fidelity of wives who were often encouraged with the most brazen lies by the Gestapo to seek divorce. They lacked all news of children whose living memory had already begun to pale. This war of nerves represented one of the most demoralizing hazards of camp life. Small wonder that even at the risk of death prisoners sought time and again to smuggle letters out of camp. Prisoner Foremen who worked in outside labor details and enjoyed a certain freedom of movement were the favorite go-betweens; or it might be necessary to find a prisoner who had bribed an SS man.

There is but one known Buchenwald case in which an SS man stood ready to accept all the risks of such intercession, from pure humanitarianism and for no material consideration. He was SS Sergeant August Feld of Lummerschied near Saarbrücken, a courier assigned to a special Buchenwald detachment rather than to the station complement. He was a man of integrity in every respect, who helped in many ways and performed deeds of valor for a large number of prisoners. During the last few days of the camp he risked his life for us.

Chapter Twelve

"RECREATION"

Concentration-camp life was a matter of unending slave labor, of a constant struggle for naked survival. The penal companies had virtually no leisure time whatever. And often the entire camp had to report for additional work after mess and deep into the night. Floodlights glared over the terrain to provide the necessary illumination for work and control. After 1939 night work at Buchenwald was a "privilege" of the Jews, until in 1942, the prisoner administration succeeded in having other prisoner categories included. Henceforth the Jews had to work only two or three nights a week. Though the efficiency of this night work was nil, of course, it succeeded in destroying not only leisure time but even sleep.

For years—in some camps, right down to the end—there was Sunday work, especially the dragging of timber and the carrying of stones, until noon or afternoon, with relatively short breaks. Regular labor details did not usually work on Sundays and the Detail Leaders were off. The Block Leaders assigned to supervise Sunday work took their revenge for the loss of their own leisure by inflicting particular atrocities on the prisoners.

Nevertheless, there was a niggling residue of leisure time, used for many forms of recreation. If the weather was fair and if it was permitted—which was not the case in all the camps and at all times—one might take a "walk." The memory of camp life floods back over me, as I write down that word, making it seem inordinately absurd. Yes, one walked, alone or with a friend, between the barracks, in the mud, always wary of SS noncoms who might suddenly appear on the scene, jostled by hurrying fellow prisoners, coarsely shunted aside by some mess carrier with a "Look out, stupid!"

Or of a Sunday afternoon one might lie down in the sun—*if* there was any sunshine, which was rare in the inhospitable situated concentration camps; *if* there was still an unoccupied spot to be found; *if* there was really no chore that had to be done . . . *if* . . . *if* . . .

Until 1941 there was still something like a stand of timber inside the Buchenwald compound, a grove where one could lie on the slope (*if* . . .), look out over the Thuringian countryside through the barbed wire between the watchtowers. Far, far in the distance were the hazy outlines of the Harz Mountains, with the Kyffhäuser peak showing on clear days. A farmer might stalk across the field, behind a plow and a team of horses. Further on lay a village with a church spire, blue smoke curling up among the roofs.

Out there—yes, out there lived the German people. Ho hum.

And then things would happen.

In 1939 an SS man answering to the fine name of Kraut-wurst happened into the grove. He became incensed that so many prisoners were lying about there in their leisure time. He reported seventy of them—most of them were "guilty" of not having "beat it" in time. For several Sunday afternoons in succession they had to carry manure for the gardening detail.

Curiously enough, there actually were athletic activities in camp. There were young men who professed to have surplus energy—and some of them, assigned to the right kind of detail, did have it. They managed to obtain permission from the SS to play soccer! The SS seems to have looked on this as a fine advertisement for camp conditions and prisoner morale. Most of the teams appeared on the field in spic-and-span uniforms, even with spiked shoes. Where did this equipment come from? These are secrets of camp corruption.

Until every available spot of ground in the compound was pre-empted for barracks, handball and volleyball were played as well as soccer. The prisoners even introduced boxing! It sounds like lunacy, but it is true. There were strapping bully boys in the camps who were quite willing to exhibit their punching prowess. And the feeble wrecks, the emaciated star-velings, half dead on their unsteady legs, gleefully came to watch the fun. There are inscrutable depths to human nature.

In the summer of 1945 Himmler issued a "Reich Directive" to the effect that brothels, chastely designated as "Special Buildings," were to be established in the concentration camps. Eighteen to twenty-four girls were shipped from the women's concentration camp at Ravensbrück to each camp where a brothel was established. Each group was supervised by two women noncoms of the SS, who frequently behaved like camp followers themselves. The girls were all volun-teers—they were promised that they would be discharged in six months. Their case histories usually listed past diseases that did not indicate a particularly stable mode of life before admission to the concentration camp. Apart from a very few exceptions, they were resigned to their fate with rather little restraint.

For men without "pull," the duration of a visit to the brothel was twenty minutes. Every patron had to undergo prior medical examination in the prisoner hospital, and sub-sequently had to take prophylactic treatment.

The purpose pursued by the SS was the corruption of political prisoners, who were given precedence. They were to be watched and distracted from political activity. The camp grapevine had passed along instructions that the brothel was not to be patronized, not merely for the reasons stated, but also for social considerations. It was regarded as shameful that wives and mothers sent money they could ill afford, only to have the prisoners pay out two marks admission to the brothel. But at the very outset camp headquarters had com-pelled the Senior Camp Inmate at Buchenwald to visit the building. The least that could have happened to him if he had refused would have been his removal from office, which might have created much trouble in camp. He yielded, after holding out for two days, and never went back a second time. By and large, all political prisoners hewed to this line, so that the objective of the SS was foiled.

The brothel brought enough corruption into the camp as it was, notably a strong inducement to parcel thievery. It was not so much "love" that was responsible for the gifts to the women in the brothel. It was the desire to gain admission outside of regular hours and to stay longer than the prescribed period of twenty minutes. Men with good sources of supply, strapping Prisoner Foremen with lingerie, brassieres, shoes and the like, were able to spend hours in this form of "recreation" when they wished. Among the thousands of pitiful wraiths forever hovering on the borderline between life and death, there were still plenty of these braggarts, provocatively regaling their fellows with tales of their prowess the previous night. There were others too who drained their last physical reserves at the brothel. Nor was the place scorned by the SS officers, who could often be found there at advanced hours of the night.

It was into this environment that Princess Mafalda, daughter of the King and Queen of Italy, was brought, when the isolation barracks for prominent prisoners at Buchenwald burned to the ground as a result of the air raid of August 24, 1944. The Princess herself was seriously wounded in the arm. Dr. Schiedlausky, Camp Medical Officer, insisted on performing the amputation himself, but his patient died of loss of blood. Her naked body, together with those of the men who had died that day, was dumped into the crematory, where the prisoner in charge, Father Joseph Thyl, dug it out of the heap, covered it up, and arranged for speedy cremation. He cut off a lock of the Princess's hair, which was smuggled out of camp and kept in Jena, until it could be sent to her Hessian relatives.

As already mentioned, there was a camp band. In Buchenwald it had been formed by Rödl's command late in 1938. At first it was the Gypsies with their guitars and harmonicas who produced a somewhat feeble brand of music. Later a trombone was added, and still later a drum and a trumpet. The prisoners had to pay for the instruments themselves. Members of the band worked by day in the lumberyard or the carpenter shop, rehearsing only after hours.

It was ghastly to watch and hear the Gypsies strike up their merry marches while exhausted prisoners carried their dead and dying comrades into camp; or to listen to the music accompanying the whippings of the prisoners. But then, I remember New Year's Eve of 1939, a night ringing with frost. Hungry and chilled to the marrow, I was walking between the first and second row of barracks below the roll-call area. It was just before taps and the camp streets were deserted. The utter stillness was caught up in a strange sense of enchantment. Ice flowered on the barracks windows, rime dusted the roofs, and the snow crunched underfoot. The night was clear, and even sorrow and terror seemed to have stiffened into frost.

Suddenly the sound of a Gypsy violin drifted out from one of the barracks, far off, as though from happier times and climes—tunes from the Hungarian steppe, melodies from Vienna and Budapest, songs from home. . . .

In 1940 Officer-in-Charge Florstedt ordered a regulation brass band to be formed. The SS Main Office was to finance the instruments. But when the instruments arrived, the SS officer found a simpler solution, "The Jews shall pay for the music!" This was done. In addition, twelve of the new instruments were immediately requisitioned for the SS band.

Members of the prisoner band were henceforth relieved of heavy labor and were able to have regular rehearsals. Their practice room, however, was a favorite hangout for bored Block Leaders who were in the habit of ordering the band to play one popular tune after another. The band was so overworked that even in this relatively light detail six prisoners had to drop out on account of weak lungs and tuberculosis. One died of tuberculosis of the larynx.

When the camp was inspected by visitors from the outside, the band regularly had to serve up sprightly tunes to enhance the show that was put on. In 1941 the band was decked out in gorgeous uniforms of the Royal Yugoslav Guard, part of SS war booty. In these resplendent trappings and with their ordinary camp insignia, the band henceforth looked like nothing so much as a group of circus ringmasters. On Sundays the band would occasionally play for the prisoners in the barracks, singly or in groups, or there might be a concert in the roll-call area.

The irrepressible human urge for life and self-expression even produced string quartets in camp. These performed many a concert on a high artistic level. This institution took a long time to develop at Buchenwald. In the winter of 1939-40 a Jewish Senior Block Inmate had given permission for the formation of a quartet and for prisoner concerts. He not only lost his job but his life.

There was radio in camp as well. The Block Leaders on duty in the gatehouse could plug the public-address system into the German broadcast network any time it pleased them, thus bringing the official programs to the prisoners. In some camps this was done regularly after hours, in others it never happened. New camps—the number of which steadily grew, especially during the war—were not equipped with radio facilities at all. The programs were generally musical, since the SS men disliked lectures of every kind, and thus the prisoners were usually and happily spared the propaganda flood that poured from the Goebbels machine. Often the programs were quite welcome, but they could also become a serious annoyance for many prisoners, especially the elder men, for the Block Leaders might not turn off the music until eleven or twelve o'clock at night, eating into the few precious hours of sleep.

From six to seven o'clock on Sunday afternoons the symphony concerts of the central German transmitter could be heard. They represented pleasure and relaxation of a high degree, impaired only by the inevitable noise and bustle in the barracks—the clop-clop of wooden soles, the clatter of mess gear, and the like. Even today, thinking back to these concerts, I can never forget the tens of thousands of victims who were gassed and tortured in so many camps during the very time that the music was on the air.

In May 1941, Buchenwald began to enjoy a unique form of relaxation—motion pictures. The Buchenwald movie theater was the first in a German concentration camp, and it seems to have remained the only one. Permission to establish it was wheedled from the SS by the Prisoner Foreman of the photo section who dwelt on the enormous profits to be made from exhibiting, at thirty pfennigs a head, ancient, worn-out films costing but thirty-five marks apiece. SS morale had already begun to disintegrate. Corruption and avarice had long got the better of any rational policies. During the very first six months of operation the camp movie theater produced a net income of twenty-three thousand marks for the headquarters fund, to be squandered on drink and revelry. Admission was later reduced to twenty pfennigs, but even so the growing number of inmates kept the business remunerative. The procurement of films from the UFA Company in Berlin was not always an easy matter. SS men had to be bribed and every stratagem had to be employed to keep on sending couriers to the capital. Both entertainment and documentary films were offered, weekly or biweekly, with longer interruptions.

Many prisoners drew strength from the few hours of illusion given them by the movies; others, faced with the ever present misery in camp, could never bring themselves to attend, especially since the theater was used also as a place of punishment. The fact that it was so used sprang from no particular sadistic streak on the part of the SS: the hall merely happened to be suitable and convenient—spacious and gloomy, the ideal place for the whipping rack, which was carried out to the roll-call area only when a special show was put on. The movie theater also provided storage space for the gallows and the posts, inserted in special holes, on which prisoners were strung up. It was a ghastly sensation to sit before the flickering screen of an evening and to realize that only a few hours ago in this same place comrades had been brutally beaten and tortured. The SS could not have been impervious to this effect, even though it was not premeditated.

Some of the camp inmates used their leisure time for reading. Newspapers and books were available in the camps. The chief Nazi newspaper, the *Völkischer Beobachter*, was permitted, as well as the regional Nazi sheets, newspapers from the prisoners' home communities and a few illustrated magazines. Here and there prison libraries were established. In starting such libraries prisoners were often permitted to have books sent from home, or they had to make appropriate financial contributions, with which headquarters then bought Nazi books. Several tens of thousands of marks were collected for this purpose in Buchenwald though a total of only 1,009 books was actually purchased. From its own resources the SS contributed 264 volumes, including 60 copies each of Hitler's *Mein Kampf* and Alfred Rosenberg's *Myth of the Twentieth*

Century. These books always stood on the shelves unread, in mint condition.

When the war broke out all books in languages spoken by nations at war with Germany were supposed to be destroyed. Representations were made that these books were of a technical character—which was by no means the case—and permission was granted merely to withdraw them from circulation. Within a few weeks they were again made available to interested prisoners.

Some of the books in the libraries were of great value and interest. In the winter of 1942–43 a succession of bread thefts in Barracks 42 at Buchenwald made it necessary to establish a nightwatch. For months on end I volunteered for this duty, taking the shift from three to six o'clock in the morning. It meant sitting alone in the day room, while the snores of the comrades came from the other end. For once I was free of the ineluctable companionship that usually shackled and stifled every individual activity. What an experience it was to sit quietly by a shaded lamp, delving into the pages of Plato's *Dialogues*, Galsworthy's *Swan Song*, or the works of Heine, Klabund, Mehring! Heine? Klabund? Mehring? Yes, they could be read illegally in camp. They were among books retrieved from the nation-wide wastepaper collections. The Nazis impounded many libraries of "enemies of the state," and turned them over to these collections, part of which found its way into the camps as toilet paper. The prisoners carefully retrieved what was of value. The bales might contain the "Pandects" of Justinian, famous law books, the Bible in new editions and old. Sometimes it was even possible to conduct salvage right in the privies, though the collector had to provide an immediate substitute, to quell any incipient revolt from his fellows. This was not easy, for paper was extremely scarce.

Only under the exceptional circumstances described was it ever possible to be alone in camp. Ordinarily it was impossible. Never to be alone—this is a hardship not easily appreciated. Yet this most important form of recreation was barred. Possibly it was just as well for many thousands. It kept them from brooding, from lapsing into melancholy. But for the few the utter lack of privacy made matters only worse.

Chapter Thirteen

SANITATION AND HEALTH

General sanitation in the concentration camps, as will be readily believed, was in the worst possible state, largely owing to the chronic water shortage in most of the camps. In the final war years, shipments of filthy and vermin-infested prisoners arrived from all sides. Thorough-going disinfestation therefore became an iron necessity. It was prisoner initiative rather than the SS that laboriously procured the necessary disinfectants and gradually saw to it that a major disaster was avoided. Buchenwald had its own Barracks Sanitation Wardens who twice a week conducted a rigid inspection for vermin. This helped a great deal in sparing the camp the scourge of epidemics which ravaged other camps, especially in the east, where there was no such systematic control.

From 1939 on, all Buchenwald inmates were immunized against typhoid fever and dysentery. There were similar programs at Dachau and Sachsenhausen. From 1943 on, certain French age groups were immunized against scarlet fever, to which they were particularly susceptible. From 1944 on, the entire staff of prisoner functionaries was immunized with the typhus vaccine produced right in camp.

141

Some of the Camp Medical Officers aided in these measures. The SS naturally feared that any outbreak of contagious disease might spread to its own ranks. Typhoid fever, typhus and other diseases reaped a toll of hundreds in the camps. The existing conditions made it impossible to prevent epidemic outbreaks altogether. The prisoners did as much as they could, in simple self-protection. But most of the camps were so infested with staphylococci that certain skin and eye afflictions, cellulitis, stubborn abscesses, etc., could scarcely be checked, let alone rooted out. The general state of malnutrition greatly contributed to the susceptibility of the prisoners to disease. Cases of edema and collapse caused by starvation were common.

Sanitary measures, like everything else, were exploited by the SS as pretexts for unspeakable brutalities and sadistic torture. The following case was reported by Heinrich Orb, with all the names involved. It is an extreme case, but no experienced camp inmates will be surprised by it.

In the summer of 1935, Koch, even then an SS Lieutenant-Colonel, was Commandant of the Columbia House concentration camp in Berlin. A group of Franciscan monks had been admitted, supposedly as foreign-exchange violators. To serve his notions of a practical joke, Koch permitted the monks to retain their brown cassocks and invented the tale that they were infested with crab lice. The monks were assembled and a SS physician issued them a salve. They were compelled to lift up their cassocks and let down their trousers, while a shrieking horde of SS bullies recited obscene jokes, read aloud from pornographic books and held up lewd pictures. The rest of the scene afforded ample opportunity for a hail of blows and kicks and other vile abuse.

Without mention of such excesses any description of sanitary conditions in the concentration camps is likely to leave a false impression. The hell of the concentration camps perverted even simple sanitary measures, and the fearful actuality must by fully known in appraising the true significance of dry statistics and regulations. To become sick in a concentration camp meant to be doomed. And thousands of prisoners, torn from their familiar lives, hurled suddenly into this wretched environment with all its terror, did fall sick. Patients were profoundly affected not only by the external difficulties that faced them, but by a sense of having become altogether useless and superfluous. The fate awaiting the sick prisoner was common knowledge. His death sentence could be pronounced at any moment, chiefly by the very figure to whom the sick the world over look for relief—the physician. "There are no sick men in my camp," Koch used to say. "They are either well or dead!" Most of the SS medical officers acted on this precept.

The prisoner hospital was called the *Revier*. It was shunned like the plague by all but those very few prisoners who were thoroughly familiar with its workings and maintained good personal connections with the staff.

Sick call was a hazardous business in many of the camps. The Buchenwald hospital, for example, from 1938 on, was located in the wooded grove remaining inside the compound. If the patient succeeded in getting time off from his detail, in the first place, he had to pick his way through knee-deep mud, over fallen trees and snags, to get to the infirmary. The single gravel path was reserved for the SS physicians and staff. Any prisoner caught using it was kicked off. Once arrived, the prisoners had to stand in long lines out in the open, exposed to every weather, their shoes nevertheless required to be immaculate. It was simply not possible to treat all the sick, and there were always prisoners among the waiting who were merely trying to shirk work, for wholly understandable reasons. A robust hospital guard therefore proceeded with the first radical weeding-out process.

In the course of the forenoon, the SS Medical Officer might condescend to put in his appearance. He was usually vociferous about how he despised the "dirty" business of prisoner practice. He would conduct his own winnowing process, dealing out slaps and kicks right and left. Those who had neither voluntarily departed nor been chased away were admitted as indubitably sick.

Before entering the building, prisoners had to remove their shoes. Shoes were often enough stolen or mixed up, another disaster. Some of the patients then appeared before the prisoner medical staff; the remaining exceptional cases were presented to the SS physician for examination. Patients had to strip in the unheated hallways. There they had to wait, naked, until their turn came. It took a hardened constitution to face this preliminary treatment, which could readily add pneumonia to what might have been a minor ailment.

Out-patient treatment itself was conducted by prisoner personnel. Within the existing limitations, everything possible was done, though often enough by the rough-and-ready maxim "Above the belly button: aspirin; below: castor oil." There were creditable exceptions, however, in every camp.

Dental treatment varied greatly from camp to camp. Generally speaking, it came into operation only at a late date—some camps never had it at all. The hospital personnel usually lacked all dental knowledge and treated the prisoners according to their lights. Aching teeth were simply pulled—if they were found! Often enough sound teeth were extracted. It was common for diseased teeth to be broken off, so that the impacted roots might have to be pulled years later.

The Dachau concentration camp got a dental clinic of its own at an early date. In Buchenwald such a clinic was established in June 1939, with the latest equipment but no trained personnel. The first SS "dentist" there was SS Technical Sergeant Coldewey who had never practiced before and who conducted his first experiments on the prisoners. His imcompetence was matched only by his sadism. Patients had to do fatigue drill before treatment! Scarcely one of his extractions succeeded, making extensive operations necessary at a later date. Whenever he discovered a gold tooth, he would extract it at once, remarking that the tooth could not be saved. There was no chance to protest, of course. A regulation was posted at the entrance to the dental clinic, making it an offense to refuse to obey the instructions of the SS dentist.

On orders from Himmler, dated September 23, 1940, and December 23, 1942, SS dentists had to remove gold teeth from the bodies of dead prisoners. They were also empowered to extract from the living dental gold "incapable of repair." Available monthly reports of the Buchenwald Camp Medical Officer show that from six to seventeen ounces of gold a month were obtained there alone from this source. Among other things, Commandant Koch had a collegiate "beer-fob" for his watch chain made from this gold. In a symbolic gesture, the birth dates of his children were engraved on it.

Prisoners plundered in this way had a ridiculously small

amount credited to their accounts. Dental gold from the dead was carefully assembled, with full data on the name, origin and number of the deceased, and sent to Berlin headquarters with a weight certificate. There it was melted down into new dental gold. The ghouls plied their trade in the most precise and bureaucratic way.

Prisoner dentists and dental aids gradually found their way into the clinics, and in the course of the years matters reached a point where not only were prisoners no longer treated by SS men, but SS men were actually treated by prisoner dentists. Such prisoner specialists were even sent around from camp to camp. They did much valuable illegal work—dentures and bridges for prisoners whose teeth the SS had knocked out or who had lost them in the general low state of health.

Ward treatment in the prisoner hospital always presented serious problems. There were never enough beds, and only the worst cases could be admitted. The main criterion was temperature. Only the Camp Medical Officers had authority to admit patients to the hospital. But since they were often unavailable or took no interest, this authority in some camps gradually slipped into the hands of the Hospital Capo (chief of the prisoner detail).

At the Auschwitz concentration camp, admission to the wards took place in the following fashion: The patients reported to the out-patients' clinic at night and were hurriedly examined by a prisoner physician. If they were in very poor condition, they were admitted at once and placed in a so-called reception ward. The others were sent away. In the reception ward the patients lay side by side without distinction—typhus, dysentery, pneumonia, fractured leg—it did not matter. Usually some of them died before they could be presented to the SS physician.

The next morning the reception-ward cases and those patients who had been sent away, although admitted in principle, returned to the out-patients' clinic, where they had to wait naked on the stone floor—arranged by nationality rather than symptoms!—until His Honor, the Camp Medical Officer, deigned to put in an appearance. When he arrived at last, each patient had to present his Sick Card. The SS man would then make his selection: right, left, right, left. One side was admitted to the hospital, the other immediately given fatal injections. No sooner was this ceremony over, than the cards of the killed were sent to the orderly room with the notation: "Scratch!"

Small wonder that the right to admit patients to a ward was a matter of extreme importance to the Hospital Capos.

Work in all the camp hospitals was difficult, and involved, above all, much responsibility. Initially hospital equipment everywhere was more than primitive, and for years it continued to be inadequate. There was a particular shortage of drugs. Wherever possible these were pilfered from the SS hospitals or straight from the crates at the SS medical depots. Only gradually could surgery be practiced—in Buchenwald not until 1939.

The SS medical staff was headed by the Chief Medical Officer of the *Waffen SS* units assigned to the camp. The Camp Medical Officer was his subordinate. Occasionally the two functions were combined. The *Waffen SS* medical officer was independent of camp headquarters, which occasionally opened the door to influence and intervention of vast significance, and also made possible co-operation between the prisoners detailed to the SS hospital and those working in the prisoner hospital. When necessary, a Second and Third Camp Medical Officer might be assigned, as well as several grades of SS noncommissioned medical personnel. In every camp a few of these noncoms achieved notoriety.

A few words on the quality of the Camp Medical Officers are in order, since their names will be mentioned time and again. Their activities were seldom limited to a single camp. They were frequently shifted or were placed in charge of several subsidiary camps. This is true, for example, of SS Lieutenant-Colonel Kirchert, SS Major Ding (who later took the name Schuler), SS Second Lieutenant Wagner, SS First Lieutenant Eysele, SS Captain Hoven,[1] SS Captain Plaza, SS Captain Schiedlausky. They differed greatly in character and professional qualifications. Generally speaking, they were more adept at feathering their own nests than at healing, and usually their skill lay in killing rather than in saving. There were a very few who could not stomach the situation and

[1] Hoven was hanged in 1948.—*Tr.*

requested a transfer from camp duty as soon as possible. SS Captain Hofer volunteered for front-line duty, even when appointed only Deputy Camp Medical Officer.

Because of their incompetence, the Medical Officers often made use of prisoner aides, recalling the employment of Greek slave scholars by Roman upstarts in ancient times.

Hoven, for example, had his doctor's thesis on the treatment of silicosis written by two prisoners, Wegerer and Sitte. Three days before the examination, he memorized the paper and then took his doctor's degree with distinction at Freiburg University. During the last two years I spent in Building 50 as medical clerk, Dr. Ciepielowski and I, in solemn contempt for Nazi science, wrote half a dozen medical papers on typhus which Dr. Ding-Schuler published under his name in the *Journal for Infectious Diseases*, the *Journal of Hygiene*, and other scientific publications. Dr. Ding-Schuler's own contributions consisted chiefly of the insertion of statistical material which was generally invented from beginning to end. In one instance—a contribution entitled "Droplet Infection in Typhus?"—he claimed to have tested ten thousand smears without having found any *Rickettsia Prowazeki*. Not a single slide had been prepared, let alone tested!

In the first years the prisoner medical detail, too, consisted of wholly unskilled men. In the course of time, however, it acquired great practical experience. The first Buchenwald Hospital Capo had been a printer in civilian life. His successor, Walter Kramer, had been a lathe hand. Krämer was a powerful, courageous personality. He was a tireless and gifted organizer. In the course of time he acquired high skill in the treatment of wounds and in surgery.

In every camp the job of Hospital Capo was associated with unusual influence on camp conditions as a whole. The prisoners, therefore, never filled it with an experienced medical man, even when that would have been possible. They always chose someone who was clearly a representative of the ruling prisoner class in camp. A medical man in the leading prisoner function in the hospital would have inevitable precipitated a crisis. He would simply not have been equal to the far-flung network of intrigue that often had a fatal outcome.

In some camps prisoner physicians were admitted to the

hospital staff. By 1945 there were some seventy prisoner physicians of every nationality among the 280 male nurses at Buchenwald. Late in 1944 special Barracks Physicians were actually installed, the result of some careful maneuvering by the prisoner administration.

The prisoner hospital was not merely the place where the sick were ostensibly cared for and cured. It was also an experiment station for the SS medical officers. These experiments are dealt with in the next chapter, merely touched on here. Dr. Neumann of the Institute of Hygiene of the Waffen SS, for example, excised sections of liver from the healthy body. All of his victims died in agony. Worst among this type of SS physicians was undoubtedly Dr. Eysele. His accomplishments between 1940 and 1943 probably outdid any of the depravities committed by other SS physicians. He too, in order to "complete his training," engaged in human vivisection, subsequently killing his victims. He would abduct them indiscriminately from the camp streets, take them to the out-patients' clinic, and inject them with apomorphine to gloat over the emetic effect. He performed operations and amputations without the slightest reason. He never used anesthesia. One of the ve: y few surviving witnesses is the Netherlands Jew, Max Nebig, whom Eysele used as a guinea pig to perform a stomach resection.

Deliberate killing of patients in the hospitals on the part of the SS was even more widespread than experimentation. There were, of course, concentration camps, such as Auschwitz, where this was done systematically. When the number of patients exceeded a certain level, the syringe was resorted to. The patient would be held down by two men and would receive an injection of ten cc. carbolic acid directly into the heart.

The SS was very liberal in its diagnosis of "disease" that in its opinion forfeited a prisoner's life. In Auschwitz it often happened that newcomers, questioned as to their health, innocently reported some ailment in hopes of drawing assignment to a soft detail. By and by they would be ordered to report to the hospital, where they were poisoned.

Groups of death victims were chosen even from among prisoners still fully capable of work. At evening roll call the order would come: "Roll up your trouser legs!" A medical

noncom or even a mere Block Leader would pass down the
rows and pick out anyone with swollen legs. These "patients"
were ordered to step forward—"Column right, march!"—to
the hospital. There they were taken straight to the morgue. At
the entrance stood another medical noncom with a syringe. As
many as a hundred prisoners might be dispatched in this
fashion in a single night. At Auschwitz it was Sergeant Klähr,
a figure of dread, who had hundreds of prisoners on his conscience.

On one occasion, at Buchenwald, Dr. Hoven had finished
off a whole row of prisoners with injections of sodium evipan.
He strolled from the operating room, a cigarette in his hand,
merrily whistling "The End of a Perfect Day."

He plied his trade for about a year and a half and there were
weeks when, with the complicity of Dr. Plaza, his assistant
and later Camp Medical Officer in Dachau, Nordhausen and
Ohrdruf, he dispatched dozens of prisoners in the manner
described. Yet at the same time he did a great deal for the
camp as a whole and for individual prisoners.

Prisoners slated for "liquidation" were placed in a special
hospital room—for some time Room 7. It held ten beds and
their occupants never knew what fate awaited them. The room
had barred windows and most of the patients thought they
were under some form of detention. When the order came to
"transfer" them, they were taken to the operating room.
They invariably landed in the morgue. Only in very rare instances did the victims include incurable cases. Room 7 was
often cleared and restocked three or four times a week in this
fashion.

But sixty-year-old Master Sergeant Wilhelm, chief medical
noncom, nicknamed "Old Bill" in the hospital, could also
adopt other methods. On one occasion a nurse was taking a
patient to the bathroom. Wilhelm saw them and roared at the
nurse: "What's the idea, bathing a wreck like that? We'll
make soap of him!" He noted down the patient's serial
number. That night the patient was promptly "transferred."

Under the conditions described no prisoner in his right
mind would have ever voluntarily entered the hospital
buildings, had he known what went on. But alas, most of the
prisoners did not know what was actually happening. This
total ignorance was one of the ghastliest facts in the con-

centration camps. Tens of thousands of newcomers had not a glimmering of what went on, nor did the old-timers who knew enlighten them. The newcomers were much too naïve and inexperienced. As evidenced by many tragic examples, they would merely have repeated the tale, boasting with the name of their informants to buttress it. That meant instant retribution.

There were only four ways of escaping danger. The first was not to fall ill; the second was to work for the underground, to represent a political asset in the fight against the SS; the third was to maintain good connections with the right people in camp; and the fourth was to be assigned to the hospital detail. None of these ways offered any guarantee that the prisoner would be spared, and all four together might not suffice to save him. But immunity increased in proportion to these prerequisites.

In every concentration camp where the political prisoners attained any degree of ascendancy, they turned the prisoner hospital, scene of fearful SS horrors that it was, into a rescue station for countless prisoners. Not only were patients actually cured wherever possible; healthy prisoners, in danger of being killed or shipped to a death camp, were smuggled on the sick list to put them beyond the clutches of the SS. In special cases, where there was no other way out, men in danger were nominally permitted to "die," living on under the names of prisoners who had actually died. Others were simply marked "sick" or "incapable of travel" whenever the Political Department sought to include them in a death shipment—until they were brought to safety by some means or other.

This, of course, meant evasion of control by the SS physicians, a matter often not too difficult, since the zeal of the Camp Medical Officers usually extended only to killing. Otherwise they were conspicuous by their absence. The tuberculosis wards in particular were suitable hiding places for concealing prisoners for months, sometimes years. The SS men stood in holy terror of infection.

A whole series of old-time inmates were saved in this way. On three occasions I myself was kept from being shipped to Auschwitz for liquidation only by submerging in the TB ward. In this ward, conversely, patients had to watch out, lest they were slated for liquidation precisely because they were there.

It was a matter of disappearing in time in the event of an SS visit. In the camp jargon this was called "being on the wire."

The so-called convalescent clinic was likewise exploited by the prisoners on their own behalf. Not every camp had such an institution. Where it existed, it was counted as a special labor detail, though assignment to it was in the hands of the hospital. It was meant for patients whose ailments were not serious enough for ward treatment, and for convalescents discharged from the wards. The Camp Medical Officers tried to keep down the number of these patients as much as possible.

A "convalescent slip" authorized a prisoner to spend several days in the barracks or in a special hospital wing. In the early years, "convalescence" frequently meant that the patients had to carry wood in any weather. Later the convalescent detail was also assigned to carrying stones, bales of prisoner clothing, and soil for the gardening detail!

In January 1942, eighty-two of the 7,964 Buchenwald inmates were assigned to the convalescent clinic. In March 1945, with some 30,000 of a total of 82,400 prisoners actually in the base camp, there were 1,542 convalescents—roughly five per cent, as against slightly more than one per cent three years earlier.

Here too a persistent campaign against the SS had resulted in many gains for the prisoners. By way of the convalescent clinic many old camp inmates were able to enjoy a kind of annual vacation. There was always the danger of a sudden check, of course. It happened at times that substitutes from the wards had to "stand in" for up to twenty-five per cent of the "convalescents," who were not sick at all. As soon as the prisoner grapevine had announced the impending inspection, the nurses would drag out the genuine patients, who had no idea of what was going on and were naturally in great fear. They simply stood in line for the required half hour, while the pseudo-convalescents "vamoosed." Camp conditions being what they were, even convalescence was not available to every prisoner who needed it. As a rule it could not be brought off without "pull."

Chapter Fourteen

SCIENTIFIC EXPERIMENTS

Among the most dreaded institutions in the large camps were the isolation wards for so-called scientific experiments. Here human vivisection, practiced without rhyme or reason in the camp hospitals generally, was put on a systematic and pseudo-scientific basis. Not that these programs were confined to the isolation wards. The camp hospitals and certain outside installations often participated.

The experiments conducted by the SS directly, or by German Air Force scientists and physicians under SS tutelage, were initiated by various central agencies. Not one of them was undertaken without the knowledge and express authorization of Himmler. Some of them he ordered himself, at the suggestion of certain official, semi-official, or private interests, through the Experimental Department V at Leipzig, which developed much initiative in these fields, from the testing of domestic and exotic plant poisons to the development of chemical protectants against burns and the use of artificial glands. Other agencies through which Himmler operated were the Institute of Hygiene of the *Waffen SS* in Berlin and even the SS Main Economic and Administrative Office.

Most of the experiments, and by far the worst, were conducted at Dachau, Buchenwald, Sachsenhausen, Natzweiler, Ravensbrück and Auschwitz. The co-operating agencies included not only the German armed services, but also great industrial corporations like I. G. Farben and the Behring Works, as well as German scientific institutes and individual scientists. Co-operation with the SS might be quite open, or it might be under some form of camouflage. When the participants learned the naked truth—namely, that the experiments were to be conducted on concentration-camp prisoners, they were officially advised that the experimental human subjects were arch criminals under sentence of death, and had been especially designated for the purpose by Himmler himself.

I myself, for more than two years, from March 1943 to April 1945, served as a so-called Ward Clerk at Buchenwald, and during this period the secret lists of prisoners selected for these experiments passed through my hands. I know of no single case in which one of these human guinea pigs had been previously sentenced to death by a court of law. I am reliably informed that the situation was no different in the other camps. The official agencies that participated, as well as the individuals, some of them men of standing, never seriously inquired whether the SS was telling the truth or not. In actual practice the human subjects were for years picked by camp headquarters by methods now familiar. They were generally convicts and homosexuals, with a sprinkling of political prisoners of all nationalities.

After 1944, when the SS in the concentration camps had already reached such a stage of disintegration that it rejected full responsibility for such undertakings, the selection of human experimental subjects was frequently left to the Reich Criminal Police Office in Berlin and its chief, SS Major-General Nebe, already mentioned.[1]

---

[1] A number of important post-war publications, especially *To the Bitter End* by H. G. Gisevius, and *Germany's Underground* by Allen Dulles, as well as testimony in the great Nuremberg trials, have described Nebe as one of the most active supporters of the anti-Nazi opposition. He was, indeed, executed after July 20, 1944. In the first German edition of this book, I called him "the least-known and most pitiless functionary of the SS machine." I said that "he later turned opportunist, trying to get off the doomed Nazi bus . . . by joining the conspiracy of July 20, 1944." So far as the man's character and motives are

It is impossible, within the scope of this book, to give a full report on all the human experiments conducted in the concentration camps. Such documented report would require another full-size book.[1] I can convey no more than a barely adequate picture of the chief experiments, merely mentioning a few of the others.

In the late fall of 1941 the Institute of Hygiene of the *Waffen SS* in Berlin opened a clinical laboratory for its "Division for Typhus and Virus Research" at Buchenwald. In 1942 this was transferred to Isolation Ward 46, surrounded by double barbed wire.

The installation was established by Dr. Joachim Mrugowsky, then an SS colonel, after consultation with Lieutenant-General Handloser,[2] German Army Medical In-

---

concerned, I now correct this judgment. Almost from the outset, Nebe had serious qualms of conscience. Especially in the later years he sought time and again, by means of flight or suicide, to extricate himself from the foul and murderous entanglements in which he had become enmeshed. His friends among the Nazi and anti-Nazi opposition always prevailed on him to remain and keep the important resources at his disposal available to them. Thus he played his dual role down to the bitter end at the hands of the executioner. Contrary to the views of many of his friends, I believe that this policy was *inadmissible*. In my own case, I successfully exploited my influence over SS Major Ding-Schuler, chief of the Buchenwald experiment station, time and again to the end of *preventing* important opposition actions from being covered by the *murder* of third persons. No matter how liberally the right of active self-defense against the immediate enemy is interpreted, the life of innocent persons puts an insurmountable limit to our actions. Nebe cannot be exculpated from having taken over command of a special liquidation unit in the east—even though he may have evaded some of its more frightful assignments—nor from having designated human experimental subjects for the concentration-camp laboratories. Such activities cannot be justified by simultaneous opposition work, nor by the avowed purpose of camouflaging such work, nor by the apparent impossibility of evading the consequences of earlier errors in any other way. I am today convinced, however, despite the light in which I came to see Nebe and his work, that he was by no means merely the pitiless SS functionary and opportunist whom I described in the first edition. His figure is invested with a certain aura of tragedy—insofar as it is possible to speak of tragedy in the case of any votary of so evil a cause. It was not by mere chance, after all, that a man like Nebe ascended to the rank of SS major-general and chief of the Reich Criminal Police Office.

[1] *Doctors of Infamy*, by Alexander Mitscherlich and Fred Mielke (New York: Henry Schuman, 1949).—*Tr.*

[2] Mrugowsky and Handloser were defendants in the so-called Nazi Medical Trial before an American Military Tribunal at Nuremberg in 1947. Both were convicted and hanged.—*Tr.*

spector; Reich Health Leader Conti, an SS major-general; the chief of the Reich Health Office, Professor Reiter; and the chief of the Robert Koch Institute in Berlin (Reich Institute for the Control of Contagious Diseases), Professor Gildemeister.

On December 29, 1941, a diary entry records the establishment of the clinic with the following unabashed comment: "Since animal experiments cannot provide adequate evaluation [of typhus serums], experiments must be conducted on men." SS Major Ding-Schuler was charged with the conduct of the experiments. By the end of 1944 there had been twenty-four series of experiments, the number of subjects in each ranging from four to forty, and even sixty—on one occasion there were 145 in a group. The tests concerned the efficacy of typhus serums of different origin: the egg-yolk-sac culture produced by the Behring Works after the process worked out by Cox, Gildemeister and Haagen; the Weigl serum, produced from the entrails of lice by the Institute for Typhus and Virus Research of the Army High Command at Cracow; the Durand-Giroud serum, prepared from rabbit lungs at the Pasteur Institute, Paris; a dog-lung serum by the process developed by Cantacuzino, Bucharest, and a Danish serum from mouse livers, both made available by Professor Rose,[1] chief of the Division for Tropical Medicine of the Robert Koch Institute, Berlin; and finally certain drugs, such as nitro-acridine and methylene-blue from I. G. Farben (Professor Lautenschläger[2]); rutenol from the same firm (a diary entry of April 14, 1944, reports that "SS Major Ding and detail at I. G. Farben, Höchst, for discussions with Professor Lautenschläger, Dr. Weber, and Dr. Fussgänger, concerning the experimental series on acridine granulate and rutenol in the Buchenwald concentration camp"[3]); and a drug

[1] Sentenced to life imprisonment in the Nazi Medical Trial.—*Tr.*

[2] Acquitted in the trial of I. G. Farben officials at Nuremberg.—*Tr.*

[3] Drs. Weber and Fussgänger, following publication of the first German edition of this book, explained to me that they had been deceived by the SS. They had been advised that the I. G. Farben drugs were to be administered to soldier-patients suffering from typhus in the hospitals of the SS divisions. When they were forced to conclude, in view of the suspicious circumstances, that the tests were being conducted at the Buchenwald concentration camp, they broke off all contact, in concurrence with their chief, Professor Lautenschläger.

named "persicol," produced by and tested for Professor Ruge, a naval surgeon then in Rumania.

All in all about 1,000 prisoners passed through Ward 46. Some of them had the good fortune to be used only in blood-bank tests, or in other experiments that, for one reason or another, stopped short of actual infection. Of the remainder of some 450 persons, 158 died, not counting groups of three and five who month after month were admitted solely as so-called carriers, i.e., who were infected with highly virulent fresh blood from typhus patients, in order to keep the germ strains alive. Virtually every one of these carriers died.

The scientific value of these tests was either nil or else of but insignificant proportions, because the method of infection bordered on lunacy. A rational approach would have called for a quantitative and qualitative determination of the threshold values of infection—those values coming closest to the situation in actual transmission by the louse (in European or so-called classical *typhus exanthematicus*), and barely sufficient to overcome or at least to modify prior immunization. But that was too much trouble for the gentlemen of the SS. Infection was attempted by subcutaneous and intramuscular injection, by scarification and by means of the vaccinating lancet. The virus strains furnished early in 1943 by the Robert Koch Institute, however, proved to be no longer virulent. Infection was then effected simply by injecting intravenously two cc. of highly virulent blood from a typhus patient. Naturally the effect smashed through all immunization measures, resulting disastrously in nearly every case. Scarcely had this method of infection been introduced, when mortality rose to above fifty per cent, not including the so-called controls, subjects who had not been immunized at all in order that the onset of the infection could be established. Almost all of these controls died.

This latter fact I can confirm, from my association with Dr. Ding-Schuler. I should like, however, to address a question to all scientists who were unwittingly caught up in human experiments or were drawn into them by the SS: Since when does the scientific or medical code of ethics permit the administration to sick soldiers, without their consent, of drugs heretofore tested only on animals? And were not Himmler and his whole SS gang in such disrepute with large segments of the German population that ordinarily no one would dream of having anything to do with them? Was not extreme caution on the part of every scientist indicated even in the most casual contact?

The quantity of injected blood was later reduced to one-tenth cc., but without forfeiting the deadly effect, since the virulence of the strain had meanwhile risen by transmission through human carriers. In but a single series of experiments was any noteworthy immunization effect observed. This was in the case of a serum produced right in Buchenwald. Of twenty subjects immunized not one died, and the course of the disease was much less severe than with subjects who had been immunized with the best serum heretofore available, the Weigl serum made from louse entrails. Of the twenty controls in this series, nineteen succumbed to the treacherous infection.

Not one of the luminaries of German medical science who were involved in these human experiments—or who, like Professor Gildemeister, actually witnessed the infection process at the concentration camp—seems ever to have taken the pains to evaluate their premises critically, to consider whether they were permissible at all, from a human and scientific point of view, and whether they should be entrusted to the SS in the concentration camps. These gentlemen accepted the finding without objection, simply credited and utilized the published reports that appeared especially in the *Journal for Hygiene and Infectious Diseases*. To my knowledge, only Professor Rose on one occasion, the Third Conference of Military Surgeons in Berlin, declared that the reported findings added nothing to the results obtained in animal experiments and therefore did not justify the use of human subjects; but that did not keep him, a year later, from suggesting similar tests with the Ipsen serum of the State Serum Institute in Copenhagen and actually having them conducted.

One wonders what Ministerial Councilor Christiansen of the Reich Ministry of Interior could have been thinking when he gave permission to the SS to test in the concentration camps a new drug of the rhodane series, "otrhomin," developed by Professor Lockemann of the Robert Koch Institute at Berlin.[1] As a result of this authorization, forty prisoners

---

[1] Professor Lockemann has declared on oath that he and his associates were responsible only for the scientific research that led to the development of "otrhomin"; that he gave Dr. Ding-Schuler, who was sent to him by the Reich Ministry of Interior, only technical data; and that he learned of the experiments subsequently conducted in the concentration camps only from the reports of the

—thirty of them immunized, with ten controls—were infected by being fed two cc. of a suffusion of typhus germ in a physiological table-salt solution, disguised in the form of potato salad. Evidently the Ministerial Councilor thought nothing of it. He merely read the fever charts and case histories sent regularly from Buchenwald to him and to the Chief Hygienist of the SS. The reports told him that seven cases had contracted the disease with light symptoms, twenty-three with moderately severe symptoms. Six were receiving out-patient treatment and four had failed to contract the disease altogether. There had been one death—Case No. So-and-So. Whether this was a former Reichstag deputy, a professional colleague of the Honorable Ministerial Councilor, a worker, or a poor wretch branded as a professional criminal; whether a mother, a wife, or children shed tears when the stereotyped letter of condolence from the SS Commandant reached them—could such questions be of interest to a medical man in the service of the Third Reich, a man who permitted men to be fed potato salad tainted with typhus germs?

Ward 46 at Buchenwald, by the way, was well equipped and a model of cleanliness. It served not merely for human experimentation but as an actual isolation ward for patients who had contracted typhus in camp by natural means, or who were admitted to the camp suffering from typhus. Insofar as such patients survived the dread disease at all, they were nursed back to health in the ward.

The responsible prisoner in charge of the ward was Arthur Dietzsch, who acquired his medical knowledge only by the experience there gained. Dietzsch was a veteran of more than twenty years in political detention. His was a hardened nature and, understandably, he was one of the most hated and dreaded figures in Buchenwald.

SS officers and noncoms stood in holy terror of typhus infection, which they believed could be contracted by mere contact, by means of the air, or by the coughing of patients. They never entered Ward 46. As a result, the SS medical officers

Ministry to the Robert Koch Institute. According to this sworn statement Professor Lockemann therefore was not the instigator of the experiments as was stated in the first German edition of this book on the basis of Dr. Ding-Schuler's notes and the SS files.

had their own way, especially Dr. Hoven who for months took the place of Dr. Ding-Schuler, frequently absent on official trips. The prisoners too exploited the situation, in collaboration with the Ward Capo, Dietzsch. On the one hand, the camp underground rid itself of persons working with the SS against the camp (or suspected of doing so, or simply fallen into disfavor!). On the other hand, important political prisoners in danger were protected from the SS via Ward 46, a matter sometimes very difficult and dangerous for Dietzsch, since his nurses and orderlies almost all wore the green triangle. These he held down with an iron hand. He never admitted prisoner physicians.

One of the most interesting and daring rescue attempts made by way of Ward 46 will be discussed further on in this book. To understand how it became possible, it is necessary to make brief mention of Ward or Barracks 50 at the Buchenwald concentration camp. This building too was assigned to the Division for Typhus and Virus Research, though its only link to Ward 46 was its common chief, Dr. Ding-Schuler. It was in Ward 50 that typhus serum was produced from mouse and rabbit livers, by the process of Professor Giroud of Paris. This laboratory was established in August 1943. The best available experts in camp were selected for the work, including physicians, bacteriologists, serologists, and chemists, notably Dr. Ludwig Fleck of Lemberg University, whom Dr. Ding-Schuler especially requisitioned from Auschwitz through the SS Main Economic and Administrative Office.

Shrewd manipulation among the prisoners at once contrived to exploit this assignment as a shelter for comrades of all nationalities who were in special danger. The SS dreaded Ward 50 just as much as it did Ward 46. From different motives, both SS Major Ding-Schuler and the prisoners fostered this taboo on the part of the SS—for example by posting warning signs on the barbed-wire fence surrounding the building. With the knowledge and approval of Dr. Ding-Schuler, Ward 50 gave refuge to such candidates for death as the Dutch physics professor Van Lingen, the Dutch physical-culture official Jan Robert, the Dutch architect Harry Pieck and other Dutchmen, the Polish physician Dr. Marian Ciepielowski (who was put in charge of production), Professor Balachowsky of the Pasteur Institute in Paris, the author of this book who had been an Austrian publicist, and seven Jewish comrades. Appropriate petitions to the Reich Main Security Office, always suggested, written and presented for signature by myself, enabled this crew to enjoy protection from threatening death shipments and other forms of imminent action.

The detail numbered sixty-five men, including twelve Russians. The valuable equipment, laboratory apparatus, microscopes, etc., came mostly from France, either as "booty," or "bought" from French firms, without payment.

The typhus strains (*Rickettsia Prowazeki*) were cultured by injecting guinea pigs with two cc. of blood from typhus patients in Ward 46. Officially two kinds of serum were produced: a standard serum for the combat troops; and a second quality, somewhat turgid in appearance, for use by the prisoners. Actually, and without knowledge of Dr. Ding-Schuler, the top-quality product, relatively limited in quantity, was reserved for prisoners in exposed positions. Considerable quantities of the second-quality product—which did no harm, nor any particular good—were made available to the SS.

In January 1942, at the behest of Professor Klaus Schilling. SS Captain Prachtl, later replaced by SS Captain Plöttner, began to select for malaria experiments Dachau prisoners in good health between the ages of twenty and forty-five. The first five men had to report to the hospital by March 1942. Subsequently there were twenty additional men each week.

The experiments were conducted in the following way: Anopheles mosquitoes, infected with malaria germs, were procured from the tropics, the Crimea and the Pontine swamps and used to infect the human subjects. One of the questions to be investigated was the relationship between human blood groups and malaria. The initial attack usually occurred three weeks after exposure. At this point the patient was again admitted to the hospital—he had had to continue working in the meantime. Fever chills occurred every two or three days—when the disease had reached a more advanced stage two or three times a day. The course of the disease was observed with all the familiar complications—heart trouble, jaundice, severe diarrhea and pneumonia. I have no information in this instance as to what drugs were tested, what

German firms furnished them, and whether any therapeutic success was achieved with them. At any rate, of two hundred human experimental subjects, seventeen died during the early test series. Later, when the initial health examinations and age limitations were dropped, mortality rose considerably. Serious losses were sustained by the Polish clerics at Dachau, who were used for these experiments.

In 1942 Dr. Grawitz, so-called Reich Physician of the SS and a man whose name bobs up in connection with virtually every experiment on human beings conducted by the SS, arranged to have women inmates of the Ravensbrück concentration camp infected with staphylococci, gas bacilli, tetanus bacilli and certain mixed germ cultures, in order to ascertain the healing effect of the sulfa drugs. Supervision over the experiments was assumed by Dr. Karl Gebhardt,[1] Professor of Orthopedic Surgery at the University of Berlin, Chief Surgeon of the Hohenlychen Medical Institution, President of the German Red Cross, and Himmler's friend and personal physician. He had most of the operations performed on Polish women by the SS physicians Dr. Schiedlausky, Dr. Rosenthal, Dr. Ernst Fischer, and Dr. Herta Oberheuser.[2] Actually there was no responsible supervision. The infections were always set in the lower leg, and the women subjects never learned their purpose. As scars on a very few survivors have shown, and as witnesses have confirmed, the incisions frequently went as deep as the bone. On several occasions, particles of wood and glass were introduced into the wounds, in addition to the germ cultures. Suppuration of the leg quickly ensued. Those victims who went untreated, merely for the purpose of observing the course of the infection, died in fearful agony. Even of the others only a small number survived. Each of the series of experiments included six to ten girls, usually the prettiest, selected from a large number ordered to report at the hospital. There were at least six series.

Dr. Gebhardt reported on the outcome to the "Third Eastern Working Conference of Consulting Specialists of the Academy of Military Surgery, Berlin," May 24–26, 1943,

---

[1] Sentenced to death in the Nazi Medical Trial; 1947.—*Tr.*
[2] Fischer got life, Oberheuser twenty years.—*Tr.*

under the title: "Special Experiments on the Effect of Sulfonamides." Actually he had visited Ravensbrück but occasionally to inspect the wounds of the patients and hear a report on the results. Each time the women had to wait for several hours, strapped in rows to operating tables, until the Herr Professor put in his appearance. The conference to which he reported was attended, among others, by Professor Siegfried Handloser, chief and inspector of the German Army Medical Service; Dr. Paul Rostock, Brigadier-General in the Medical Corps Reserve, chief of the University Surgical Clinic, Berlin, consultant to the German Army and chief of the Office for Medical Science and Research; Dr. Oskar Schröder, Lieutenant-General in the Medical Corps, chief and medical inspector of the German Air Force Medical Service; Reich Health Leader Dr. Conti; Dr. Karl Genzken, chief of the Medical Service of the *Waffen SS*; SS Colonel Helmut Poppendick, chief of the Personal Staff of the SS Reich Physician; Professor Karl Brandt,[1] a Major-General in the *Waffen SS*, Reich Commissioner for Health and Sanitation, and Hitler's personal physician; as well as a number of very well-known and eminent German professors. In his address Gebhardt made no secret of the fact that the experiments had been conducted on concentration-camp inmates, indeed, he expressly assumed full responsibility for them. Not one of his listeners protested.

Dr. Sigmund Rascher, a captain in the German Air Force Medical Service and subsequently a second lieutenant in the SS, was a special favorite of Himmler. As early as 1941, after Rascher had consulted with an air surgeon from the Air Force Ground-Level Testing Station for Altitude Research at Munich, Himmler authorized him to conduct certain experiments at the Dachau concentration camp. These experiments were marked by bitter rivalry and cross-intrigues with Dr. Hans Wolfgang Romberg of the Division for Aviation Medicine of the German Experimental Institute for Aviation, and Dr. Siegfried Ruff,[2] chief of the Institute for Aviation Medicine of the same agency. Purpose of the ex-

---

[1] As a result of the Nazi Medical Trial, Karl Brandt was hanged, Schröder and Genzken got life, Poppendick ten years (for SS membership only). Rostock was acquitted.—*Tr.*

[2] Romberg and Ruff were acquitted in the Nazi Medical Trial—*Tr.*

periments was to ascertain human reactions and capacity to sustain life at high altitudes, during rapid ascent to such altitudes (up to twelve miles and higher), as well as in rapid descent. A suitable decompression chamber belonging to the air force was shipped to Dachau. As reports that have been preserved show, the death of the human experimental subjects deliberately entered into the calculations from the very outset. Himmler had originally designated "arch criminals" under sentence of death (such as Poles and Russians of the resistance movement!) for these experiments—a provision never observed in practice and dropped altogether after 1942. The survivors were supposed to have their sentences commuted to life (except, of course, Russians and Poles).

A mobile unit was set up at Dachau in the camp street, between Block 5 and the adjacent barracks. The area was isolated from the other hospital buildings so that outside observation was impossible. The unit consisted of a high enclosed box on wheels, with built-in instruments for the measurement of pressure, temperature and altitude. The equipment made it possible to simulate conditions during an ascent to high altitudes and during rapid descent. Heart action of the subjects was measured by an electro-cardiograph. Autopsies were conducted immediately upon death ("the blood does not yet boil at an altitude of 70,000 feet" reads the final report of the three "experts," dated July 28, 1942). On one occasion, during an autopsy, Rascher found the heart of the victim still beating. He thereupon instituted a whole series of killings, solely for the purpose of establishing the length of time during which the human heart remained active after death.

Naturally the "Sky Ride Wagon," as it came to be known in camp, inspired panic among the prisoners. The first victims had been requisitioned from the Labor Utilization Office as a special detail to be granted supplementary rations. Some innocents had actually volunteered. But within a few days sinister rumors were heard. There were no more volunteers. Thereafter the victims were simply taken from the barracks on one pretext or another. Newcomers were especially popular as subjects. Frequently "The Captain," as he was known in camp, went stalking for suitable victims himself.

In reply to a detailed intermediate report, Himmler wrote

Dr. Rascher on April 13, 1942, that he was deeply interested in the matter, wishing "continued success in the experiments." (In the passage immediately following he wrote: "Kindest regards to your dear wife as well. Heil Hitler!") Rascher replied, saying among other things that "the productive interest of the Reich Leader SS" deeply stimulated his "energy and resourcefulness." The results of this productive interest and resourcefulness were some eighty killings. These were reported by Dr. Ruff to Professor Hippke and Dr. Schroder, both of them major-generals in the Medical Corps and Air Force Medical Inspectors. Neither of them raised any objections, even at a time when there had been only a few fatalities. On the contrary, on October 10, 1942, Professor Hippke wrote to Himmler:

> DEAR MR. REICH LEADER SS:
>   *In the name of German aviation medicine and research I express my obedient gratitude for your great interest and aid in connection with the Dachau experiments. These experiments supplement our knowledge to an important and valuable degree. . . . Freezing experiments along different lines are still under way in Dachau. As soon as the work requires your further kind support I hope I may be permitted to appeal to you again through Captain Rascher.*
>   *With Heil Hitler!*
>
> PROFESSOR DR. HIPPKE.

A letter by the Reich Air Ministry's official in charge of aviation medicine, dated October 8, 1942, shows that as early as February 24, 1942, Professor Holzlöhner of Kiel had been asked by the Medical Inspector of the German Air Force to investigate "The Effect of Chilling on Warm-Blooded Organisms." This was scientific jargon for the plight of fliers crashing into icy seas. Dr. Rascher proposed to the air force that experiments be conducted on concentration-camp inmates. The result was a collaboration between Rascher and Holzlöhner, who supervised the experiments up to late October 1942. Rascher then continued them until May 1943.

During the first period the subjects, clothed or stripped, were immersed in water of 39 to 48° F. until they grew stiff.

Temperature was measured rectally by thermo-electric means. There were fifty to sixty subjects and fifteen to eighteen fatalities. During the second period Rascher also used another method. Prisoners were exposed to the cold winter air (4 to 13° F. below zero) overnight. When their screams created too much of a disturbance, Rascher finally used anesthesia. According to the testimony of an eyewitness, the former inmate Walter Neff, Rascher immersed two Russian officers, brought from the camp prison, naked in ice water. It took them five hours to die. During the third hour a Polish orderly who was also present heard one of the Russians say to the other: "Why don't you ask the officer to shoot us!" The second replied that it was no use expecting any mercy from this Fascist dog.

The total number of human subjects from November 1942, to May 1943, was between 220 and 240. Some underwent experiments two or three times. There were 65 to 70 deaths.

Himmler was especially interested in methods of warming persons who had been severely chilled. In a number of series this was done by means of naked women, brought from Ravensbrück for the purpose. "Personally I believe," Himmler wrote Rascher, now promoted to SS captain, "these experiments may bring the best and most sustained results, but of course I may be mistaken." He was not mistaken. Rascher was able to report in detail how revived subjects practiced sexual intercourse at 86 to 90°F. and that this proved to be the equivalent of a "hot bath." When placed between two naked women, the subjects did not recover as rapidly as with one woman. "I attribute this to the fact that in warming by means of one woman personal inhibitions are avoided and the woman clings more closely to the chilled person (cf. Curve 4)."

The SS leadership insisted that these experiments were of great importance to German aviation, and that the gentlemen of the air force were not supporting them with sufficient enthusiasm. Professor Hippke defended himself against these charges in a letter of March 6, 1943, directed to SS Lieutenant-General Wolf, chief of Himmler's personal staff:

You are mistaken, however, in assuming that I, the responsible head of all medical-scientific research work, ever offered the slightest opposition to the freezing ex-

*periments on human beings, thus impeding their progress.
I instantly assented to these experiments, because our own
preliminary tests on large animals had been concluded and
required supplementation. It would seem rather im-
plausible that I, who am responsible for every kind of
rescue method for our airmen, would not do everything
possible to promote such work. When Rascher first presented his plans to me, I agreed with him at once. . . .*

Apart from the gruesome deaths, there were no practical
results from these experiments. They contributed nothing that
was helpful to German fliers.

Three separate series of experiments were initiated by the
SS leadership in its efforts to find a method by which large
numbers of human subjects could be quickly and permanently
sterilized without their own knowledge.

The first experiment in this line was based on the published
results, in a German scientific magazine, of certain animal experiments conducted by the firm of Madaus & Co., Dresden-
Radebeul, with extract from the South American plant
Caladium Seguinum ("Animal Experiments on the Question
of Sterilization by Drugs," *Zeitschrift für die gesamte ex-
perimentelle Medizin* [*Journal of Experimental Medicine*,
109, 1]). Himmler's attention was called to this publication
from two sides at once. In August 1941, the Deputy *Gauleiter*
(Provincial Governor) of Lower Austria wrote that Dr.
Fehringer, chief of his regional Office of Racial Policy, had
taken up the subject of sterilizing men and women by means
of drugs. He proposed to conduct "the necessary investigations and human experiments . . . on inmates of the
Gypsy camp at Lackenback in Lower Danube Province, by
means of an appropriately selected medical staff, on the basis
of the animal experiments of Madaus, and in collaboration
with the Institute of Pharmacology of the Vienna Medical
Faculty." He could only hint at "the vistas opened up by the
possibility of sterilizing an unlimited number of people in the
shortest possible time and the simplest possible way."

The Munich dermatologist and urologist, Dr. Adolf
Pokorny,[1] was more blunt. In October 1941, after having read

----

[1] Acquitted in the Nazi Medical Trial at Nuremberg.—*Tr.*

the Madaus report, he wrote to Himmler:

> *If we were to succeed, on the basis of these researches, in producing as soon as possible a drug that would within a relatively short time, imperceptibly bring about sterilization in man, we should have a new and extremely effective weapon at our disposal. The thought alone that the three million Bolshevists presently in German hands could be sterilized, making them available as workers while excluding them from procreation, opens vast perspectives.*

The perspectives were set forth in detail:

(1) Dr. Madaus must not be allowed to make any further publication (the enemy is listening!). (2) Cultivation of the plant (readily cultivated in hothouses). (3) Immediate experiments on human beings (criminals!), to establish dosage and duration of treatment. (4) Intensive research into the effective chemical substance, leading to: (5) Synthetic production, if possible.

Himmler immediately mobilized the resources of the SS Main Economic and Administrative Office, through SS Lieutenant-General Pohl, and those of the Reich Physician SS, through SS Lieutenant-General Grawitz. A hothouse for the cultivation of *Caladium Seguinum* was built. "Sterilization experiments in the concentration camps" were set in motion, "using whatever supply of the plant may be available." According to a statement by SS Colonel Rudolf Brandt,[1] Himmler's personal adjutant and chief of the Ministerial Office in the Reich Ministry of Interior, such experiments were actually conducted, but I have been unable to learn in which camp. The difficulties encountered in cultivating *Caladium Sequinum* on German soil, and other methods of mass sterilization that had opened up in the meantime, caused SS initiative along this line to slow down.

A certain Dr. Horst Schuhmann, who had been active as a consultant and head of an institution in 1939, during Hitler's so-called euthanasia program, had investigated the effect of X-rays on the human generative glands. In 1941, when the gassing of mental patients no longer occupied all his time, he

---

[1] Rudolf Brandt was sentenced to death in the Nazi Medical Trial.—*Tr.*

communicated with Reich Leader Bouhler who, according to SS Colonel Victor Brack,[1] Chief of Service in Hitler's own Chancellery, proposed "to solve the Jewish problem by means of mass sterilization." In 1942 contact with the SS Main Economic and Administrative Office was established. Himmler gave his personal support to the plans "by making available suitable material in the Auschwitz concentration camp." Dr. Schuhmann got hold of able-bodied Jews, aged twenty to twenty-four, and exposed their sexual organs to X-rays for fifteen minutes. Subsequently the men had to go straight back to work. Those who could not keep the pace because of the ensuing burns and abscesses were gassed. Two to four weeks later the remaining victims were castrated, so that their testicles could be dissected and examined under the microscope. Between times Dr. Schuhmann traveled to Ravensbrück, where he sterilized Gypsy children without anesthesia.

A report by Brack to Himmler on the completed preliminary work contained the somewhat premature conclusion:

> *The following results can claim certainty and an appropriate scientific foundation: if persons are to be rendered permanently sterile, this can be accomplished only by X-ray dosages so high that castration with all its consequences ensues. These high X-ray dosages destroy the inner secretions of the ovaries and the testicles. . . .*
>
> *Theoretically, with top voltage, thin filter and close proximity, an exposure of two minutes for men and three minutes for women should be sufficient. But another disadvantage must be taken into account. Since it is impossible to screen other parts of the body with lead without attracting attention, the tissues are affected and radiation sickness ensues. If the radiation has been too intense, the skin reached by the rays will, in the ensuing days or weeks, show symptoms of burning, varying with the individual.*
>
> *One practical method, for example, would be to have the persons to be processed step up to a window where they would be asked certain questions or have to fill out certain*

[1] Brack was sentenced to death in the Nazi Medical Trial.—*Tr.*

forms, detaining them for two or three minutes. The official behind the window could operate the equipment in such a way that the switch simultaneously turned on two X-ray tubes, since exposure must be from two sides. A two-tube installation thus could sterilize 150 to 200 persons a day, twenty installations some 3,000 to 4,000 persons a day. A larger daily load is out of the question anyway, in my estimation.

The method was to be applied primarily to the two to three million European Jews, both men and women, who were still "well able to work," the report concluding

that even now it has become a matter of small moment whether the persons affected know from the effects in a few weeks or months that they have been castrated. If you, Reich Leader, in the interests of preserving manpower should decide to choose this way, Reich Leader Bouhler is prepared to place at your disposal the physicians and other personnel required to do the work.

Dr. Schuhmann, on the other hand, on the basis of his experiments at Auschwitz and Ravensbrück, insisted that in all likelihood castration of men was not feasible by this method, besides being far too expensive. Castration by operation, he said, was cheaper and took no more than six to seven minutes. The method, however, could not be adapted to large numbers of subjects, nor was it really "fast and inconspicuous." Yet it was precisely mass sterilization in which Himmler, the "Commissioner for the Strengthening of the German National Character," was interested.

In 1942 Professor Clauberg, an SS brigadier-general of Königshütte in Upper Silesia, had suggested a third method for rendering women sterile—the injection of chemical irritants into the uterus. On July 7, 1942, in the presence of Himmler, a conference took place between Professor Gebhardt, SS Lieutenant-General Glücks, Pohl's deputy in the SS Main Economic and Administrative Office, and Professor Clauberg. Auschwitz concentration camp was "made available" to the latter for his "experiments on humans and animals" (these were the very words used!). It was also proposed to assign the German X-ray specialist Professor Hohlfelder, chief of the so-called SS X-ray Battalion, so that work on men could be included in the program. Only three days later Clauberg was notified that Himmler "desired" him to go to Ravensbrück to conduct sterilizations by his method on Jewish women.

Before you start with your work, the Reich Leader SS would appreciate learning from you the approximate time that would be required to sterilize one thousand Jewesses. The Jewesses themselves are to know nothing about it. In the opinion of the Reich Leader SS, you should be able to administer the injections in the course of a general examination. Extensive tests would have to be made to show the effectiveness of the sterilization. For the most part, these could perhaps consist of X-ray photographs, to be made after a certain period of time, to be determined by yourself, which would establish what changes had taken place. In some case or other, however, there might have to be a practical test, conducted in such a way that a Jewess is locked up with a Jew for a certain period of time, any success attained to be observed.

Clauberg went to work. On June 7, 1943, he reported that his method was "virtually complete." A "single injection into the cervix" was sufficient, and it could be administered "during the usual gynecological examination familiar to every physician." To Himmler's question he replied: "An appropriately trained physician, using appropriate equipment and perhaps ten assistants (the number depending on the speed to be attained), can very probably handle several hundred women a day, if not, indeed, one thousand."

To work out the last "refinements" in his method, he had another three hundred women shipped from Ravensbrück to Auschwitz. Those who did not die of the experiment were subsequently gassed. X-ray photographs made during certain preliminary tests at Ravensbrück showed that Clauberg's injections "penetrated to the end of the ovarian duct; in several cases even to the abdominal cavity."

In 1944, as the Nazi regime began to disintegrate, the whole SS sterilization program came to a halt in a welter of documents that refused to admit failure and hoped for better results. The actual results were hundreds of dead and maimed.

I believe it will be sufficient to give a mere enumeration of other "scientific experiments" conducted by the SS on defenseless prisoners.

In Buchenwald and Neuengamme, "Experimental Section V" conducted work in counteracting homosexuality by gland implants and synthetic hormones. These experiments were suggested and executed by the Danish SS Major Dr. Vaernet, who was stationed at Prague. The report went to SS Colonel Poppendick. In Buchenwald a total of fifteen inmates were treated, of whom two died. Vaernet also tried his hand with men who had been castrated. The matter became the butt of many jokes on the part of the SS Medical Officers as well as the prisoners. No positive results were obtained.

In Buchenwald, experiments were conducted with yellow fever (results reported to the Behring Works, Marburg-on-Lahn, and the Army Medical Inspection Service, Berlin), smallpox, typhoid, paratyphoid A and B, diphtheria, combat poison gases, other poisons and phosphorus-rubber incendiary bombs. Tests were also made for the Academy of Military Medicine at Berlin, to show whether blood stored for some time could still be transfused; and typhus convalescent serum was prepared for the SS from the blood of patients in Ward 46. Further experiments were conducted on "the experimental physiology of nutrition" (SS Major H.D. Ellenbeck) and on the preservation of blood for the SS base hospital at Berlin. At intervals of three or four weeks, two SS medical noncoms would arrive to bleed hundreds of hospital inmates. A slice of bread and a piece of sausage were offered in return for 200 cc. blood; but often as much as 400 cc was taken.

At the Natzweiler concentration camp, experiments with typhus and yellow fever were conducted by Dr. Eugen Haagen, Professor of Hygiene at Strassburg University. His liaison man to the Institute for Military Scientific Research of the *Waffen SS* was Professor Hirt, Strassburg anatomist, to whom Haagen on one occasion complained that of one hundred prisoners transferred to Natzweiler for the experiments eighteen had died in transport, while only twelve were in a condition that made them suitable for the tests.

Professor Hirt, on his part, late in 1942 suggested to Hitler that a collection of skulls and skeletons of "Jewish-Bolshevist commissars" be created. The SS Main Economic and Administrative Office immediately instructed Auschwitz to make concentration-camp inmates available for this purpose, and 115 persons were selected—seventy-nine Jewish men, thirty Jewish women, two Poles and two Asiatics. They were shipped to the Natzweiler camp, where they were gassed with cyanide which Professor Hirt gave the Camp Commandant for the purpose. Some of the male victims had the left testicle removed (evidently a private project at Natzweiler). The bodies were shipped to the Institute of Anatomy at Strassburg University for Professor Hirt. There they were preserved in basins containing a fifty-five per cent alcohol solution and stored for a year, until the approach of the Allied front caused Hirt to order the bodies dismembered and burned.

At the Sachsenhausen concentration camp, blood was banked regularly from 1944 on, for the SS base hospital at Berlin (SS Major H.D. Ellenbeck). From 1942 to 1945 there were various experiments with combat agents. For this purpose Dr. Mrugowsky, Chief Hygienist to the SS, in company with other SS officers, actually inflicted gunshot wounds on Russian prisoners of war with poisoned bullets. From 1939 on tests were made in this camp with liquid war gases (mustard or yellow cross). The substance was applied to the skin of inmates and the symptoms recorded until death supervened. Reports on these tests went to Himmler, who had similar experiments on a large scale—up to 150 prisoners—conducted at Natzweiler by Professors Hirt and Bickenbach (the latter an internist at Strassburg University). Some of the victims went blind before they died in agony.

At the Dachau concentration camp in 1942 and 1943 abscesses were artificially induced, in order to test the efficacy of allopathic and homeopathic drugs. The subjects were chiefly Catholic clerics and Poles. SS Chief Surgeon Wolter selected them, while Dr. Laue, another SS physician, set the infections. Mortality was high and no cures were effected. Of one group of fifty priests a report to Himmler from Dr.

Grawitz, Reich Physician SS, stated (August 29, 1942): "One case was evaluated as positive and four as positive with reservations, as opposed to thirty-five failures, including ten deaths. The tests at Dachau are being continued.", Results continued to be negative. Most of the clerics died of blood poisoning induced by severe suppuration.

At the Ravensbrück concentration camp and at Hohenlychen there were experiments in muscle regeneration and bone transplants. Women inmates had a section of muscle excised from the thigh from time to time, to establish whether and how regeneration might take place in the cast. Other women had healthy legs or arms or shoulder blades removed. These parts were wrapped up by the SS physician involved and taken by car to Professor Gebhardt at Hohenlychen where Drs. Stumpfegger and Schulze transplated them to patients at the clinic. The concentration-camp "donors" were killed by injection.

Chapter Fifteen

REPRISALS AGAINST THE JEWS

I must again emphasize that it is impossible to present here anything like an exhaustive picture of the Jewish mass tragedy. A fully documented story would far transcend the scope of this book. The reader will have to rest content with a mere inkling of the character and extent of the fate that engulfed the Jews in the concentration camps proper, as well as in the eastern ghettos.

There are three major periods in the tragic story: action against individuals until the fall of 1938; organized liquidation campaigns beginning about that time; and after 1942 the systematic extermination of the Jews, especially in the east.

The Jews in Germany were *not* arrested as a matter of general policy in the early years of the Nazi regime. Merely a portion of them were picked up and sent to the concentration camps, on criteria determined by the Gestapo. The number was probably below twenty thousand. Their treatment was fairly uniform throughout the camps and, as we have already seen, dreadful enough.

On June 15, 1938, five hundred Jews arrived at Buchenwald, chiefly from Berlin and Breslau. They were subjected to the usual admission ordeal and then assigned to the so-called sheepshed, a blockhouse that contained neither tables, benches nor bunks. The earth floor was skimpily covered with tanbark. There was no water, despite the warm season, and as much as one mark was paid to convicts for a single sip. Mess was out in the open regardless of the weather. There was one loaf of bread a day for every five Jews, and a pint of soup for each man. The Barracks Orderlies were convicts, and they withheld most of the food, subsequently selling it. Reveille was at three o'clock in the morning, with roll call beginning two hours later and frequently lasting until seven o'clock. It is hard to believe, but because of the wretched footgear of the prisoners, the march through the quagmire to the roll-call area took as much as an hour, though it was only about two-thirds of a mile. All the men had sore feet, and there was no dispensary treatment. At five o'clock in the afternoon the Jews returned from work. After evening roll call, night work began for all those engaged in the construction of masonry barracks. This lasted until eleven o'clock at night. Physical abuse was a daily matter of course.

A large proportion of the newcomers quickly died of exhaustion. Others grew desperate and committed suicide. Within two months there were 150 dead, while most of the rest were unfit for work. The other camp inmates were strictly forbidden to give any aid to the Jews, indeed, even to talk to them. The Second Officer-in-charge, Hackmann, was particularly virulent in his incitement: "Any man who takes even a single thing from a Jew will choke on it!" This did not keep him from accepting eight thousand marks for the "purchase of books" two days later, and a similar amount two weeks later, for "charity"—actually for himself and his fellow officers. The surviving Jews were not transferred from the sheepshed to a wooden barracks for another two months, after a Jewish inmate who had been released and had emigrated described the situation over the British radio.

In August 1938, some 2,200 Jews arrived at Buchenwald from Dachau; they were mainly Austrians.

In November 1938, the assassination in Paris of the German Embassy Secretary Vom Rath at the hands of Grynszpan, a Jew, led to a wave of arrests of Jews throughout Germany. In Buchenwald alone 9,815 Jews were admitted.

These arrests were made without regard for age. Ten-year-old boys could be seen side by side with septuagenarians and octogenarians. En route from the Wiemar railroad station all stragglers were shot down, while the survivors were forced to drag the bloody bodies into camp. A great jam ensued at the gatehouse, when each batch of one thousand men arrived. The SS refused to open the big gate, except for a narrow gap through which but one man could pass at a time. Inside stood the Block Leaders, wielding iron rods, whips and truncheons, and virtually every Jew who got into the camp sustained injuries.

The events that took place at the time are not easily described in a few words. Let me merely mention that sixty-eight Jews went mad that very first night. They were clubbed to death like mad dogs by Sommer, four men at a time. The Jews were assigned in batches of two thousand to the notorious Barracks 1a to 5a (later torn down), primitive shelters intended for four or at most five hundred men. The sanitary conditions in these buildings grew unimaginable. Hundred-mark bills were used as toilet paper—the Jews had brought along a great deal of money, in some instances tens of thousands of marks. SS noncoms pushed the heads of some of their charges into the overflowing latrine buckets until they suffocated.

The arrivals had come in such large numbers that the SS had initially been unable to take down personnel records. The Roll Call Officer therefore announced over the public-address system: "If any more of the Jews string themselves up, will they kindly put a slip of paper with their name in their pocket, so that we know who it is."

A Jew from Breslau named Silbermann had to stand by idly as SS Sergeant Hoppe brutally tortured his brother to death. Silbermann went mad at the sight, and late at night he precipitated a panic with his frantic cries that the barracks was on fire. Hundreds threw themselves out of the upper windows and whole bunks collapsed. The SS men shot into the crowd and prisoner henchmen wielded their clubs freely, but it took much effort and time to restore order. Officer-in-Charge

Rödl chose to interpret the incident as a Jewish mutiny. He had seven hostages taken from the building and handcuffed together. Three Block Leaders then let loose trained dogs on the unfortunates, who were torn to pieces.

The SS exploited the Vom Rath reprisal campaign shamelessly for purposes of blackmail. One day the public-address system announced: "All millionaires to the gatehouse!" They were required to sign for large financial contributions, up to several hundred thousand marks. All the Jews were suddenly permitted to write home for money, ostensibly to pay for the trip home for their poorer comrades. Those who owned cars or motor-cycles were likewise called up. They had to transfer their vehicles to the SS.

The Nazis in Weimar got in on the deal. Their champion was SS Sergeant Michael. He brought into camp every kind of shopworn merchandise—old books and notebooks, thumb tacks and hairpins, which were sold to the Jews at fancy prices, with a few cigarettes or some food as bait. Michael and his cronies carried bills out of camp by the bushel basket.

Two Jewish physicians, Drs. Margulies and Verö, who later got to America, performed prodigies in tending these Vom Rath Jews. But in less than three weeks there were several hundred dead among them.

Suddenly, for reasons that never became clear, most of the Jews were set free on orders from the Reich authorities. They were actually taken to the border or to ships that took them into exile. One asks in vain whether the Nazi leaders were not afraid of the inevitable factual publicity that resulted abroad. Possibly they sought new pretexts to proceed against the Jews that remained behind.

The discharge announcement was always the same: "Attention, Barracks 1a to 5a! The following Jews report to the gatehouse at once with all their things. . . ." It sounded at every hour of the day and night and naturally became famous throughout the camp. Only those Jews who had travel money were released. A special "Travel Fund" was created for this purpose. It was kept in a blue valise and every day had to be taken to Officer-in-Charge Rödl and Roll Call Officer Strippel. This loudspeaker call likewise became famous: "Herzog with the diamond chest to the gatehouse!" (Gustav

Herzog was a Viennese journalist.) Even the Jews who were released were first thoroughly plucked.

By the time this Little Camp was dissolved on February 13, 1939, the remaining 250 inmates being transferred to the camp proper, there had been some 600 deaths in the five barracks.

No additional Jews arrived until September 1939, when some 500 of them were admitted from the Protectorate of Bohemia and Maravia. They were victims of another large-scale campaign that brought thousands into the concentration camps. In October they were followed by 200 inmates of the Jewish Home for the Aged in Vienna, together with some 2,000 other Austrian and German Jews who had originally immigrated from Poland. The Jews at this time lived in seven different barracks.

On the night of November 8–9, 1939, an alleged attempt on Hitler's life was made in the Bürgerbräu Cellar at Munich. During the morning of November 9, all Jews were suddenly recalled from their details and confined to barracks. One by one, each barracks had to line up, and SS sergeants Planck, Jänisch and Warnstedt picked out twenty-one Austrian and German Jews, entirely at random, without any list. Most of them were vigorous young men. A lad of seventeen who happened to be coming back from the post office was included without further ado. The SS took the group out through the gatehouse and shot them at close range in the quarry. The remaining Jews were kept in their quarters for five days, with blacked-out windows and neither food nor drink, and in constant, gnawing uncertainty as to what was to happen to them. On the fourth day they were put on half rations. This effort then got lost in another program of reprisals directed against the entire camp, ostensibly because of some stolen hogs.

In February 1941, the Jews in the Netherlands were cleaned out, and 389 of them, from Amsterdam and Rotterdam, arrived at Buchenwald. This measure was based on the Dutch general strike against the occupation authorities. The rough climate at Buchenwald severely affected the Dutch Jews. In addition, Dr. Eysele suddenly barred them from the hospital. Those who already happened to be in the hospital at the time were either given fatal injections at once or discharged as recovered in the nick of time.

A short time later, when 341 of them were still alive, the Dutch Jews were ordered transferred to the Mauthausen concentration camp. Two political prisoners from Mauthausen who were later transferred back to Buchenwald—Adam Kuczinski, a Pole, and Ludwig Neumaier, a German—gave the following account of what happened to the Dutch Jews.

The shipment from Buchenwald arrived around midnight. In the morning the inmates at Mauthausen were not permitted to leave their barracks. Fifty of the newly arrived Jews were chased from the bathhouse naked and driven into the electrified fence. All the others were herded into a barracks in which George Glas, a political prisoner from Landshut in Bavaria, was the clerk. The First and Second Officers-in-Charge—the latter was named Ernstberger—told Glas that the barracks would have to be "cleared" in six weeks at the latest. Glas replied that he would sooner resign his function than lay hand on a prisoner. He was instantly relieved, got twenty-five or thirty-five lashes, and was assigned to the sock-mending detail, a favorite source for injection liquidations, when such were "needed." Glas, however, was successfully smuggled to another camp, and in his place a convict became clerk.

The second day after their arrival, the Jews where shunted into the quarry. There were 148 steps leading down to the bottom of the pit, but they were not permitted to use these. They had to slide down the loose stones at the side, and even here many died or were severely injured. The survivors then had to shoulder hods, and two prisoners were compelled to load each Jew with an excessively heavy rock. The Jews then had to run up the 148 steps. In some instances the rocks immediately rolled downhill, crushing the feet of those that came behind. Every Jew who lost his rock in this fashion was brutally beaten and the rock was hoisted to his shoulders again. Many of the Jews were driven to despair the very first day and committed suicide by jumping into the pit. On the third day the SS opened the so-called "death-gate" and with a fearful barrage of blows drove the Jews across the guard line, the guards on the watchtowers shooting them down in heaps with their machine-guns. The next day the Jews no longer jumped into the pit individually. They joined hands and one man would pull nine or twelve of his comrades over the lip with him into a gruesome death. The barracks was "cleared" of Jews, not in six but in barely three weeks. Every one of the 340 perished by suicide or by shooting, beating and other forms of torture.

It should perhaps be mentioned that the civilian employees at the Mauthausen quarry requested that these suicides by jumping be stopped, since the fragments of flesh and brains clinging to the rocks afforded too gruesome a sight. The quarry was thereupon hosed down and prisoners were posted to prevent men from jumping. The survivors were simply clubbed across the guard line to their death. When new batches of Jewish prisoners arrived, the SS had its fun by dubbing them "parachute troops."

Only one member of this group of Dutch Jews was saved—Max Nebig of Amsterdam. Dr. Eysele, Buchenwald Medical Officer, had arbitrarily performed a stomach resection on him. Subsequently he was to be given a fatal injection, but the Hospital Capo substituted a harmless water syringe and had the dying man carried away before Eysele's eyes—to the TB ward, where he was secreted until the liberation of the camp.

The Jews began to be transferred to the death camps as a general policy in October 1942. This phase lasted until the summer of 1943 and created a state of intense agitation which even men who had survived all previous ordeals were hard put to withstand. Reports that trickled through, together with the experience already gained, left no doubt as to the character of these new shipments. Actually only a very small percentage survived them, and often it was largely a matter of quick wit, presence of mind, resourcefulness and determination whether a man succeeded at the last moment in catching a life line by means of which he might be dragged back into the saving solidarity of his comrades.

With the exception of 200 Jews who were exempted and retained as skilled construction workers—they included lawyers, writers, physicians, and artists!—all Jews were removed from Buchenwald at that time. This was a nationwide policy. Virtually all the eastern ghettos were likewise emptied at this time—Kielce in July 1942, Warsaw on July 22, Lemberg in August, to mention but a few. At the same time a steady stream of Jews slated for annihilation reached the various ghettos and concentration camps from the remnants of the Jewish population in Germany and the other European countries under Hitler's domination. This campaign continued until the Nazis were reduced to their last manpower resources and preferred using the surviving Jews as labor slaves to stuffing them into the gas chambers or mowing them down with machine-guns. It is to this circumstance that certain Polish and Hungarian Jews owe their survival. Some 18,000 Bulgarian Jews, on the other hand, were handed over to the German authorities and gassed, a fate also suffered by many Greek Jews. As late as the summer of 1944, 6,115 Hungarian Jews reached Buchenwald alone. They were followed in January 1945 by 5,745 Polish Jews, all of whom had to slave in the outside labor details to the point of exhaustion.

The best picture of what happened to the Jews at this time comes from the reports of those few who were in the shipments but managed to escape death.

Dr. Ludwig Fleck, a college instructor, reports:

The Lemberg ghetto originally comprised as much as one-fifth of the city. There were 140,000 Jews in Lemberg, or thirty per cent of the population. The ghetto lasted from the fall of 1941 to August 1942, every day involving fearful abuse. Whenever the armed forces or the SS needed anything, whether it was furniture, clothes or other articles, they would simply requistion it from ghetto headquarters which had to provide it free of charge.

In August 1942, the Jewish mass liquidations began, under the command of SS Major-General Kazmann. The first phase took about two weeks. Some 50,000 Jews, mainly the aged, sick and children, were carried off to Belze where, as later transpired, they were gassed. They included the entire personnel of the hospital for contagious diseases—physicians, nurses, orderlies. The operation was carried out by a special SS detail and was repeated every few weeks.

The ghetto was shifted to the outskirts of the city, where there were practically no stone houses. Assignment was on the basis of about twenty square feet of living space per head. There were no shops—all food had to be smuggled in. Sanitation was dreadful. Some seventy per cent of the

*Jewish population contracted typhus. Every day saw
pillage and robbery on the part of the SS, while individual
reprisals and murders took place at night. A forced-labor
camp was set up and healthy young Jews were sent to it.
The aged and the sick, as well as women and children, were
sent to a concentration camp near Betrec to be gassed. By
the fall of 1942 there were still some 15,000 Jews left in the
ghetto—replacements were constantly shipped in from the
countryside—and some 12,000 in the labor camp. It is
known from reliable sources that the ghetto inhabitants at
Lemberg continued to dwindle away under great
deprivations, until the survivors were all massacred in
March 1943, all the buildings being burned down.*

Soon after the ghetto was liquidated the inmates of the
labor camp were mowed down with machine-guns to the last
man. A special detail of one hundred Jews is supposed to have
survived and, curiously enough, to have been well treated
later on. Nothing is known of their further fate. The Commandant of the labor camp was SS Lieutenant Colonel
Willhaus.

Oskar Berger, a merchant, lived with his wife and boy in
Kattowitz. At the outbreak of the war he fled eastward and
when Poland had been subdued he was put in the Kielce
ghetto. In July 1942, the Jews there were "resettled" and
taken to Treblinka. Berger reports:

*I was separated from my wife and never saw her again.
Just before the resettlement all the sick, in homes as well as
the hospital—some four or five hundred persons—together
with the inmates of the homes for the aged and the orphans
in the orphan home, were either shot or killed by injection.
I was a strong young man and was detailed to recover the
bodies and bury them in a large garden in Okrej Alley.
There were about sixty Jews in this detail. The bodies were
flung into the pit dressed as they were, after we had
searched them for jewels, gold and money, which had to be
delivered to the SS. When the work had been done, we
were assembled in the synagogue and Gestapo Chief
Thomas picked some of us for shipment to Treblinka.*

The trip was a nightmare. We crouched in the cars,

*crowded together, children crying, women going mad. We
arrived toward three o'clock the next afternoon. There was
a big sign at the railroad station: "Treblinka Labor
Camp." The train was shunted to a siding which led into
the woods for two or three miles. A ghastly scene greeted
us at the end. Hundreds of bodies lay about, together with
scattered luggage and clothes, all in wild confusion. We
were herded out of the carriages, as German and
Ukrainian SS men mounted to the roofs and began to
shoot indiscriminately into the crowd. Men, women and
children writhed in their own blood; screams and sobs rent
the air. Those who were not shot down were ultimately
driven across the mounds of dead and wounded through an
open gate into a barbed-wire enclosure. Two wooden posts
flanked the open area.*

*Together with several other men, including a certain
Gottlieb of Kielce, I was chosen to clean the cars, to pick
up the bodies of the new arrivals and take them to great
pits that had been dug by steam shovels. Into these the
bodies were flung, regardless of whether they were dead or
still twitching. The work was supervised by SS men who
held pistol or truncheon in one hand, whisky bottle in the
other. Even now my memory stands aghast at the picture
of small children seized by their feet and dashed against
tree trunks.*

(There were sergeants, incidentally, who carried photographs of such scenes as souvenirs.)

*We got no food, though for weeks our detail had to per-
form the most exhausting labor. Two or three shipments
arrived every day. We lived on the food we found in the
luggage of the victims.*

*Sometimes there were shipments that held only corpses.
I believe these people must have been gassed in the cars,
for I never noticed any wounds. The bodies were con-
vulsively intertwined, the skin blue. Curiously enough
there were isolated instances of small children, from three
to five years old, who survived these shipments. They were
deaf and incapable of speech, and their eyes were haunted.
We were never able to conceal them for very long. The SS*

would discover them and put an end to them. There were also shipments that consisted exclusively of children or old people. They would crouch in the clearing for hours, until they were liquidated by machine-gun fire.

During the weeks I worked at Treblinka a small brick building was constructed off to one side in the woods. The path leading to it was marked with a sign reading "To the Bath-House." Another sign requested that gold, money, foreign exchange and jewels be deposited in a bundle at a bath-house window. From this time on new arrivals were gassed rather than shot. A special detail like ours took care of burying or cremating the bodies.

Many of us made isolated attempts to escape. I belong to the very small number of fortunates who succeeded. Together with my friend Gottlieb and a thirteen-year-old boy, I hid between blankets and bundles of clothing and luggage which we had to load into freight cars. We took along a plentiful supply of jewelry, gold and money, mostly American dollars. It was September 1942 when we made good our escape. Unfortunately my freedom was only short-lived. On January 5, 1943, I was again arrested in Cracow, as a "partisan," together with Gottlieb. We were brutally tortured and had to confess that we were Jews. We were shackled and taken to the ghetto prison, where we remained until March 14, 1943. In company with one hundred other Jews we were then taken to the Auschwitz concentration camp in closed buses, and from there to Birkenau. Most of the group were at once selected for the "left side" and gassed. I had the good luck to be placed in the Clothing Room.

On October 21, 1944, we were transferred to Oranienburg near Berlin. This transfer was limited chiefly to those who had enjoyed good jobs and working conditions at Birenau. At Oranienburg we were quarantined for two weeks in the Heinkel Works, miserably dressed and suffering great hunger. We were then herded on foot to the Sachsenhausen concentration camp, and from there only two days later by rail to the notorious Buchenwald Subsidiary Camp S III at Ohrdruf. More than half the prisoners died within a short time from the effects of the strenuous work in the mines. Every two months or so those

*who were feeble or unfit for work were picked out and sent
to Bergen-Belsen near Hanover.*

The stories of some survivors are marked by hair-breadth
escapes. Motek Strigler of Zamosc, Poland, had been in
ghettos and in labor and concentration camps since 1939.
Buchenwald was his twelfth camp! He was able to tell of the
extermination camp, Skarzisko Kamienno:

> *On the eve of the Day of Atonement, October 1943, the
> guard leader Schuhmann visited us in camp. He was
> looking for my comrade, Mendel Rubin, a well-digger of
> Cracow, and took him away. A few days later there was a
> report from the Gestapo at Radom that Rubin's name was
> to be scratched, since he would not come back—he had
> been discharged. We heard nothing for a long time. In
> April 1944, two cars with German police arrived. They
> requisitioned straw originally allotted to us for our bunks.
> This was taken to the woods, near sheds 96 and 97 of C
> Plant. There it was woven into mats, and an area was
> marked off and surrounded with a six-foot wall of the
> mats, making it impossible to see what happened inside the
> enclosure. We found out, nevertheless—through Mendel
> Rubin.*
>
> *He was among those who worked there for about a
> month. The area was always surrounded by a heavy cor-
> don of German police. One day one of the policemen came
> to us and asked for my comrade Henoch Edelmann of
> Cracow, a mechanic who worked with the German master
> plumber Corosta. The policeman gave Edelmann a small
> piece of soap. It contained a little glass tube in which there
> was a slip of paper with a message from Rubin. He had im-
> portant news for us, he wrote, but would send it only when
> he was certain that communication had been established.
> By way of confirmation he asked that he be sent certain
> pictures of his wife and child which he had left behind. He
> got the pictures.*
>
> *News from Rubin now began to arrive. The German
> policeman gave the messages to Regina Rabinowicz of
> Warsaw and Fela of Samosc, girls who worked with us.
> We got four or five letters. Enclosed with one was a slip of*

*paper from a Polish friend of Rubin's. It bore the heading:
"Katyn, Government General." We buried all these reports—it was Henoch Edelmann who took care of that. In
essence they reported the following:*

*At Radom, Rubin had been assigned to a detail of sixty-
seven men whose job it was to cremate the bodies of
Gestapo murder victims and to erase all traces. The victims
often numbered hundreds a day. We got a list of
prominent persons who had been killed in this way. The
detail itself consisted only of candidates for death, i.e., of
men who were permitted to live only as long as they were
left to this service. They were shackled hand and foot and
had to sleep in their clothes. They were given plenty of
food. They turned over to the Gestapo only part of the
money and jewelry they found, giving a share to the
policemen, who returned the favor by providing food and
drink.*

*Contact with Rubin was broken off when the policeman
who was acting as go-between fell in a skirmish with partisans. We had learned from him that the men in the
special detail were shifted from place to place, as they were
needed.*

*In our own plant the detail, during its sojourn, had to
dig up the thousands of bodies that had been buried on the
rifle range and cremate them. The site of the mass graves
was filled in, graded and planted with grass, but we were
still able to find tell-tale traces—fragments of bone, fingers
cut off for their rings, melted down gold. The exhumed
bones were not burned but loaded into a truck containing a
bone mill.*

*Members of the detail were themselves shot and
cremated after a few weeks. Rubin, however, spent almost
seven months there.*

There is a wealth of testimony on similar operations in the
east. The SS, the Secret Military Police and certain army units
never tired in their efforts, though the reader is likely to in
listening to the recital.

The Lublin district was the stamping ground of SS
Lieutenant-General Globocnig, an Austrian who, following
the murder of a Jewish jeweler in Vienna in 1933, had fled to

Nazi Germany and in 1938 had returned to Vienna as *Gauleiter*. A year later he was involved in a huge foreign-exchange scandal. Public prosecution, however, was quashed and Globocnig was shifted to the SS. Among countless others, 1,150 Viennese Jews fell into his clutches in 1942. Only three or four of them survived "resettlement"! I hope that some day there will be an exhaustive documentation of the awful fate the Nazis prepared for the Jews of eastern Europe. It is likely to be one of the ghastliest records in the history of the world. To spare the sensibilities of those who need suffer nothing worse than the reading, I confine myself to two final reports.

A young German Jew, Hans Baermann of Cologne, was forced out of school at the age of fourteen and on December 7, 1941, was carried off to the east with his parents.

We were notified of our evacuation three weeks beforehand by the Cologne Gestapo. We were enjoined from selling any of our personal property, all of which except for the furniture, was to be packed. Every family affected by the evacuation also had to prepare a washtub full of foodstuffs. With six trunks and three knapsacks, grips and briefcases, my family arrived at the Cologne fairgrounds at the appointed time. There were about 1,000 persons in the shipment. Our luggage was examined for valuables, and jewelry, watches, wedding rings and all identification papers were confiscated. Another physical examination left each person with but ten marks. We were then herded into the main hall on the fairgrounds, which had been enclosed with barbed wire, and we were left on the wet wood shavings for twenty-four hours.

On December 8, at four o'clock in the morning, only a single trunk having been left to us, we were taken to the Deutz railroad station. The trip lasted eighty hours and ended at Riga. There was no food on the way, and water on but one occasion. At the Skirotava freight yards we were driven from the cars by Latvian SS men armed with whips and iron rods. There was no question any longer of taking anything along. At 11° F. below zero we started out on the painful march to the Riga ghetto. Two days before we arrived there had been 34,500 people there. We saw only corpses and pools of blood and frightful devastation in all the homes.

Together with 177 people, my parents and I were herded into a room about 150 square feet in area. Here we had to live. That night some 4,500 Latvian Jews came looking for their families but found no one. This was the surviving remnant of the ghetto. The other 30,000 had been escorted to a valley where they were mowed down by machine-guns. After the massacre the hills on either side had been blasted, burying the bodies under mountains of rock.

We lived for two days on the food we found in the room. Another shipment of 1,000 Jews from Cassel had meanwhile arrived. Two days after our arrival 200 Jews, aged eighteen to forty, were taken to Salaspils camp, twelve miles from Riga. I was among them. Frozen and starved, we reached a snow-covered clearing that held but a single, large, roofless barracks of wood. Some 4,000 Jews from southern Germany already lived in it, and they attacked us like wolves for food and drink. Our hair was shorn and we were then assigned, three men to a bunk eighteen inches high, six feet long and less than five feet wide. It was bitter cold and the slats were covered with ice. On the third day after our arrival we saw our first bread and a horse-drawn sleigh loaded with potato peelings from the SS kitchen at Riga. An SS sergeant named Nickel introduced himself as the Commandant, and immediately assigned us to work, to be performed without overcoats and without fires. The construction program embraced forty-five barracks in which Latvians and Russians were later quartered. This program was fulfilled, all but five barracks. Watch towers also had to be constructed and the entire area enclosed with barbed wire.

I spent seven months starving in this death camp. In the end I weighed only eighty pounds and was infested with lice. Reduced virtually to a skeleton, I was photographed for the Stürmer.[1]

Of 15,000 men who passed through this camp in time, virtually all wasted away. Only 192 survived. I was among

---

[1] A violently anti-Semitic and semi-pornographic magazine published by Julius Streicher, who was convicted by the International Military Tribunal at Nuremberg and hanged.—*Tr.*

them. On August 2, 1942, camp construction having been completed, I was taken back to the Riga ghetto.

Food and shelter in the Riga ghetto were not quite as bad as at Salaspils. The atrocities, however, were not far behind the abuse and arbitrary terror practiced in the camp. Details of young men were promptly assembled who had to dig mass graves in the Bickernick Forest. These pits were fifty feet long, thirteen feet wide and six and a half feet deep, and they were intended for shipments from Bielefeld, Düsseldorf, Hanover, Berlin, Vienna, Dresden, Leipzig, Cassel, Dortmund, Stuttgart, Nuremberg, Munich, as well as from Czechoslovakia and Austria. Immediately on their arrival, the victims were taken to the woods in trucks of the air force, the army, the SS and the Security Service. These operations were all in the hands of Major Arreis of the Latvian SS. At the pits, twenty men were picked out for each pit, then another two hundred were brought and stripped without regard to age or sex and shot down with machine-guns. The twenty who had been previously selected had to see to it that the bodies landed in the pits; then they shared the same fate. These atrocities were quite generally known. Air force personnel who witnessed them often talked about them.

After November 1942, a simpler method was chosen to get rid of the people. This was a closed truck with trailers, into which a total of two hundred persons could be crowded. En route a gas valve would be opened. The trucks always headed into the Bickernick Forest and came back an hour later with only the clothes.

Mail communication with the outside world and the possession of money were punished by death. Occasionally starving Jews tried to trade a garment for a sandwich. Ghetto inmates caught in such an attempt first received twenty-five lashes and then were hanged.

At a later date the Commandant, SS First Lieutenant Krause of Leipzig, had all persons over fifty segregated in the ghetto. There were 2,200 men and women. My parents escaped only by falsifying their birth dates. This selection process also affected children under thirteen. Mothers who refused to part from their children were permitted to accompany them. The destination of the shipment was given

Dünamünde. That was deliberate deception. The goal of the shipment was never reached.

A week later, in November 1943, the ghetto was dissolved. Russian refugees were quartered in it. The remaining 1,500 inmates were transferred to the Kaiserwald concentration camp near Riga. They included my parents. The Commandant there was SS Lieutenant-Colonel Sauer. Some of the inmates were parceled out to special army installations—the commissary depot, the motor pool, the clothing office, etc. I was among the latter. On orders from Berlin all women and girls had their hair shorn.

As luck would have it, I managed to get news of my parents two months later. They were tortured by hunger. My assignment permitted me to save up some of my food, and I found a way of getting small quantities to my parents. Both my father and my mother worked on the banks of the Düna River. They had to drag logs out of the water and up to a sawmill. This transport had to be accomplished entirely by human labor. The Senior Camp Inmate at Kaiserwald was Xaver Apel, a convict under sentence of life who had been a member of the Sass gang in Berlin. He was called Mr. X in camp. He was assisted by another inmate who wore the green triangle, Hannes Dressler of Hamburg. Both of them were on an excellent footing with SS Lieutenant-Colonel Sauer, who supported and approved their every act. Mr. X was in the habit of throwing inmates no longer able to do a full day's work into the Düna and preventing any attempt at rescue. They were then scratched from the rolls with the notation "heart failure." One inmate, who had fallen ill of dysentery, gave away his food. Mr. X got wind of it and had the man thrown in a large kettle of boiling water, intended for preparing coffee for the camp. The sick man was scalded to death, but the coffee was prepared from the water all the same.

SS Major Krebsbach of Cologne was always picking on the sick and feeble. In May 1944, my father too was purged for this reason, because of a slight leg injury. The destination of the shipment was again given as Dünamünde. My father managed to get a farewell message to me. It said that the gas truck was parked in his immediate vicinity. He appealed to me to continue assisting my mother as much as I could. In less than an hour, he said, his own torments would be over.

Early in July 1944, I was taken to the Stutthof concentration camp, with 1,350 men and the same number of women. There again the sick and feeble were picked out and taken to the crematory, after first having been killed by means unknown to me. My mother is supposed to have come to Stutthof, two months later. I never heard anything more of her. I myself, together with others, was shortly afterward transferred to Buchenwald.

And now for a picture of the heroic struggle of the Jews in Warsaw, as reported by Vladimir Blumenfeld, who reached Buchenwald on April 5, 1945, after an adventurous pilgrimage.

The entire Jewish population of Warsaw was registered immediately after the occupation by the German armed forces. Those who refused to register were liable to capital punishment. Resettlement resulted in the creation of a great ghetto in which initially some half a million Jews lived. Additions from the countryside swelled the number to three-quarters of a million. The situation continued essentially unchanged until July 22, 1942, the day the extermination of the Jews began.

On July 20, companies of the SS regiment "Reinhard Heydrich," part of the extermination detail at Lublin, reached Warsaw under the command of SS First Lieutenant Tumann. On July 22, 1942, the ghetto walls were surrounded by Ukrainian SS. A notice was posted: "All Jews—men, women and children—who do not work in German factories or armament plants or in the ghetto administration must leave the ghetto." They were to be shipped to the east to help in rebuilding the devastated areas. The office of the Civilian Commissioner was abolished. His place was taken by an SS Resettlement Staff under SS Second Lieutenant Brand, who established his office at 103 Eisengruber Street in the ghetto.

Every day whole blocks were surrounded and whoever

was inside the line, whether in the houses or the streets, had to come along to the railroad station to be herded into freight cars. If the required quota of ten thousand Jews had not been assembled by six o'clock, the SS resorted to other measures. They began to shoot and kill until the quota was full.

Signs called on the Jews to volunteer for shipment to the east, where life was pictured as much easier than in the confined ghetto. The ghetto food supply was choked off, while six pounds of bread and half a pound of marmalade were issued to every volunteer. To break the spirit of the Jews, the water supply was also cut off. These measures were not without success. The Jews began to "volunteer."

The SS established a Property Administration under SS First Lieutenant Conrad and District Governor Fischer, who employed two thousand young Jews and had them temporarily exempted from resettlement. Everything that was left behind—furnishings, valuables, clothing, linen—was collected, sorted and stored in the SS depot at 51 Wild Street, formerly Dr. Sonnenhofer Street. The SS members of the Resettlement Staff got rich on the loot. What was left went to the Nazi welfare organization.

Many of the Jews tried to hide, since they foresaw the fate that awaited them. True, postcards arrived from Maljinka near Treblinka, reporting that the settlers were faring well. But the cards were almost identically worded, and it was instinctively felt that they could not correspond to the truth, merely representing the only chance to show a sign of life. There was no possibility of escape from the ghetto, however, and resettlement was continued.

On August 9, 1942, there was a sudden official declaration that the program had been completed. Those that were still left were to be permitted to remain in the ghetto, on condition that they submitted to another registration. They were to assemble within the area bounded by Ostrowska, Dr. Sonnenhofer, Mila and Nalevki Streets. Absentees were threatened with death.

A glimmer of hope pervaded the wretched ghetto inmates. Some 200,000 men, women and children answered the call and appeared at the appointed hour. In rows of five they had to march past SS Second Lieutenant Brand

and his staff. The muster went on for six days—and 50,000 new victims were selected! They were shipped off to the east. The others were issued a pass and were permitted to return to their homes.

The selection process was a nerve-wracking ordeal. I was forbidden to leave the area. Day and night the people cowered on the ground, without food or drink. On August 14, it was my family's turn. We passed before the lord over life and death. Suddenly the lieutenant's glance fell on my father. A wave of the hand ordered him to step out of ranks. Before he could even shake hands with me or say a word, an SS corporal shot him down with two bullets from his pistol. I stood paralyzed for a moment, then caught my father in my arms. There was a small disturbance. I dragged away the dying man, accompanied by my mother and two sisters. At least my father was spared the "trip to the east."

There was no news from those who had departed. We were prepared for the worst. Meanwhile, however, there were isolated fugitives who had succeeded in escaping from Treblinka. At a Jewish youth meeting, reports were made of what members of the recovery squads had seen and experienced at Treblinka—massacres, shootings, gassings. It was decided to establish secret communication with members of the Polish Socialist Party. As a result some Polish Socialists went to Kossuv near Treblinka and confirmed what we had been told. The trains of settlers with their Polish escort went only as far as the gate. No one except the victims got inside the barbed-wire enclosure. The smoke could be seen and the pungent odor smelled at considerable distance.

Clandestine leaflets in Jewish advised the Jews of Warsaw of the deeds of their "protectors." The Polish National party spread the news in Polish circles. The impact of these dreadful accounts gave rise to but a single thought: The next selection and shipment must be resisted!

Dr. Izaak Schipper, leader of the Polish Zionists, became the soul of the resistance movement. At a secret youth meeting he said: "If history and destiny have decided on our extermination, we shall die fighting. We shall not voluntarily go to our death in the east!" With the aid of the Polish Socialist party, rifles were obtained. A resistance group was created under the leadership of Laib Rodal of Kielce. The metal manufacturer Abraham Geppner was the first to contribute one million zloty for the purchase of arms. Many millions were collected. We paid 5,000 zloty for a pistol, 12,000 for a machine-gun. We obtained hand grenades; we built dugouts in the cellars. We succeeded in evacuating old people into the city, keeping mainly they young people and some of the women and children who were determined to die at the side of their husbands and fathers. My mother and one sister remained in the ghetto. My younger sister went to the non-Jewish part of Warsaw. She was fair and blue-eyed and unlikely to attract attention. I never saw her again. We formed small combat groups. Assassinations were carried out—of the prison warden, of the chief of the Property Control Office, of Gestapo collaborators seeking to save their own lives at the expense of the Jews.

January 18, 1943 became a milestone in the martyrdom of the Warsaw ghetto. The German police were given orders to exact revenge for the assassinations. Again the ghetto was surrounded and the entire population was required to report. No one answered the call. The Jewish Council went into hiding. Instructions were issued by word of mouth to offer no resistance for the time being. A search was conducted for four days. Many Jews were picked up with arms and shot out of hand, as were those found in hiding in the houses and nooks. Some 18,000 men, women and children were killed. There was more work for the Property Control Office. The Jewish Council was ordered to provide burial for the "bandits." We were but 40,000 Jews left in the ghetto, most of us young people organized into small combat groups of the Jewish youth organizations.

Passover was approaching—April 19, 1943. We learned from friends in the Polish camp that several SS companies had arrived in Praga, the eastern suburb of Warsaw. On the second day of Passover at four o'clock in the morning, they surrounded the ghetto. Our boys hurried from house to house and a state of alarm was announced. Everyone descended to the cellars, with arms and food. Groups of the SS began to enter the ghetto. At the corner of Nalevki Street, at No. 42, a young man stepped from a door and halted a group of twenty-five SS men commanded by a sergeant. He pointed to the third courtyard and said that ten Jews were hiding there. The SS detachment followed him. It had scarcely reached the third courtyard, when the young man drew his pistol and shot down the sergeant. The signal for battle had been given. Shots crashed from the windows, hand grenades began bursting, and hell broke loose. The young man who fired the first shot was Mordechai Nutkowicz of Ripin. He fell dead, but not one of the invading SS men left the courtyard alive. The entire section flamed into revolt and fighting broke out at every corner. The SS had not expected this reception. They hastily withdrew from the ghetto. Quiet prevailed until the next day. Then tanks moved up and fired incendiary shells at the houses. We tried to put out the flames and to fight the tanks with hand grenades, but our forces were far inferior. In the end we crawled into our dugouts. SS infantry pushed their way into the ghetto. They were received with a hail of bullets and hand grenades. It was then decided to strafe us from airplanes. The ghetto began to burn at every corner. The fire lasted for four days. The dugouts were located by means of listening devices and then blasted and destroyed one by one with mines and shells. Within two weeks the mopping-up operation had been completed.

The survivors were shipped to the Lublin concentration camp, including myself, my mother and my sister. The shipment offered the familiar picture: one to two hundred persons herded into cattle cars, with neither food nor water; detrainment at Lublin; women and children to the left, men to the right. I can still see my mother and sister being led away with many others between Fields I and II. A small house swallowed them up. I never saw them again. They died by gas.

I remained in the Lublin concentration camp until July 24, 1943. From there I was shipped to Auschwitz. I soon contracted scabies, a harmless skin rash, was selected for liquidation, taken to Block 20 to be gassed the next day. I owe my life to Jusek Kenner, who somehow got hold of a diamond ring and gave it to the Senior Camp Inmate. The

*latter took me from the barracks at night. From Auschwitz
I was sent to Camp S III at Ohrdruf in Thuringia, and on
April 5, 1945, to Buchenwald.*

In view of the descriptions that have been given, it will be
readily understood what it meant for the Jews remaining
behind in Buchenwald when one morning in 1943 the Commandant's personal barber, a political prisoner named Franz
Eichhorn, while waiting as usual for the Commandant to
emerge from his bath, found an order on the desk which read:
"to: All Camp Commandants. All Jews in Europe to be
shipped to Koch at Lublin. Himmler." Two hundred Jewish
"bricklayers" nevertheless remained in Buchenwald, marked
indispensable for certain important defense construction
work.

Many Jews, especially if they were not German, lived in the
camps unrecognized—i.e., the SS never identified them as
Jews. True, they were not in constant danger of death, but
theirs was by no means an easy life, for they were forever exposed to the risk of being discovered or denounced by their
fellows. Initially the SS went far beyond the Nuremberg racial
laws and stigmatized anyone as a Jew who had even one
Jewish grandparent and was unable to conceal the fact in his
record. Sometimes the mere shape of the nose was sufficient
evidence for the SS men. Anyone whom they did not like
became a Jew. At a later day "quarter-Jews" and "half-
Jews" were in part "aryanized" and no longer wore the
yellow triangle. For most of those affected it was already too
late.

Chapter Sixteen

REPRISALS AGAINST OTHER "INFERIOR RACES"

Almost as soon as the Polish campaign in 1939 was over, members of the Polish minority in Germany were sent to the concentration camp. In October they were followed by partisans and later by Poles in large numbers. Not until August 1944, after the uprising in Warsaw, were Poles again sent to the concentration camps on a large scale.

In general the Poles adapted themselves relatively well to the situation. They did not have an easy time of it, however, even among the prisoners, who regarded them with little affection. Thus most of them were intent on mutual aid. In the course of the war years they came to fill some important prisoner offices in some of the eastern camps and to some extent in other camps as well. They were often very strongly represented in the ranks of the Barracks Orderlies and also not infrequently in privileged details, for as a group they pursued a systematic policy of pushing their own people. There were fine valiant comrades in their ranks, as a rule with a strongly developed national and religious sense, which was much more wide-spread among them than Communism. The majority were highly adaptable and managed to get by. With all their virtues and faults the Poles in the concentration camps reflected their national character rather faithfully.

Some seventeen hundred of the Poles sent to Buchenwald in October 1939, including Polish Jews, chiefly from Austria, were placed in the Little Camp in the roll-call area, already described. The partisans were allowed to starve and freeze to death in the "Rose Garden." The others had to slave in the quarry. As early as the second half of October an epidemic of dysentery broke out among the Poles. It spread so rapidly that camp headquarters was compelled to exempt the inmates of the Little Camp from labor and to quarantine them.

The SS officers, led by Commandant Koch and SS Captain Hüttig, then Second Officer-in-Charge, and the special commissioners for the Little Camp, Master Sergeants Planck and Hinkelmann, were inexhaustible in contriving new torments to fill the enforced leisure. And every now and then Hüttig provided "extra fun." He had the whipping rack set up in the Little Camp, moved in with a number of Block Leaders, and indiscriminately had twenty-five lashes administered to every tenth inmate. In one instance a prisoner volunteered to take the punishment for his brother. Hüttig showed his impartiality by having both brothers beaten.

Master Sergeant Hinkelmann delighted in leaving a pot half filled with soup on the roll-call area. When the hungry inmates crowded around it to get a share, he would set upon the whole group with a heavy club until heads were beaten bloody.

It grew colder as the season advanced, but there was no change in the situation in the Little Camp. Each prisoner kept his single blanket. No one undressed any longer, all sleeping in their clothes and in consequence becoming more and more infested with vermin. Food grew even scarcer. The bread ration was cut. The soup issue was reduced to less than a quart, and it seemed to have been put through a filter. Even this scanty fare the inmates of the Little Camp did not get every day, since Commandant Koch liked to impose a fast upon the entire camp for every alleged infraction and Master Sergeant Planck imposed his own additional ration withdrawals. This took on such a scope that in November 1939, for example, there were twelve days on which no rations were issued. In other words, the prisoners were "fed" on only eighteen days!

The bestialization which this barbarous treatment induced is seen from the following practice which became general: when an inmate had died in the tents, the fact was concealed and the dead man was dragged or carried by one or two men to the bread issue point, where the ration was issued to the "helpers." The body was then simply dumped anywhere in the roll-call area.

There was no issue of winter clothing in the Little Camp. The men continued to wear what they had. Even during the period of intense cold—December and January—neither overcoats nor sweaters, mufflers, ear protectors and gloves were available. When quarantine was imposed, treatment at the dispensary automatically stopped, and frostbite of the feet as well as other afflictions inexorable led to death. During morning roll call, fifteen, twenty and even twenty-five bodies could be counted each day in the snow. On one occasion, when the Commandant received the daily report on deaths in the Little Camp, he replied, "That's much too slow to suit me. Can't we let the men work?"

Fear of the spread of dysentery prevented that, but there were other methods. Early in December, camp headquarters professed to see danger in the increasing vermin infestation in the Little Camp—it was not uncommon for an inmate to harbor as many as fifty lice. Delousing was ordered and carried out on December 8. The inmates enjoyed the bath, but their clothes were withheld for two days and they were issued only thin summer clothes. The blankets, of course, were also retained, and no replacements were issued. There followed a dreadful night in which no one was able to sleep because of the cold. The next morning, on their way to the roll-call area, the other prisoners in the camp anxiously looked for the result. There it was, laid out neatly in the snow: six rows of ten each, and one row of seven—sixty-seven dead.

For unknown reasons camp headquarters, in mid-January 1940, decided to dissolve the Polish Little Camp and transfer its remaining inmates to the camp proper. Of the 1,700 men who had been placed in the Little Camp in October, 600 still survived. Most of them emerged in a state that made their further survival seem improbable. Their average weight was below ninety pounds, and even convalescent status at the hospital was unable to save many of them. Several hundred died in short order.

All in all, an estimated forty men of the original 1,700 may have survived, including Felix Rausch, a reliable witness of the events that have been described—events that were, of course, witnessed by the entire camp through the inner barbed-wire enclosure.

In addition to this operation, which was merely one aspect of the general reprisals the Poles suffered immediately after the conclusion of the campaign, they became the victims of two other special measures.

In 1938–39, the Jews, chiefly those in Vienna, had been forced to sign over their houses and property to Nazis and their creatures. The "sales prices" ranged down to ten marks! In the case of the Poles an even simpler procedure was adopted. They received no payment whatever. They were simply notified that they and their families had to leave their homes. To refuse to give the required signature was tantamount to suicide. Dozens of letters testified that the German conquerors and their henchmen allowed the Poles not even an hour to clear out, and that nothing could be taken along except a single handbag and thirty marks for each person.

When tens of thousands of Polish labor slaves, branded with insulting emblems, had been carried off to inner Germany, instances arose in city and country in which Polish men entered into relations with German girls. Under orders from Himmler, the Poles were hanged, while the German girls were sent to Ravensbruck, the concentration camp for women, where they received twenty-five lashes on the naked buttocks three times in succession. Frequently the local population, incited by notorious Nazis, had already "spontaneously" pilloried the poor women by cutting off their hair and parading them through the streets.

Suddenly, in the year 1941, the Poles at Buchenwald began to be grilled for such cases of "race defilement." Denunciations, both inside the camp and out, played a large part in the process. Young Poles were pressed into service as executioners of their fellow countrymen. These Polish hangmen were sent out from Buchenwald over a large area of Thuringia to do their work. Equipped with a double-armed gallows, each arm providing space for three victims, they visited cities and villages under SS escort, conducting public executions in order to deter the eastern slave workers. Whenever any act of violence attributed to Poles occurred in the region where the camp was located, as many as thirty Polish inmates would be taken to the scene of the incident and hanged as an example.

The youthful Polish hangmen who had been pressed into this service were enjoined to the strictest silence and did not know the countryside. It was therefore impossible to get reliable data on the cities and villages where such executions took place—though for months I myself sat in the immediate vicinity of one of these Poles in the prisoner tailor shop at Buchenwald.

The Russians in the camps fell into two groups that were sharply distinct: Russian prisoners of war and civilians; and Ukrainians. The second group constituted the preponderant majority. The prisoners of war, Communists proudly standing up for their cause, were a well-disciplined body that was skillfully and rightfully intent on protecting its collective privileges. As for the mass of the Ukrainians, they were a rather motley crew. In the beginning they were favored by their German party comrades in a way that made it almost impossible to make even the slightest complaint against a "Russian." But the insolence, sloth and lack of solidarity among many of them soon brought a thoroughgoing change that no longer permitted them to gain leading positions. In the final year at Buchenwald the Russian prisoners of war, together with a few outstanding Young Communists from the ranks of the Ukrainians, undertook the task of training at least the useful members of this group, which was marked by utter lack of restraint, in order to fit them into the whole structure. Occasionally this difficult task succeeded in part.

Late in the summer of 1941, mass shootings of selected Russian prisoners of war began in all the large German concentration camps. Before "Detail 99" had been formed, the first executions at Buchenwald took place on a rifle range to one side of the camp, in the area of the German Armament Works, right behind the tailor shop. To drown out the crack of the rifles, the entire camp had to assemble in the roll-call area and sing songs, often in the middle of the work day. By the second time this happened everyone knew what was going on, since the bodies appeared at the crematory within the hour. After several weeks, matters proceeded without this rather ridiculous camouflage, until the stable had been appropriately equipped.

There was no chance to do anything for these victims, since they were marked for "special treatment" by the Political Department immediately on admission and there was no possibility of establishing contact with them. The executions took place by day as well as by night. In Buchenwald they ran to at least 7,000, probably more. There are well-reasoned estimates that run as high as 9,500. After the executions, the trucks with the bodies drove from the stable to the crematory, where it was possible to make a rough count. In the Sachsenhausen and Dachau concentration camps these liquidations likewise ran to about 10,000 each.

The executions affected primarily officers, political commissars, Communist youth leaders and other Communist party officials. To ferret these out there were Gestapo informers in every "Stalag" (prisoner-of-war base camp) and in every concentration camp admitting prisoners of war. In Buchenwald this sorry job was performed by an alleged former Czarist general named Kushnir-Kushnarev, to whom I shall revert in still another connection.

I have in my possession a document marked "Top Secret," the transcript of an address delivered by two Weimar Gestapo officials to a selected group, on their activities as informers of this kind in Stalag District IV E, embracing Dresden, Altenburg, Halle, Lützen, Merseburg, Naundorf and Weissenfels. The document was found among the papers of a Weimar Nazi judge, and may be the only surviving copy. Unfortunately it does not give the names of the lecturer—his accomplice was named Pause. The two informers expressly state that the directives and decrees under which they operated were issued "with the concurrence of the Army High Command." In the introduction we read:

The custody, care and utilization of 2,500,000 Soviet Russian soldiers in the Reich territory confront the Government and the Army with new tasks. A number of considerations enter into the question. As far as can be seen from directives and decrees issued so far, a large part of the territory we have conquered will be opened up to German colonization. Obviously we need people for the conquered territory who (1) are acceptable for the reconstruction of the country and (2) are able to put agriculture and industry back on their feet. At the present time there is no German population excess available for this purpose. We are thus compelled to resort to the Russians themselves.

Naturally not every Soviet-Russian can be considered for this work, for since the early twenties the Russians have been systematically indoctrinated and incited along Bolshevist lines. Thus all unacceptable elements among the prisoners of war who might be used in the occupied territory must be discovered and eliminated. These politically unacceptable elements include chiefly important government and party functionaries, professional revolutionaries and Comintern functionaries, all leading functionaries of the Communist party and the Soviet Union and their subsidiary organizations from the Central Committee down to regional and local soviets, all People's Commissars and their deputies, all former Red Army political commissars, leading personalities at the top and intermediate level in government, industry and culture, all Jews and all persons known to be agitators and fanatical Communists. All persons, furthermore, must be detained who might be useful in further investigations and in clarifying questions of general interest.

To achieve these objectives as quickly as possible, the Reich Main Security Office, in co-operation with the Army High Command, utilized the inspectors of the Security Police and Security Service at nearly all the regional Gestapo offices to form so-called Emergency Squads (*Einsatzkommandos*) that were detailed to the prisoner-of-war camps. How they proceeded is seen from a single paragraph in the lecture:

There is not the slightest reason for allowing sentimental considerations or other emotional factors to prevail in the case of the Russians. For this reason the Soviet-Russians classified as suspect by the Emergency Squads were immediately reported to the Reich Main Security Office, ac-

cording to its directive of July 17, 1941, and shot upon receipt of an execution confirmation. It was necessary for this purpose that the Soviet-Russians in question be released by the Army High Command and turned over to the Security Police. Under agreements entered into by the agencies in question, this was done in every instance. On receipt of the confirmation, execution of the measures ordered is always instituted at once. Extended detention of the Soviet-Russians in question in the camps is avoided. Execution itself must not take place in the camp nor in its immediate vicinity. Furthermore it must not be public; indeed, no spectators whatever are to be admitted. According to instructions from the inspector in Dresden, the Soviet-Russians classified as suspect are shipped to a concentration camp as quickly as possible, and execution then takes place there.

From the moment they fell into German hands, Russian prisoners of war underwent a whole series of such weeding-out processes.

The first examination takes place in the front-line Stalags, where screening and classification along every line are conducted. This process is repeated in the rear camps, through the medium of the labor details. For this reason it is easy to see that the remaining Russians have for the most part already been winnowed from the suspect elements. Only in the last few days has the Army High Command issued detailed instructions to subsidiary commands concerned with the treatment of Soviet-Russian prisoners of war in all prisoner-of-war camps. . . . These instructions merely underline the importance of political and other screening of Soviet-Russian prisoners of war. They are motivated by the idea that the Russian prisoners are not prisoners of war in the ordinary accepted sense, but that they are, as the Führer emphasized in his latest speech inaugurating the 1941–42 Winter Aid Campaign, composed exclusively of beasts and brutes. They must be primarily treated as such.

The two Gestapo agents represented themselves to the

Russians as commissioners charged with selecting personnel for especially desirable labor details, and according to their own statements they were able to pick out, from 1,650 prisoners of war, "three political commissars or their assistants, five unacceptable elements, five civilians, three Asiatics, seven members of Turki races, three officers, and twenty-four potential undercover agents."

In 1943, the mass liquidation of Russian prisoners of war gradually subsided, apparently because of international complications. It was ended early in 1944. Shootings of individual Russians or smaller groups often occurred even subsequently.

Quite apart from these measures, other Russian prisoners of war were admitted to the concentration camps by the thousands. In the middle of 1941, the first three thousand arrived in Buchenwald. The whole camp was tense in anticipation of what the SS would do as a result of the incitement which they had undergone. Virtually the entire headquarters staff, led by Officer-in-Charge Plaul, waited at the gatehouse. When the Russians arrived, they were subjected to no more than verbal abuse. The figures that limped in looked too wretched for anything more. They had been on the march for many months, had traversed hundreds of miles on only a minimum of food. They were in rags and tatters and they were utterly exhausted. Tottering through the gate, they resembled shadows of men. Emerging from the bath-house, they looked like skeletons.

The army and the SS tried to create the impression that the Russians had been ill-fed and ill-clad at home. The purpose of the long march across Germany was to demonstrate this to the German population. In the concentration camp the effect was precisely opposite. There was an immediate demonstration of solidarity such as had not been experienced before. Everyone who had the time and opportunity ran to his barracks to get food and cigarettes. Many men surrendered their last crust of bread.

When headquarters learned of this, three well-known Communist Senior Block Inmates were at once relieved. The three, Karl Wappel, Kurt Leonhardt and Josef Schuhbauer, were treated to twenty-five lashes by Sommer and were sent to the quarry. The entire camp was penalized by having rations withdrawn for a day. "If I ever catch any of you Germans giving anything to these sons of bitches from the east . . ." roared SS Major Schobert, First Officer-in-Charge, over the public-address system. Of course aid continued, but in secret.

In the months from March to June, 1942, more than six thousand Russians were admitted, some of them prisoners of war, others displaced persons. They too generally arrived in a state of complete exhaustion. The prisoners of war in the concentration camps were segregated from the rest of the camp by a barbed-wire enclosure, and the separate section was designated "Prisoner-of-War Camp." The sign was the only thing in which the enclosure differed from the regular concentration camps.

In February 1942, the bulk of the Russian prisoners of war at Buchenwald were shipped to Sachsenhausen, some 4,200 perishing en route. After late 1942 there were only about 1,200 Russian prisoners of war left at Buchenwald, and shootings, disease and malnutrition gradually reduced the figure to 800. These 800 managed to maintain themselves well, playing an important part in camp, without the knowledge and against the will of the SS.

If the Nazi regime had had its way, not a single Russian would have survived imprisonment and the concentration camp. "We were able to see with our own eyes," says the above-cited lecture, "that they devoured leaves, tubers, roots, worms and mice in the fields. The guards at the Klausa air-force base near Altenburg told us that the prisoners picked up moldy food and inedible offal from the garbage heaps and devoured them." One wonders whether this could have been from pure enthusiasm or because they had been subjected to severe starvation! The Gestapo informer gives this cold-blooded reply:

The diet of the Russian prisoners is worse than that of the others. The reason is that Russia never subscribed to the Geneva Convention on the treatment to be accorded prisoners of war, and there is thus no cause for us to treat the Russians according to international law. We do not know how the Russians treat our own prisoners, but it must be assumed, from such reports as are available, that few of them will survive.

It must be assumed . . . the mere "assumption" was once again sufficient to justify the murder of hundreds of thousands of men of alien nationality, thereby exposing the Germans in enemy hands to reprisals.

The almost two thousand Danes, mostly police officials, who came to Buchenwald in 1944, formed a close-knit unit living under somewhat more favorable conditions than other special groups and pretty much to itself. There were never any conflicts between the Danes and the other prisoners. They rejected participation in illegal activities against the SS, probably from distrust. Time and again they contributed a certain share of the Red Cross supplies that were available to them in relative abundance.

This was even truer of the 350 Norwegian students who likewise spent some time at Buchenwald. They brought a spirit of sportsmanship with them and were excellent comrades.

The Czechs who were not exterminated at Auschwitz came to the concentration camps as so-called "Protectorate Prisoners" and originally enjoyed certain privileges. They lived in barracks of their own, wore their hair long and for months were not required to work, which earned them much envy and dislike. Yet their readiness to help, especially in distributing surplus food and sharing their smokes, smoothed over many conflicts with the other prisoners. By and by a growing number of them volunteered for labor—before the whole group was summarily deprived of its privileges—and thus had a chance to pick out good details. In the long run few of the Czechs held heavy labor assignments. They stuck together systematically and helped their fellow countrymen wherever they could. When party conflict within their ranks had been overcome, their relations with other nationality groups among the prisoners were in part friendly, in part correct.

Central directives affected not merely Russian prisoners of war but also Dutch, French and Belgians. They resulted in the so-called NN shipments. The SS had a matchless way of attaching romantic-sounding labels to their murder operations. "Operation Whitecap" and "Operation Zephyr," for example, were names for the round-ups of Frenchmen to be sent to the German concentration camps. The state in which these men sometimes arrived can scarcely be pictured. In the summer of 1943, hundreds of Frenchmen, scantily dressed or completely naked, were unloaded at the Weimar railroad station together with their dead, from cars into which they had been herded since Compiègne. They were then marched to Buchenwald in a group that included high government officials, professors, officers (especially of the French police) and engineers.

By virtue of their temperament and their generally smaller physical resistance, the French suffered more from the hardships of camp life than other groups. Their marked individualism and usually high intellectuality involved them in many avoidable difficulties with which their fellow prisoners then often showed little patience. A number of Frenchmen managed to establish excellent connections in the camps. But by and large they were badly off. It proved impossible to unify their ranks in order to make them more capable of resistance, to increase their value to the prisoners, for politically they were incredibly divided. Only the minority group of the French Communists had close contact with the camp underground at Buchenwald. Like their German comrades, they never mustered the strength to purge their ranks of politically camouflaged criminals and other dubious elements, so that the protection afforded by the group often remained a one-sided affair. The preponderant majority of the Frenchmen in the camps were helplessly exposed to every hardship—except the French physicians, many of whom gained noteworthy positions in the prisoner hospitals.

Soon after the influx of French prisoners in 1943, the label "NN shipments" began to trickle through from the Political Department in camp. At first this was interpreted as a special campaign directed against Netherland nationals. The true meaning soon transpired—"Never-Never Shipments."[1] These affected several hundred Dutch, Belgians and French. They were to be given a "race-biological examination" and then shipped to other concentration camps, notably the notorious Natzweiler camp. By what criteria selection for these shipments was conducted never became clear.

The prisoners slated for NN shipments were forbidden to

[1] The German words are actually *Nacht und Nebel*, night and fog.—*Tr.*

write their families. According to news that was received, their fate at Natzweiler varied. Poison gas experiments, originally planned, do not seem to have been conducted with them. All the same, it is likely that only a few survived these shipments.

The Dutch prisoners at Buchenwald exhibited a sturdy endurance. In the beginning, there were sharp conflicts between them and the other prisoners, but in the course of time these were greatly ameliorated and bridged. They were freedom-loving men who hated every form of compulsion, no matter from what source. Their native virtues enabled them time and again to overcome such difficulties as arose. The relationships between them and the other nationality groups in the camps were not only correct but often warm.

The Luxemburg nationals were also the victims of special Nazi measures. Most of the men from Luxemburg were young policemen. Several hundred of them had been arrested by the Gestapo and carried off to various places in Germany. In the end they were shipped to the concentration camps in groups of thirty to sixty. After the summer of 1940, most political prisoners from Luxemburg were shipped to the special SS camp Hinzert near Trèves, originally a so-called Labor Disciplinary Camp for "loafers," where prisoners spent only up to two months. Hinzert never had more than six or eight hundred prisoners, and the SS was therefore able to exercise extremely close control. The Commandant was a certain Sporenberg, given to inciting his SS men against the inmates in every possible way. He was aided by the Senior Camp Inmate, Eugen Wipf of Switzerland, who murdered and maimed many inmates. The labor details were without exception very hard, and all of them were located outside the camp. On moving in every night the columns would drag a cart behind them, loaded with their injured comrades. Outside the hospital barracks the cart would be overturned by a Block Leader, hurling the injured men to the ground. The Medical Officer was an SS sergeant named Brendel, a bricklayer by profession. He was a notorious alcoholic. The treatment of the patients often enough consisted only of blows with a club or a poker on the naked body.

I do not know the total number of victims among the Luxemburg prisoners in the Hinzert camp. Frenchmen admitted to this camp, by the way, had two large letters painted on their clothes—HN, the German initials for "Nation of Dogs."

For about half a year, until late in 1944, 167 English pilots were at Buchenwald. They had a well-disciplined military organization and maintained close liaison with leading non-Communist personalities among the prisoners. They observed an attitude of loyalty toward the German Communist leadership and also had useful contact with the Russian prisoners of war. Like the Danes they were rather reserved, which may have been a matter not only of their national temperament but of their calling. During the later period at Buchenwald, many excellent plans of action were based on the assurance of their aid.

The regional Gestapo office in Paris sent a number of Allied secret agents from the west to the concentration camps in 1944. Forty-three of them, English and French, arrived at Buchenwald on August 17 and were quartered in the admission barracks No. 43.

Their stories were full of the exciting incidents usually associated with secret services, and especially so at that particular time. They ranged from adventures with the French Maquis to open warfare against Gestapo agents. At Buchenwald these colorful careers moved toward their tragic climax.

On September 9, 1944, without any advance knowledge in the camp, sixteen of them were called to the gatehouse and immediately hanged in the crematory. An effort was made at once to save as many as possible from the ranks of those that remained. Together with my friend Heinz Baumeister of Dortmund, who worked with me in Ward 50, of the prisoner hospital, I offered to carry out the operation by way of Ward 46, though the Ward Foreman was my enemy. My chief asset was that I had SS Major Ding-Schuler under my thumb, a situation still to be related. Unfortunately only a very limited number of the doomed men could be included. There was a tragic scene, when Squadron Leader Dodkin (whose real name, Yeo-Thomas, was known to no one) had to make a selection from among his comrades and put them in a sequence of priority. Because of his own importance, his comrades insisted that he head the list. These Britons and Frenchmen exhibited sterling morale. Only three of them could be saved: in addition to Dodkin, the British Captain

Peuleve and Lieutenant Stephane Hessel of General De Gaulle's secret service.

Under dramatic circumstances we succeeded in wresting authority for the rescue operation from Dr. Ding-Schuler. As a cover we staged a pretended typhus epidemic in Barracks No. 17, placing the three officers named in isolation, an action that had to be kept not only from the camp but even from Ward 50. The three men were admitted to Ward 46, where Dietzsch, the Capo, was made privy to the plot by Baumeister, insofar as this was necessary. At this particular time, "unfortunately," there did not happen to be among the prisoners or the incoming shipments any fatal cases of typhus with whom the agents might have traded identities. We could not use the convicts who were experimental subjects in the typhus experiments—not only as a matter of principle but also because the men to be saved would only have been exposed to additional dangers as wearers of the green triangle. Furthermore, only Stephane Hessel spoke German. This language difficulty limited our search to Frenchmen. Both Dodkin and Peuleve spoke fluent French.

But where were we suddenly to find Frenchmen dying of typhus?

As early as October 5, another twenty-one members of the group, including Peuleve, were called out. Twenty of them were shot. Twice on that day the SS came to Ward 46 to pick up Peuleve, who had been reported to the Roll Call Officer as sick. The first time Dietzsch, warned by our excellently functioning intelligence service, deliberately absented himself, and the SS men were afraid to enter the ward, because of the supposed danger of infection. The second time Dietzsch refused to surrender Peuleve, citing his orders that no one could enter Ward 46—except with the permission of Dr. Ding-Schuler.

While Heinz Baumeister and I administered an injection of milk to Peuleve in order to have him run a high temperature, Dr. Ding-Schuler actually paid no less than three visits to the Commandant. The first time he insisted that it was impossible to execute a dying man running a fever of over 105° F. (SS Colonel Pister replied: "Why not shoot him down with a revolver while he's on the litter?") The next time Dr. Ding-Schuler tried to have the execution delegated to himself as chief of Ward 46—which Pister declined to do.

Baumeister regarded any further attempt to use the SS major to outwit the Commandant as futile; but Dr. Ding-Schuler went to Pister a third time, to ask him to delegate the execution to Dr. Schiedlausky. It was an uncertain and hazardous expedient, threatening the very lives of all concerned. Pister's suspicions, however, were not aroused and he assented. Dr. Ding-Schuler was dispatched to see Dr. Schiedlausky. We knew that since his sojurn in Buchenwald, Schiedlausky had discarded the habits he had acquired in other camps. He no longer liked to administer fatal injections in person. It was Dr. Ding-Schuler's job to persuade him to delegate the execution to SS Master Sergeant Wilhelm. We knew enough about the sergeant to have confidence that we might use him as an unwitting tool.

It was late afternoon and night was beginning to fall. Dietzsch prepared a magnificent repast for Wilhelm, with plenty of *Schnaps*. Every phase of the operation had to be carefully timed, and no one except the five who were in on the plan could be permitted to have even an inkling of what was going on. When the master sergeant was deep in his cups, Dietzsch showed him a dying patient who happened to be in the ward and told him this was the man to be executed. Since the man was obviously on the verge of passing away, Dietzsch said, there was no use in wasting an injection on him. Wilhelm actually left and reported to the Camp Medical Officer that the execution had been carried out.

During this entire incident Captain Peuleve with his comrades sat concealed in an adjoining room of Ward 46, momentarily expecting execution.

To disarm any suspicion on the part of the Gestapo office that had issued the order for the execution, a separate report on Peuleve had to be prevented. Some keen-minded Security Service man might have come to know the practice of exchanging the living for the dead from other camps, even though it was rare enough. A report of a single execution in an isolation ward might arouse his suspicions. All that would be necessary to discover the evader would be to line up all the convalescents discharged from Ward 46 during the time in question. For a while I actually considered the possibility of a second change of identity. But by dispatching Dr. Ding-Schuler to the Commandant we succeeded in having all twenty-one executions reported to Berlin in a single teletype message.

During these very days a "heaven-sent" shipment arrived at Buchenwald. It included dozens of Frenchmen suffering from typhus. The first death among them occurred almost immediately. The dead man's age, appearance and background corresponded somewhat to those of Peuleve's. The transaction was promptly carried out. Henceforth Peuleve's name was Marcel Seigneur.

Another week had elapsed and we stood in daily fear that execution orders for the two other men who were to be saved might arrive. There were nerve-wracking days of waiting. Would any additional patients die, and when? All the while Baumeister and I had to maintain the sharpest vigilance, lest Ding-Schuler or Dietzsch accelerate any such deaths by means of poison. Finally we succeeded in effecting exchanges for Dodkin and Hessel.

How simple it all sounds today! We obtained the personnel records of the dead men from the Political Department, though only the Prisoner Foreman working there was supposed to have access to them. We saw to it that "regulation autopsies" were performed by Father Thyl on the supposedly dead men, even sent pathological typhus specimens from the bodies to the Institute of Hygiene of the *Waffen SS* in Berlin. For two full weeks a glass bottle labeled: "Dodkin, No. 10844. Specimens from spleen, liver, heart, brain—typhus" stood on the table before me.

Then we proceeded to smuggle the three officers—who had become a carpenter, a policeman and a student, respectively—into appropriate outside labor details, for they had of course become known in camp. Numberless dodges were adopted to mislead the personnel in the Orderly Room, the Labor Record Office, the Personal Property Room, to overcome obstacles, to checkmate possible enemies. Our heads were always in several nooses at the same time.

The reader may get a picture of the atmosphere in which this operation was conducted from the letters that were smuggled back and forth between Buildings 46 and 50 during those critical October weeks, since open communication was out of the question. I have managed to save some of these notes, scribbled on slips of paper in English, French and German.

On October 6—the day the SS twice came to take Captain Peuleve to his death—the officers wrote us about 2:30 P.M.:

You can imagine how we feel! D. [Dietzsch] remarked this morning it might be best if he infected us with typhus at once so that we would really be sick if they called us up. Later he proposed that he exchange us for two Frenchmen who are about to die, according to his statement. This proposal did not apply to P. Could not methods one or two be applied to him, to make sure that he is safe? I should regard one as the better.

If we could only talk to you for at least five minutes! It would mean a great deal to us to see the situation more clearly and to avoid tactical errors toward D. [All three men lacked camp experience and knowledge of the personalities involved, which immensely complicated the situation, since the slightest mis-step could mean the immediate end of all of us.]

Have you any accurate information about our comrades? Does the fact that those who were shipped out are being recalled mean that they too are to be shot? What a mess the whole thing is. . . . Your fighting spirit and tenacity are amazing. You know what they mean to us!

STEPHANE.

I should like to thank you from the bottom of my heart for everything you are doing for us. If I must go, it will not be because you have failed to do everything possible to save me.

With sincerest gratitude, your H.P.

Like Stephane, I should be only too happy to talk to you for a few minutes. We should be clearer on a few important points, and it just isn't possible this way. Many, many thanks for all your efforts. There's no point at all in my even beginning to tell you how grateful we are.

D. [*Dodkin*].

The next day the Peuleve switch was carried off.

Dear friends!

I can't hope to find the proper words for telling you how grateful I am to you for your magnificent achievement. . . . I only hope that the day may come on which I can repay at least a small part of the debt I owe you.

Forever your
MARCEL SEIGNEUR.

On October 13, Hessel wrote:

Well, D. [Dodkin] died today, which was a great relief to all of us. My turn will be next Monday, if all goes well. However, if the execution order should arrive before then (things happen so quickly that we must be prepared for such an eventuality any day), I ask myself whether it would not be more sensible to organize my escape, to take place at the moment the execution order arrives. Such a solution would, of course, be even more difficult, but at least it would hold an added element of safety for all of us, for there wouldn't be two simultaneous cases of sudden death just before execution under such suspicious circumstances. I leave the decision entirely up to you. Please give me instructions what to do. I place myself in your steady hands with complete confidence.

STEPHANE.

Two days later:

Since it is quite likely that we shall shortly be shipped out, it is essential that we learn certain details of our new identities. Can you try to get them for us? [This request crossed our message that the data had already been obtained.] The names are: Marcel Seigneur, No. 76,635; and Maurice Chouquet, No. 81,642. We must know where they came from and where they lived. Where did they work before they got to Buchenwald? Were they admitted with a large or small group? What was their work assignment at earlier detention places? When and where were they arrested? Why? What was their profession, religion, birth date and birth place? Whatever you can find out about their private and public lives will be of the greatest value to us.

I myself am still waiting to see what will happen to me. [Since no suitable Frenchman died from natural causes and since, in agreement with Hessel, we refused to have anyone killed for purposes of effecting the exchange, an alarming number of days elapsed, during which we considered one plan after another to save Hessel.] You can imagine the effect on me of every announcement over the public-address system.

Some three days later it appeared as though the Frenchman who had figured in our exchange plans and who had been hovering between life and death would recover. Dr. Ding-Schuler, moreover, had had enough excitement and began to lose interest in assuming any further risk. He was satisfied with having helped to save the two Britons. He had less liking for Hessel as a Frenchman, and wanted to drop him. I fought tenaciously against this trend in Schuler's mind during the brief periods in which I could talk to him without attracting the attention of the prisoners' intelligence service in Building 50, which was always distrustful of non-Communists, no matter how loyal they had proved themselves to be.

De Gaulle's officer wrote us:

The man with whom I was to change place seems to be coming through, thank God for him. There is no other dying Frenchman in prospect. I therefore believe that we can't lose any more time. I must take advantage of the next chance to stage an escape, even if that doesn't seem as safe and useful as the new solution you are contemplating, which surely sounds splendid. [By extremely devious means we proposed to smuggle Hessel into Building 50 and to conceal him for the duration of the war in a certain spot in the attic, while officially pretending that he had escaped and taking part in the search in camp and all the other consequences.]

Today is Wednesday and there is a strong likelihood that the execution order will arrive tomorrow (unless we are "lucky" enough to get it today). Please make all the necessary arrangements for having me assigned to an outgoing shipment for tomorrow. [Only a doomed man could have made such a proposal on twenty-four hours' notice, ignoring the enormous internal difficulties it involved!] And give me a good address on the outside! Anything else you can do for me over and above this would, of course, be of the greatest value. But even so I fear I must simply take my chances. It would be utter folly to wait any longer.

I am deeply indebted to you and have full confidence in you.

S. H.

The nerve-wracking ordeal had to be endured all the same. Two days later the Frenchman who was to figure in the exchange died after all. On October 21, Hessel was able to write:

Your good instincts did not deceive you. [During a night visit to the three I had expressed the conviction that the affair would come to a good conclusion, that God would not abandon those who put their trust in His mysterious workings; who maintained vigilance of heart and mind without doing wrong; who tried to serve a good and important cause with every ounce of human intelligence and devotion.] Thanks to your care, everything has come out all right. My feelings are those of a man who has been saved in the nick of time. What relief!

Now, on the question of shipping out. Cologne seems very good to us, because we might escape from there—indeed, even en route—to establish contact with the Allies as soon as possible. This might hasten matters for Buchenwald as well. Our plan would be to head for the front from there. It would be less than one hundred miles from there. If we could "beat it" from anywhere near Hamm, it would be only a little more than fifty.

Of course the whole escape plan would become much more airtight, if we had some money, civilian clothing and an address in the Ruhr region or the Rhineland. Can you get this for us? If the escape plan is abandoned, one shipment would be as good as the other, in my opinion. In-

deed, because of the air raids it would be better not to head for Cologne. Of course we are very strongly for Cologne, for a whole series of obvious reasons which are not all merely selfish!

We are still awaiting further details about Maurice Chouquet and Michel Boitel [Hessel's new name]. God, how happy I was when I learned that he wasn't married!

There are ten Royal Air Force men in the hospital at the present time. If one of them should die, please consider the possibility of another switch! This would open the way to write to England by way of the Red Cross, which likewise might advance the cause considerably. Of course the decision lies with you.

All three of us are now in fine shape and very optimistic—in view of the news from the front and the German speeches that augur well for the speedy victory of our side!

Forever yours,

S. H.

The rescue succeeded. Yeo-Thomas and Peuleve are today in London, Stephane Hessel in New York with the United Nations.

In the second half of October another member of the group, a Frenchman and the father of four children, was led off to be executed. As in the case of the others, there simply was no possibility of rescue under the prevailing circumstances, especially if the men who had already assumed new identities were not to be further endangered. Week after week the three remaining men lived in fear of the arrival of the execution order from Berlin—it usually came on Wednesday and was complied with on Thursday. Fortunately the order never did arrive. In this way the British Major Southgate survived. The two surviving Frenchmen were assigned to outside labor details. One of them, by the name of Guillot, escaped early in April 1945, but was recaptured and incarcerated in the Buchenwald prison, where he was liberated.

Suddenly, on April 5, 1945, an execution order for Dodkin was received from Gestapo headquarters! Evidently the report of his execution the preceding October had not reached the appropriate central office. In the evening the Roll Call Officer in person appeared at the prisoner Orderly Room—we had been instantly notified by out liaison man. He asked to see the file cards for all the Britons in camp. They included the cards for men who had died. He took out the card for Dodkin—which showed a variant spelling, by the way, namely *Dodkins*—and kept on searching until he found the card of a certain *Perkins*, a very popular British officer who had already been in Buchenwald for a year and a half and was not a member of the group of agents. The Roll Call Officer compared the two cards and finally took them away. We thought the Gestapo must have got on the trail of the Dodkin(s) affair, perhaps suspecting that Dodkin(s) and Perkins might be identical, because of a certain similarity in names. We feared there would be an investigation. Perkins himself seemed to be in no danger whatever, for he knew nothing about the affair and was not, in fact, Dodkin.

What had actually happened was that an execution order for *both* men had been received, a fact we could not have anticipated, since we had no idea that the report of Dodkin's execution had never reached Berlin, or Prague, whither Gestapo headquarters had moved meanwhile. Because of these fateful complications no one thought of at once admitting Perkins to the hospital, where he might have "submerged," a distinct possibility at this particular juncture. Perkins was executed that very day, a bare week before the camp was liberated by American troops.

For several months in 1944, 167 British Commonwealth pilots were in the Buchenwald concentration camp. Shortly before Christmas they were shipped out to an unknown destination. Their leader was Squadron Leader Lamason, an Australian who always maintained close liaison with Dodkin. No one knew why fliers should have been sent to a concentration camp, certainly not the fliers themselves. They lived the hard life of the Little Camp.

Chapter Seventeen

LIQUIDATION OF OTHER
"UNDESIRABLES"

As is by now well known, Hitler, at the conclusion of the Polish campaign issued a predated (September 1, 1939) secret decree authorizing "mercy death" for patients designated as incurable by physicians. The program was put into effect by Hitler's personal chancellery and a special department in the Reich Ministry of Interior. Apprehension and unrest among the people were, however, anticipated. (These fears proved well grounded, and as late as November 1942, Himmler, in a letter, casually disposed of them in the following words: "It will take at least a decade to root out these narrow-minded prejudices from our people.") To camouflage the killings, three innocent-sounding organizations were therefore created: The Reich Association, Hospital and Nursing Establishments, which located the victims; the Charitable Foundation for Institutional Care, which financed the killings; and the Non-Profit Patient-Transport Corporation, which shipped the death candidates to the murder plants. The program, however, did not remain a secret. In 1940, when the wholesale extermination of inmates of mental institutions, purely by "medical" selection from questionnaires, was under way, a tremendous underground turmoil arose in Germany. There was wild fear, entirely justified, that the plan was to include not merely the "incurably sick" but also other categories of "socially unfit life" in succession: persons unable to work, the sick, aged and feeble, serious war casualties, and finally every kind of Nazi opponent. The German nation, especially its Christian and humanitarian sections, proved to be "narrow-minded" enough to offer a serious threat to the common war effort. As a result Hitler was constrained, in August 1941, to slow down the main aspects of his euthanasia program for the time being. It continued to be enforced to the end of the war against children, "half-Jews" and eastern slave workers.

Naturally Herr Himmler could not forego letting his SS murder machine loose in this special field. In the concentration camps the operation was camouflaged under the code number "14 f 13," so designated by the SS Main Economic and Administrative Office. It was to winnow out prisoners who were mentally ill or unfit for work and, of course, Jews—in actual practice any prisoner who had run afoul of anyone with influence. A medical commission was entrusted with the task of selection. Some of its members were the very doctors who had previously been Hitler's euthanasia emissaries, traveling over the countryside like avenging angels. It took them only a few hours on each occasion, early in 1942, to compile lists of prisoners at Dachau, Sachsenhausen, Buchenwald, Mauthausen, Auschwitz, Flossenbürg, Gross-Rosen, Neuengamme and Niederhagen, and to set their fatal medical seal on the lists. The lists consisted simply of prisoners herded into the clutches of the medical commission by camp headquarters, and soon afterward the prisoners would be shipped out to an unknown destination. A short time later—six hours to three days, depending on the location of the camp—the personal possessions of the prisoners, including the contents of their pockets and their dentures, would be returned to the camp. We soon learned that new poison gases had been tried on the prisoners. The gases had been previously tested on cattle. Among the very first to be shipped out of Buchenwald to be gassed in this way were a whole series of political prisoners, such as the Austrian Security Director from Salzburg, Dr. Bechinie. According to reports, the mental institution at Bernburg, near Köthen, was the scene of these special gassings.

A few surviving letters give a picture of how the operation was conducted:

Buchenwald Concentration Camp
Office of the Commandant
Weimar-Buchenwald, February 2, 1942
Subject: Jews unfit for work in Buchenwald concentration camp.
Reference: Personal discussion. Enclosures.
2. To Mental Institution, Bernburg-on-Saale, P.O. Box No. 263.

With reference to personal discussion, enclosed herewith for further action two copies of a list of Jewish inmates of the Buchenwald concentration camp who are sick and unfit for work.

> *The Camp Medical Officer*
> *Buchenwald concentration camp*
> *signed HOVEN,*
> *SS First Lieutenant (Res.).*

The reply:

Bernburg Mental Institution
Bernburg, March 5, 1942
File reference: Be go-Pt
To: Buchenwald concentration camp, near Weimar
Attention: The Commandant
Reference: Our letter of March 3, 1942
Subject: Thirty-six prisoners, twelfth list of February 2, 1942

Our letter of March 3 requested you to make the remaining thirty-six prisoners available to us on the occasion of the final shipment on March 18, 1942. Because of the absence of our Chief Medical Officer, who must issue medical certificates for those prisoners, we now request that you ship the prisoners on March 11, 1942, rather than on March 18, together with their records which will be returned on March 11, 1942.

> *Heil Hitler!*
> *(signed)* GODENSCHWEIG.

●   ●   ●

The Gross-Rosen concentration camp had sent a list of 214 names of prisoners. The doctors of death at Bernburg replied:

> *March 24, 1942, seems to us the most suitable date of arrival, since we are being supplied from other concentration camps in the meantime and we need an intermediate period for technical reasons. If you can deliver the prisoners by bus, we suggest two shipments of 107 prisoners each, on Tuesday, March 24, and Thursday, March 26. We request your reactions to our proposal and your final decision, so that we may make further disposition.*

Dr. Eberl and his assistant Godenschweig had a long history of association with the SS and they continued to "make further disposition" on its behalf. As shown by a letter of March 19, 1943, from Dr. Hoven, dealing with the Buchenwald subsidiary camp at the Junkers Works, Schönebeck-on-Elbe, they had a little sideline of cremating the bodies of prisoners without death certificate:

> *Contractual obligations of physicians and negotiations with cemetery authorities have often led to insurmountable difficulties. . . . For this reason I immediately communicated with Dr. Eberl, Medical Director of the mental institution at Bernburg-on-Saale, P.O.Box No. 252, telephone number 3169. He is the physician who carried out 14 f 13. Dr. Eberl showed unusual understanding and courtesy. All current bodies of prisoners from Schönebeck-Wernigerode were shipped to Dr. Eberl at Bernburg, where they were cremated even without a death certificate.*

After January 1943, the SS Main Economic and Administrative Office sought to have Operation 14 f 13 limited entirely to mental patients. But this had little practical significance in the concentration camps, where at this time one gas shipment after another was being assembled. Auschwitz, gas-chamber headquarters of Europe, had the easiest time of all. The death candidates merely had to be taken to nearby Birkenau, where ninety per cent of all incoming prisoners were immediately exterminated as a matter of routine.

No one familiar with Nazi aims and government policy will be surprised that the Nazi overlords extended their extermination program to persons suffering from tuberculosis. They had figures to show that in Poland there were some 25,000 cases of open tuberculosis and some 130,000 patients whom treatment might be able to cure. For the first group *Gauleiter* Greiser of Posnan and Heydrich in the summer of 1942 proposed to Himmler that a "radical procedure" be adopted. Professor Blome, Deputy Chief of the Nazi party's Main Office of Public Health, likewise favored the plan, but in a communication dated November 18, 1942, he added:

> *Since some time ago the Führer halted the program in the mental institutions, it occurs to me that he may not regard "special treatment" of the hopelessly sick as politically feasible at the moment. In the case of the euthanasia program, German citizens afflicted with hereditary diseases were involved. This time it would be infected members of a subjugated nation. There can be no question that the proposed method represents the simplest and most radical solution. If there were the assurance of complete secrecy, all reservations, regardless of the reason, could be withdrawn. But I regard such secrecy as downright impossible.*

Blome proposed another solution—"strict quarantine and institutionalization of all infectious, hopeless tubercular patients. This solution would tend to make the patients die off fairly rapidly. The necessary inclusion of Polish physicians and nurses would to some extent rob such institutions of the character of death camps."

On December 3, 1942, Himmler instructed Greiser to "select a suitable area into which incurable tubercular patients can be sent." What happened to the plan in detail is unknown.

In some manner the number of tubercular patients in the concentration camps seems to have been limited by some central agency in Berlin. At any rate, in the summer of 1941, Dr. Eysele suddenly announced that there were "enough t.b.

patients'' at Buchenwald. He proceeded to kill whole groups of them by intravenous injections of sodium-evipan or by injecting the drug directly into the heart. Eysele killed at least three hundred men in this operation. Most of the victims—there were whole wards at a time—were given a sedative before the fatal injection was administered. Occasionally patients with particularly vigorous hearts survived as many as two injections, succumbing only to the third.

As were so many SS measures, this program directed against the tubercular was shot through with contradictions. It was limited to definite periods of time and was never truly comprehensive. For example, a so-called X-ray Battalion organized by the SS under the direction of Professor Hohlfelder traveled all over Germany to lay the scientific basis for an all-embracing anti-tuberculosis campaign among the German people. It even visited the concentration camps. X-ray photographs were made of every prisoner, and the cases that were diagnosed, far from being killed on the spot, were actually given medical treatment. But again, extreme caution was indicated in submitting to such treatment, in view of the arbitrary actions of certain Camp Medical Officers and contradictory directives from headquarters! A great many prisoners, especially Russians, did die of pulmonary tuberculosis. In all the camps autopsies showed that tuberculosis was among the most common diseases. The proportion of the Russians afflicted ran as high as seventy per cent.

Department D of the SS Main Economic and Administrative Office had a peculiar policy of consigning, from time to time, prisoners who were disabled or unfit for work, to special camps where they had little work or none at all. Dachau concentration camp had such an invalid camp for a long time. Not until the third year of the war did the SS, at first sporadically, then systematically proceed with the extermination of aged and enfeebled prisoners, perhaps because it thought this might relieve the food situation. Wherever there were gas plants in the camps, these were used to liquidate the supernumaries; otherwise it was done by injections. At Bergen-Belsen, which at times was actually and shamelessly referred to as a "recreation camp," the murder weapon was starvation. Late in 1944, Buchenwald was advised by the SS Main Economic and Administrative Office to make no further shipments of prisoners to Bergen-Belsen. Like other concentration camps, Buchenwald would "have to solve its overcrowding problems itself."

This is what the solution looked like:

There was a certain Building No. 61 in the Little Camp, a wretched wooden barracks released for hospital purposes after a long struggle with the SS. Building 61 was occupied by more than 800 patients from the Little Camp alone. SS Captain Schiedlausky gave orders that all invalids and weaklings from incoming shipments were to be taken there. From early 1944 to April, 1945, some 100,000 prisoners passed through the Little Camp, and from the fall of 1944, 20,000 and more were always quartered in its seventeen emergency barracks, while the rest were shipped on to subsidiary camps.

The Senior Block Inmates of the Little Camp were instructed to pick out men "incapable of survival." As a rule they picked those men whom they had reason to believe medical aid would be unlikely to keep alive. These selections took place two or three times a week, and from November 1944 to March 1945, they accounted for several thousand men. The precise number cannot be established, since the bodies were lumped together with those from the whole camp in the crematory.

These men were escorted behind the special barbed wire enclosing Building 61, where they had to strip to the skin out in the open. They were then ushered into the building. Inside they were either sent to the ward, where they got the customary medical treatment, or into a small room behind a door marked B, where SS Master Sergeant Wilhelm or a prisoner administered a fatal injection immediately. The bodies were put aside and taken to the crematory on carts in the evening, during roll call. At times Wilhelm took his pick when the incoming shipments were still in the bath-house.

The camp underground saved hundreds of prisoners of every nationality from Building 61—Communists standing the best chance of rescue. On the other hand, dozens of men who were by no means seriously ill—who might even be in good health—were eliminated by way of Building 61, once they had been caught in the meshes of personal or political camp intrigue. The blame, if any, attaching to the prisoners who actually made the selection is less than that of the dictatorial intriguers in the various barracks and among the various nationality groups, who were not above perverting for their own selfish purposes the machinery organized by the prisoners to protect themselves against the SS.

The "normal" daily death quota in Building 61 ran between 15 and 30, but when special operations were under way it would rise as high as 500 a week. In most other concentration camps the problem of the disabled was "solved" in similar fashion after 1943.

Special programs directed against pregnant women were carried out in the concentration camps as a result of general directives. Whenever women prisoners in outside labor details showed signs of pregnancy, they were shipped to Auschwitz, if they were Jewish, otherwise to Ravensbruck. They were told that only these camps had suitable maternity wards and nursery schools.

The following incident shows just what these nursery schools were. A Dutch physician who was Jewish had a non-Jewish wife, and the couple had a five-year-old girl. He was scheduled for shipment to Auschwitz from the Vught camp near Herzogenbusch. Entirely ignorant of the implications, he asked whether wife and child might accompany him. The SS gleefully assented, praising the "nursery school" that was supposed to be available at Auschwitz. The wife immediately agreed to go, and actually departed with her child ahead of the husband. When the doctor reached Auschwitz, his first act was to inquire for the women's home and the nursery school. With satanic laughter, the SS men pointed to the gas chambers. Wife and child were already dead. The husband himself perished within a few days.

When the gassings at Auschwitz were halted because of the impending evacuation of the camp, pregnant Jewish women, and later all other pregnant women, were shipped to the "recreation camp," Bergen-Belsen, where they were allowed to starve to death.

Such things could not be kept altogether secret, and as a result pregnancies were covered up by every possible means. If a birth actually took place, mother and child suffered the same fate.

Chapter Eighteen

SPECIAL PLACES OF EXECUTION
AND DISPOSAL OF THE DEAD

I am not exaggerating when I say that a separate book would have to be written on the concentration-camp prisons, called "Bunker." It would be a blood-curdling collection of documents. Each bunker in each individual camp had its own gruesome story, and it would be impossible for me to tell them all here, even if I knew all the details. They ranged from the "dog cells" at Dachau where the prisoners could only lie huddled on one side and had to bark for their food when it was passed to them; to unlighted solitary cells where German intellectuals were kept until they went almost blind; to the stand-up cells at Sachsenhausen, barely large enough to hold a man in upright position—it was impossible for him to wipe off the spittle if he was spat upon; and to every other imaginable form of torment.

It happened occasionally, though very exceptionally, that a prisoner was permanently kept in the bunker without being mistreated. Such an exception was Pastor Niemöller at Sachsenhausen. He spent his more than seven years in the concentration camps in solitary confinement, and saw virtually nothing of the rest of the camp. When it was necessary for him to visit the dental clinic, he had to climb into a wheelbarrow across which a tarpaulin was spread. The dental clinic was cleared and he was wheeled there and back in the same fashion. Niemoller, it is true, was visited by his wife. But the fact that he was for years kept in solitary confinement is significant enough.

Officially the bunker was called "The Cell Block." It was generally located in one wing of the gatehouse and consisted of a series of small concrete cells with raised bunks of stone and high window embrasures.

It was against this background that the prison wardens for years plied their dreadful trade. In Buchenwald it was Master Sergeant Sommer, a man who can be described only as a beast in human form—every camp knew his kind. Arrested in the course of the trial of Koch and Dr. Hoven, he admitted some 150 murders within a single half year. He tortured and killed during grillings, sometimes with the knowledge of the Political Department, as a form of "punishment," or simply "for fun." There are few methods that he failed to use. In the end the SS feared him no less than did the prisoners, for he was in a position to "rub out" anyone who got into his clutches.

Grillings in the bunker took place in the following manner: on admission the prisoner had to strip to the skin and his clothing was carefully searched. He was then taken to an unlighted cell and shackled to the radiator so that he was unable to move. At night the trusty Fischermann, a former Storm Trooper, made his rounds in felt-soled slippers. If he found the prisoner asleep, he would set upon him with a rubber truncheon. The prisoner's screams would bring Sommer, who would wield his whip until the victim was unconscious.

In the middle of the night Leclaire, an official of the Political Department, would arrive. The prisoner was revived with cold water. Leclaire would first of all beat him about the head, to refresh his memory: "You know, don't you, that you'll never leave this place alive? If you lie, we'll give you something to laugh about all right!" If the prisoner still refused to talk or did not tell enough, Commandant Koch would be requested to issue a written authorization that has become notorious: "The prisoner is to be examined until he confesses."

On the basis of this authorization Sommer would, for example, force the stripped prisoner to immerse his testicles in ice-cold and boiling water in turn, painting them with iodine when the skin came off in strips. Naturally this caused the most agonizing pain. Or Sommer would tie the prisoner's hands on his back and string him up by them from a set of rings mounted in a barred door in the central corridor of the cell block. The prisoner would hang suspended, his feet a foot or two off the floor. Sommer and Leclaire together would, in addition, place a rope around his neck and throttle him from time to time. Sometimes they would suspend themselves from the prisoner's legs. Few prisoners stood this treatment for more than twenty minutes without losing consciousness. They were then let down and revived with cold water, and the procedure was repeated. These tortures sometimes extracted confessions no man would have made under ordinary circumstances. Yet there were prisoners who never uttered a word. Food and water would be withdrawn and the examination repeated every day. There might be as many as three suspensions and starvation might be extended to as much as ten days. If the prisoner still failed to talk on the tenth day, there came the ultimate ordeal—suspension head down. If there were still no results, Sommer might release the prisoner or, if the Political Department regarded it as a "difficult case," he might offer the man a cup of tea that put him to sleep, whereupon Sommer would administer a fatal injection.

The next morning the public-address system would announce: "Corpse-carriers to the gatehouse!" The Camp Medical Officer would certify: "Death by circulatory failure." If the prisoner refused to drink the tea, Sommer would peer in through the peephole to see whether the man had fallen asleep yet. The next day poisoned food was brought to the cell. If this too failed, Sommer would affect a curious gesture—but only if the prisoner had not squealed on another! He would apply for the prisoner's discharge, which was always authorized—that is, in those few cases in which a prisoner actually survived the tortures that have been described. When the prisoner was discharged from the bunker, Sommer would even present him with tobacco!

Fritz Männchen of Dresden, Kurt Leeser of Aachen, the bunker orderlies Richard Gritz of Antonienhütte near Kattowitz, Alfred Miller of Leonberg near Stuttgart, and Roman Hädelmeyer of Vienna all had long experience in the bunker and have recorded a wealth of factual information, all of which tallies.

The "simplest" death Sommer would pick for a prisoner was to hang him with his own hands from the window frame or radiator. Many prisoners, however, were simply beaten to death by Sommer with an iron bar. One case has become known, in which he applied an iron clamp to his victim's temples, screwing it shut until the skull was crushed.

To look out of a cell window meant certain death to any prisoner. If he was caught, Sommer would beat him to death or give him a fatal injection. The same punishment threatened anyone caught reading even the smallest fragment of newspaper issued as toilet paper. He was forbidden to pace the cell. The prisoner had to stand at attention from five o'clock in the morning to ten o'clock at night, staring at the door. The peephole in the door held a magnifying lens through which the slightest movement could be observed. Any violation was punished with twenty-five lashes. Food, when issued at all, consisted of half rations. In the wintertime, prisoners were commonly drenched with water, the clothing being allowed to dry on the body while the prisoner slept on the concrete floor.

One of the cells held seven Jews. One day Sommer appeared with a tin pail with which he beat two of the prisoners to death. He then ripped a piece of iron from the radiator and used it to kill the others. Of at least one hundred Jews who passed through the bunker between 1940 and 1941, not one left alive.

It was also customary to feed the prisoners cathartics in their food, until they fell sick with bloody stools. Of course there were no antidotes. There were two toilets in the bunker, one for the prisoners, the other for the SS. Whenever a prisoner received his twenty-five lashes, he had to bend over and immerse his head into the excrement-filled toilet bowl.

When the punishment had been administered, he was not permitted to wipe the excrement from his face.

On one occasion Sommer shackled seven young Polish prisoners to their cots. Their diet was reduced to salt water and pickles, until they perished. Bunker orderly Gritz describes how their fearful screams, and finally moans, pierced his eardrums. A Czech Communist in Cell 11 was kept without food by Sommer for seven days. He was fond of inflicting death by starvation. He was in the habit of issuing the food himself, and would withhold it wholly or in part from his victims until they had slowly starved to death.

Some of the tortures inflicted by Sommer were nightmares of sadism. He liked to strangle prisoners with his bare hands. His greatest sport was to herd all his prisoners into the corridor, about four feet wide, where he had them do kneebends and hop about until they dropped from exhaustion. He would then trample them with his heels, until the blood spurted from ears and nose and at least a few were left dead. On one occasion he crowded fifteen prisoners into a single cell, giving them only a children's chamber pot which they were not permitted to empty for some ten days. The floor of the cell was ankle-deep in excrement. Subsequently Sommer murdered all fifteen men.

His own quarters were decorated with an illuminated skull. At night he would sometimes summon a victim from one of the cells and leisurely do away with him in the room. He would then place the body under his bed and fall asleep peacefully, his work well done.

And why were prisoners committed to the bunker? For any offense at all, big or little. It was largely a matter of caprice, like everything else in camp. A Jew might be admitted because he had smoked during working hours; another for alleged loafing, a third in order to be questioned by the Political Department or camp headquarters. If a prisoner looked up from his work as the wife of the Commandant, Ilse Koch, passed by, she might jot down his serial number. The hapless wretch was committed to the bunker, for having "stared shamelessly" at the Commandant's wife. He could almost count himself lucky if he got off with a fatal injection. The use of injections was, of course, properly the prerogative of the SS Medical Officers, but Sommer could not keep his fingers off this specialized medical field. Air, chloral hydrate and evipan were his favorite agents and he used them to kill many prisoners.

An illustration of Sommer's collaboration with the SS physicians and the abysmal hypocrisy which the system combined with its barbarities, is the martyrdom of the Confessional Minister Schneider.

Pastor Schneider was brought to Buchenwald in September 1937. At the time there was a daily flag-raising ceremony, and when Schnieder refused to take off his cap before the Nazi emblem, he at once received twenty-five lashes and was thrown into the bunker. He remained there for more than eighteen months, until he was finally murdered, having suffered indescribable agonies. Fritz Männchen, a Communist who spent some time in the same cell with Schneider, reports that the minister was beaten by Sommer each time the door was opened. Later on, Schneider's cell was kept perpetually dark. Water stood two inches deep on the floor and the walls were forever wet. During his entire period of incarceration, the minister was not permitted once to wash, was never escorted to the shower, as was customary with other prisoners. As a result his clothing became infested with lice. His body was covered with festering sores, inches across, the result of beatings. Of course he never received dressings or treatment. It is almost beyond comprehension that a man could survive such treatment for so long a period of time. It was this very endurance that seems to have provoked Sommer to fury. He could not bring himself to kill his victim outright. He had to torture the man to death slowly. Schneider was fed only at irregular intervals and faded away to skin and bones. In the end even Sommer grew impatient and one day he fed Schneider poison. As always when he received food, the minister ate only very little, and the poison failed of its effect. During the final period Schneider had actually been taken to the hospital on several occasions to receive heart stimulants. On the pretext of obtaining treatment for him, Sommer had the Camp Medical Officer apply ice-cold compresses until the minister died of heart failure. The very day before his death he received a beating at Sommer's hands.

Schneider's wife and children requested permission of the

Commandant to see their husband and father once more. For propaganda reasons, Koch assented. To conceal the frightful mutilations that disfigured the body, an SS barber applied make-up to the face and covered the head with a wig. The minister then lay in state in the troop garage, decorated with flowers for the occasion. The family took a tearful farewell of its head and was escorted out by Koch himself. "Your husband was my best prisoner," he told Frau Schneider. "I was about to tell him of his discharge, when he died of heart failure!"

Apart from the places of execution already spoken of, the Buchenwald SS also used at times the dog kennels, where a portable, collapsible gallows made quick work possible. Buchenwald also had a liquidation plant of its own beyond the barbed wire, beside the riding academy. This was strictly a shooting affair. Buchenwald headquarters had a code number for this detail—"99." The SS noncoms were assigned to it in rotation, unless they volunteered.

The unsuspecting victims were almost invariably Russian prisoners of war. They were herded into the stable, where the SS officer in charge of the murder detail delivered a brief address that was translated: "You are now in a collecting camp. To avoid the danger of contagion, you are to be examined, disinfected and bathed. Take off your jacket first, then fold your trousers neatly and place your shoes at the side. Put your dogtags inside your shoes, to avoid confusion."

The SS noncoms went about in white smocks, pretending to be physicians. Then came the command: "The first six men, ready for bathing!" One loudspeaker blared out music at full volume, while through another names and numbers were called. The bloody tragedy itself took place at the other end of the building. The victims selected for "bathing" were taken to a small room with soundproof doors and walls. It was tiled and otherwise equipped like a shower room. An embrasure about a foot wide and an inch high was cut into one door. Through this an SS man shot down the victims with a machine pistol.

Sometimes the men were not all mortally hit; but when all were down they were thrown into a truck that was lined with galvanized iron. The showers were turned on to wash away the blood—and the next contingent lined up. Sometimes this went on from nine o'clock in the evening to five o'clock in the morning, with some five hundred men being "bathed."

Initially the SS had used a killing machine, but this was superseded when it did not work fast enough. It operated as follows: there was a raised wooden platform, with a vertical beam, ostensibly for measuring body height. The beam, however, concealed a truncheon suspended at shoulder height. When the victim stepped on the platform the truncheon was tripped, smashing the skull or breaking the neck.

This machine did not always kill. Those who were merely injured were nevertheless carted off to the crematory, where the coup de grace was administered with a big oaken club. Zbigniev Fuks, an assistant in the crematory, had the harrowing experience of having a Russian prisoner of war, brought in with a batch of bodies, actually address him: "Give me your hand, friend!" He had been lying, naked and bloody, atop a whole heap of corpses. SS Technical Sergeant Warnstedt, chief of the Buchenwald Crematory, instantly leaped up and killed the man with a shot from his gun.

When the execution shipments grew too large, the prisoners had to strip in the open air outside the stable. They were then lined up in big batches in the riding hall and mowed down with a machine-gun. Sawdust was sprinkled over the blood and the next batch admitted. Unlimited quantities of liquor were available for the killers.

The victims were not always ignorant of the fate awaiting them. On occasion one of the naked men would try to escape and run through the guard line drawn up around the area. In one such case the Ukrainian SS man refused to shoot. Henceforth only German SS men were employed as guards.

Civilians too were liquidated in the stable. One day a bus from the Apolda Transportation Company arrived, bearing a number of well-dressed Germans and a few officers. This was about four o'clock in the afternoon. The arrivals entered the stable, engaged in animated conversation. As soon as they were inside, a guard line drew up. Two hours later the crematory received a new batch of bodies.

The entire SS crew of "Detail 99" was decorated with the War Merit Cross.

Only a very few camps had gas chambers of their own. But

there were mobile gas chambers, vans that somewhat resembled the closed "Black Marias" of the police, for emergency use in exterminating prisoners. Gassing in these cars seems to have been slow, since they usually drove about a good deal before they stopped to discharge the corpses.

At Auschwitz, however, there was a huge gas plant—actually at Birkenau, a part of Auschwitz—which embraced five crematories together with four gas bunkers built into the ground. Each of these had an average capacity of twelve to fifteen hundred persons. The fifth crematory had no furnaces. It was only a huge fire pit.

In all the eastern camps and ghettos, designation for death in the gas chamber was known as "selection"—understandably a term that came to spread panic. In Auschwitz proper the "selectees" were assigned to special barracks, where they were kept under sharp guard. They often remained in isolation for two or three days, generally without food, for they were already considered "scratched." At the Auschwitz hospital patients of all kinds were never permitted to exceed ten per cent of the camp strength. Any excess numbers were automatically sent to the gas chambers. The personnel servicing this plant numbered about one thousand prisoners, all of them Jews. The victims were lined up before the pit naked and shot down by the SS, the bodies—or the wounded!—toppling directly into fire. The Camp Commandant, SS Captain Kramer, never missed these mass executions. He generally stood by beaming, slapping his thighs with glee when the scene grew especially exciting. Not all the prisoners were what came to be known as "Moslems," men who were physically and mentally broken, who allowed anything to be done to them. There were prisoners who went on their death march with militant songs on their lips, shouting to the SS, "We today, you tomorrow!" As for those who were neither apathetic nor militant, no one will ever know what went on in their minds.

The gas chambers were simplicity itself, yet they were planned with diabolical ingenuity. Each chamber had the appearance of a public bath, and was so represented to the victims. In the dressing-rooms there were signs, in all the principal languages of Europe, instructing the prisoners to tie their shoes together and fold their clothes neatly to avoid loss.

Hot coffee was promised after the bath. From the dressing rooms the way led directly to the "bath," where hydrocyanic acid gas was admitted through the shower heads and ventilator outlets as soon as the doors had been closed. Death took as long as four or five minutes, depending on the amount of gas available. During this time the most dreadful screams could be heard from the men, women and children inside, as their lungs slowly ruptured. Any bodies that showed signs of life when the doors had been opened were clubbed into quiescence. The prisoners of the service squad then dragged out the bodies, stripped off any rings, and cut off the hair, which was bundled into sacks and shipped to plants for processing. (In 1944 a young Jew from Brno, Yanda Weiss, was a member of this squad. He is the source of the details here presented, which have been confirmed from other sources.)

The bodies were then stacked in piles of ten each. SS Technical Sergeant Moll, in charge of the Auschwitz crematories, made his tour of inspection, after which the bodies were thrown into the furnaces or the fire pit. Moll was fond of placing naked women against the edge of the fire pit and watching them fall into the flames when they were shot in the abdomen. On one occasion he found a prisoner from the service squad in possession of a ring. He had the man drenched with gasoline and then set afire. Another man he suspended by the hands, shooting at him until the arm parted. He then repeated the process with the man's feet.

On another occasion Roll Call Officer Schillinger made an Italian dancer perform naked before the crematory. Taking advantage of a favorable moment, the woman approached him, siezed his gun, and shot him down. In the ensuing struggle she herself was killed, at least escaping death by gas.

Early in 1945 Auschwitz was evacuated and the gas chambers blown up. Some of the SS fiends who had done this work were transferred to Buchenwald, where they went about boasting of their foul deeds. They were plentifully supplied with valuables. They kept reminiscing about the "wild life" at Auschwitz, with its "strong medicine and constant alcoholic indulgences."

The chief victims of Auschwitz were Jews from all the countries of Europe that had come under Hitler's rule. But there were also Poles, Russians, aged and decrepit prisoners of other nationalities, and a contingent of the sick. The highest "output" attained by Auschwitz was 34,000 bodies, in one continuous day and night shift. According to the confession of Camp Commandant Höss, during his reign alone, from 1942 to early 1944, some 2,500,000 persons were gassed at Auschwitz.

In a number of camps the SS, for reasons of "efficiency," carried out the executions ordered by Himmler or the Main Economic and Administrative Office immediately in or at the crematories. As a rule the prisoners were garroted, clubbed or hanged. Strong hooks were set into the crematory walls for this purpose. In Buchenwald there were forty-eight such hooks. The bodies thus had to be carried but a few paces to the furnaces. These executions were carried out by SS non-coms with the aid of the Prisoner Foreman of the crematory.

Time and again persons were brought in from the outside, or prisoners were called to the gatehouse, only to be taken straight to the crematory and butchered, always in the presence of the Camp Medical Officer and a headquarters representative. There was no distinction as to age, sex, profession or nationality. The victims included Russian prisoners of war, German and Polish women, British and French parachutists, slave laborers from the East, Jewish businessmen, Italian anti-Fascists and camp inmates. Their full number is unknown.

The prisoner registry at Buchenwald secretly maintained a list covering ten months (from March 28, 1944, to January 30, 1945) for Buchenwald itself and eight and a half months (from January 28, 1944, to October 11, 1944) for Camp "Dora" near Nordhausen, then a Buchenwald subsidiary. This list, which has been preserved, contains all the names that were available, together with number, birth date, profession, nationality, and date of execution. It lists 288 names, including 10 Czechs, 1 Yugoslav, 47 Poles, 169 Russians, 1 Latvian, 1 Italian, 4 Germans, 1 Netherlands citizen, 12 Belgians, 22 Frenchmen, 9 Britons, and 1 Canadian. All in all perhaps 1,100 victims were hanged in the Buchenwald crematory.

It happened on occasion that some Gestapo branch had already done the dirty work, merely sending on the bodies to be cremated. They were generally packed in straw sacks. In the fall of 1943 the remains of two old people—man and wife—thus arrived. One of the garments bore an identification: "Hirschmann, Arnstad." In this instance the Weimar Gestapo itself had indulged the pleasure of torturing a defenseless Jewish couple to death.

Himmler prescribed cremation for the disposal of the dead in all the concentration camps. There were such enormous quantities of bodies, however, that frequently difficulties arose in keeping them until cremation. Before there were special morgues, the bodies were piled in heaps, sometimes like cordwood, in various camp buildings such as the privies. Initially it was not uncommon for some of the bodies still to show signs of life.

There were special corpse-carrying details. In many of the camps they were originally composed of Jews. Later they were chiefly Poles. These squads were generally well fed—they were on constant call and the work was hard. At almost any hour of the day or night the public-address system might ring out: "Corpse carriers to the gatehouse!"

It goes without saying that no ceremony of any kind attended the handling of the bodies. Only actual witnesses to such scenes can do them justice. One of the carriers would forcibly turn up the rigid arms of the naked corpse. The other would take hold of the feet. They would swing it back and forth—one, two, three!—and the body would hurtle atop a dozen others on the cart.

Until 1940 Buchenwald bodies were cremated at crematories in Weimar and Jena. Bodies were supposed to be dressed in a shroud bearing name and number, and to lie in a coffin. Actually the number was often simply penciled on the skin and the bodies placed in a primitive box—two to a box if they were emaciated enough. On one occasion a hearse dropped a coffin en route to the crematory, and the bodies of two prisoners, reduced to skin and bones, fell out. This happened directly outside a Weimar café.

In 1940 and before the permanent crematory was installed in 1941, a mobile crematory, borrowed from somewhere, was installed at Buchenwald. The combustion chamber was small, and there were so many bodies that they had to be stuffed in.

Occasionally limbs were not burned up and lay scattered in the roll-call area.

An autopsy was supposed to be conducted on every body before cremation, the findings to be embodied in a report. The prisoners charged with this job were anything but anatomists. For years Buchenwald autopsies were in charge of a former baker, pimp and homosexual, a man with a long prison record. The fellow's name was Stöckel and he was later killed by other prisoners. His successor had once been a carpenter. During the final year, until the fall of 1944, the Buchenwald autopsy room was under the supervision of a Czech Premonstratesian monk by the name of Thyl who time and again was saved from Dachau transports because of his extraordinarily humane character and his shining spirit of fellowship.

SS physicians rarely performed autopsies, though occasionally medical men from university clinics would come to conduct studies on the bodies of prisoners. As for the dissecting-room personnel, even had it had the desire and a sense of responsibility, it would have been utterly unequal to its assigned task. Post-mortem reports were simply fabricated. They then served as the basis for falsified hospital reports, especially after mass liquidations. The autopsy, of course, would instantly establish the mode of murder. Killing was often done by injection with air, so that air embolisms would be found; or by means of carbolic acid, the odor of which would at once pervade the room; or by means of evipan. Strychnine, morphine and other alkaloids were used to kill prisoners, as was chloral hydrate. As many as thirty bodies of prisoners poisoned thus might arrive in the post-mortem room in a single day. In every case the post-mortem report had to agree with the instructions received from the hospital beforehand. The following specimen is reasonably representative of all the camps:

Prisoner's Serial Number _____ *First and Last Name* _____ _____ *Date of Death* _____ *At the* _____ *Concentration Camp Hospital.*

Admitted to the hospital on _____ [*this was dated back an appropriate period*], *complaining of fever and pain in the left side of the chest. Careful clinical and X-ray examination established pneumonia of the lower left lobe. Despite intensive therapy, all efforts to improve the condition of the patient failed. Heart disease, treated with cardiac drugs, further complicated the clinical picture. The patient died after prolonged suffering on _____ at _____ o'clock.*

Cause of death: cardiac weakness complicated by pneumonia.

(Signature of the Camp Medical Officer.)

In the case of men officially executed by the firing squad, the report would always read, notwithstanding the frequent signs of mistreatment: "No other marks of violence except those hereinbefore described were noted." The "marks of violence" were wounds from rifle bullets fired at close range.

In order to evaluate the bodies of prisoners scientifically, a Pathology Section was installed in the large concentration-camp hospitals. It was given supervision over the post-mortem room. It prepared all kinds of specimens for the study of pathology. They were sent to the Institute of Hygiene of the *Waffen SS* in Berlin or to the SS Medical Academy in Graz, and sometimes even exhibited in a local showroom. By and large the whole idea of these Pathology Sections was arrant nonsense. Only in the rarest cases were they run by qualified men.

The first man in charge at Buchenwald was SS Captain Neumann, later sent to Shanghai on government orders. From the fall of 1940, SS Captain Müller ran the Pathology Section. He was later assigned to Hitler's headquarters near Berchtesgaden.

Müller collaborated with Dr. Wagner, a Camp Medical Officer who was writing a doctor's dissertation on tattoo markings. Both of them searched the whole camp for tattooed men, whom they ordered photographed. The prisoners were then called to the gatehouse by Commandant Koch, selected according to the magnificence of their tattoo markings, and sent to the hospital. Soon afterward the finest skin specimens would appear in the Pathology Section, where they were prepared and for years exhibited to SS visitors as particular treasures. Koch himself had an "artistic" table lamp fashioned of human bones for his own use, with a shade of human skin. The business got to be so popular among the SS that Müller received detailed suggestions about it from Berlin. Hundreds of human skins, prepared in different ways, were sent to Berlin, at the request of the Chief Medical Officer for concentration camps, SS Colonel Lolling. Müller also instructed Stöckel and another prisoner working in the Pathology Section to prepare penknife cases and similar articles from human skin. Lolling, on his part, requested a written report on methods of shrinking human heads to the size of an orange, the art once practiced by South Sea cannibals. There was source material on this subject in American literature, which was located and sent to Lolling. The SS physicians then proceeded to prepare a number of heads by this process. There were three of these at Buchenwald, of which two were still in existence when the camp was liberated.

Bodies that had not been dissected, together with those that had served "scientific purposes," were cremated. The service personnel for the actual combustion chambers always consisted of convicts. When cremations did not take place daily, huge mountains of bodies sometimes accumulated. The crematory was fueled with coke, and the "unholy flame of Buchenwald" sometimes leaped up three feet beyond the smokestack. The prisoners regarded the spectacle with a mixture of horror and apathy. It was a common subject for jokes in the roll-call area. Conclusions were drawn from the shape of the escaping smoke clouds as to the type of prisoner being cremated. "That must be a Jehovah's Witness, snaking up like that!" "Well, well, that foreign-legion man seems to be having a hard time shuffling off this mortal coil!" . . . "You'll be hitting the grate" or "You'll be going up the stack" were common phrases in camp. During roll call the Roll Call officer would often shout over the public-address system to the convicts who worked in the crematory and who never appeared in the line: "You birds in the crematory, stick your heads out the windows!" Whereupon the crew would pick up bodies and hold them out the windows. Such scenes were typical of the atmosphere in which the final rites for thousands were enacted.

Nor was there any dignity attending the shipment of the ashes to the families, which was sometimes requested. One of the convict attendants would simply scoop up a handful of ashes from the great common pile, drop it into a box and send it to the post office. At Auschwitz the crematory ashes were in part used for surfacing the roads in camp, or they were sold near by as fertilizer.

When cremation had been accomplished, the Political Department was notified and the cremation certificate made out by the Camp Medical Officer was forwarded. The local county registry would make out a death certificate, unless the victim happened to be a Russian, a Pole or a non-German Jew. In the final phase only German citizens and Czechs rated such certificates. Some staff member of the Political Department would then have the standard "letter of condolence" typed:

> *Dear Mrs. _____*
> *Your husband, _____, died in the Camp Hospital on _____. May I express my sincere sympathy on your bereavement.*
> *_____ was admitted to the Hospital on _____ with severe symptoms of exhaustion, complaining of difficulty in breathing and of pains in the chest. Despite competent medication and devoted medical attention it proved impossible, unfortunately, to keep the patient alive.*
> *The deceased voiced no final requests.*
> *The Camp Commandant: _____*

During the final months at Buchenwald there was a critical shortage of coal. Bodies began to pile up in large numbers, and the rats got into them, holding out a serious threat of epidemic. Himmler gave special authorization for emergency burial in mass graves. Cremation continued at a greatly reduced volume. It was generally limited to German citizens. As one sentimental crematory sergeant put it, Germans could hardly be expected to lie in the same graves with Jews.

Chapter Nineteen

STATISTICS OF MORTALITY

Statistics of mortality in the concentration camp hospitals would be of extrordinary interest. Unfortunately records were kept only incompletely, if at all—and not on valid scientific principles. (Camp statisticians, too, were selected by political and personal criteria rather than because of their technical qualifications.) Only a portion of the records from the concentration camps has been preserved at all. Perhaps the best insight would be afforded by the statistical material collected in Section III of Department D of the SS Main Economic and Administrative Office—if the SS did not succeed in burning it. Even this can be accepted only with reservations, and none but a few old camp inmates would be able to evaluate it accurately. But the Chief Medical Officer for concentration camps did receive monthly and quarterly reports from all the Camp Medical Officers, even though it must be noted that these statistics were compiled by prisoners.

The fragmentary material at hand may, nevertheless, serve as the basis for a first effort to arrive at an approximate calculation of the total number of deaths in the concentration camps.

A circular letter signed by SS Brigadier-General Krüger

from Section III of Department D of the SS Main Economic and Administrative Office, dated December 28, 1942, was written at Himmler's orders and dealt with war manpower considerations:

> *Mortality in the individual camps must be sharply reduced. The number of prisoners must be brought up to the level ordered by the Reich Leader SS. Chief Camp Medical Officers must exert every effort to this end. . . . The best Camp Medical Officer is not he who believes he must draw attention by inappropriate harshness, but he who maintains work capacity at as high a level as possible, by supervision and exchange among the various details.*

The letter was directed to the Camp Medical Officers and Commandants of Dachau, Sachsenhausen, Buchenwald, Neuengamme, Ravensbrück, Flossenbürg, Lublin, Stutthof, Gross-Rosen, Natzweiler, Hinzert, Moringen, Herzogenbusch, Mauthausen and two others I am unable to identify from the abbreviations "Bu" and "Nied." Enclosed with it was an illuminating table, covering the months from June to November, 1942.

I have corrected four errors in addition involving several thousand prisoners one way or the other. It should be noted that the outright death camps, such as Auschwitz and Maidanek, are not included in the tabulation.

STRENGTH TABLE
June to November 1942

Month	Additions			Subtractions				
	Admissions	Transfers in	Total	Discharges	Transfers out	Died	Executed[1]	Total
June........	10,322	2,575	12,897	773	2,903	4,080	243	7,899
July.........	25,716	6,254	31,970	907	4,340	8,536	477	14,260
August......	25,407	2,742	28,149	581	2,950	12,733	99	16,363
September...	16,763	6,438	23,201	652	6,805	22,598	144	30,199
October.....	13,873	5,345	19,218	1,089	6,334	11,858	5,954	25,235
November...	17,780	4,565	22,345	809	5,514	10,805	2,350	19,478
Totals.....	109,861	27,919	137,780	4,711	28,846	70,610	9,267	113,434

[1] In the original this column is coyly designated simply as E.

Statistical evaluation of this table is not as simple as the SS Main Economic and Administrative Office may have thought. The accompanying letter states that the table "shows some 70,000 deaths (the executions are omitted!) of 136,000 admissions (should be more than 137,000!)." As stated this is incorrect, since old prisoners died as well as newcomers and transfers. To obtain the absolute and relative values, it would be necessary to add the monthly strength figures for the camps concerned. The table does show that in sixteen large and medium-sized German concentration camps, during six months of 1942:

(1) There were 109,861 prisoners newly admitted.

(2) Only 4,711 were discharged during the same period.

(3) Of all the inmates, 9,267 were officially executed.

(4) About 28,000 were transferred between camps.

(5) A total of 70,610 prisoners were marked off the books as having died.

It is certain that a considerable number of the deaths were among the prisoners transferred. There were few ordeals that affected prisoner health as severely as these transfer shipments between camps. Assuming that half of the transferred prisoners died during the period in question, i.e., around 14,000, this would leave more than 56,000 old and newly admitted prisoners who perished. Almost 80,000 deaths as compared to scarcely 5,000 releases, and this in only part of the existing camps—here we catch a glimpse of the balance sheet of Nazi mass murder.

Within this narrow scope of time and camps, the net gain in SS slaves therefore was:

Additions	Subtractions	
	4,711	Discharges
	9,267	Executions
	70,610	Deaths from Other Cause
Total....109,861	Total........84,588	
	Net Gain.....25,273	

Something had to be done about this small increase, expecially in view of the shrinking front which was steadily reducing the area from which new slaves might be levied. This explains the motives for the circular letter cited, with its injunction against "inappropriate harshness" and its warning to improve food and working conditions for the prisoners.

These data from the SS Main Economic and Administrative
Office are supplemented by statistics from the Buchenwald
Prisoner Hospital, which on the whole were reasonably well
kept. It is impossible to publish the full material here; and
besides, up to December 1939, the data are quite incomplete.
But mortality figures were noted since 1937. They show the
following picture:

Year	Admissions	Deaths
1937	2,912	48[1]
1938	20,122[2]	771[3]
1939	9,553	1,235
1940	2,525	1,772
1941	5,890	1,522
1942	14,111	2,898
1943	42,177	3,516
1944	97,866	8,644
1945[4]	43,823	13,056
Totals	38,979	33,462

[1] An imperfect reporting system began only in December.
[2] Figure swollen by mass admissions of Jews in November 1938.
[3] Still incomplete.
[4] January 1 to April 3.

Thus at least 33,462 prisoners died at Buchenwald from
beginning to end, not counting those who were executed or
sent away in outright death shipments, or those who were
transferred to other camps, often in a moribund state, only to
die en route or soon after their arrival. In all likelihood it is a
fair estimate to put the total of Buchenwald dead over seven
and a half years at 55,000, an average of about 7,300 a year.
This means that up to and including the year 1941 virtually the
entire camp strength was "turned over" each year. (Not until
1942 did camp strength permanently rise to about the 10,000
mark.) But for the constant influx of new admissions, the
camp, from a statistical point of view, would have become
nothing but a morgue in eight months of a given year.

Figures covering wards and out-patients' clinic—in other
words, all the sick who were treated—are available for
Buchenwald from April 1941 on. They rose and fell as conditions fluctuated in camp, a number of different factors
playing their part in determining how many or how few
patients were actually in the hospital at a given time. While
mortality averaged between one half of one and eight per cent

of total camp strength per month, that of out-patients ranged from two and a half to fourteen per cent, of ward patients from one and a half to eight per cent.

From the fall of 1942 onward, when the influx into the camps began to take on staggering proportions, hospital figures got more and more out of step with the number of new admissions. In absolute terms, figures continued to grow, but relative proportions declined, since hospital capacity was not increased. The supernumerary sick simply had to die a natural or unnatural death.

Taking each concentration camp by itself, it would scarcely be fair to blame only deficient sanitation or the Camp Medical Officers for the high mortality figures. Shipments were constantly arriving with prisoners in such weakened condition from their ordeal that they died like flies in the ensuing days. "They've sent us all the scrap again," the SS used to say.

But conditions actually were much the same in all the camps. The real guilt lay with the top leadership of the SS, with the common design underlying all camp administration. The individual Camp Medical Officer could not escape this system, even if he tried to do better.

In my estimation we shall never have an altogether reliable tabulation of all the victims of the Nazi concentration camps. It is not purely a matter of the sick. They either got well or died—most of them, of course, died, or rather, were killed. But even the prisoners who left the camps at all almost always had some permanent health impairment. True, this scarcely counts, compared to the vast hosts of outright dead.

To the Nazi government, of course, the number of the sick was of considerable importance, since it directly affected labor output. Through SS Major Ding-Schuler of Buchenwald, we know of a letter addressed by the Reich Physician of the SS and Police to the Chief Hygienist of the SS, reporting that in the final phase of the Nazi regime around twenty per cent of all camp inmates had to be written off as unfit for duty (about 120,000 of 600,000). This figure cannot possibly refer to hospital patients alone, who were far less in number. Nowhere were there even approximately that number of beds. This estimate of March 1945 may have been no more than a rough guess of the part of the top leadership of the SS. Or it may have included wards, out-patients, convalescents, and all of the "scrap" slated for extermination, SS style. It is hard to say.

In making a first, approximate, critical estimate of the total number of victims who died in the German concentration camps, a number of factors must be taken into account. I expressly emphasize that in any event only attempts at *estimates* are made in the following:

(1) From 1933 to 1939 the number of concentration camps was relatively limited. Among the hundred-odd camps in existence by the end of this period at most half a dozen had a permanent strength of more than 10,000 inmates. The rest numbered no more than 500 to 1,000 each.

(2) Beginning in late 1939, both the number of camps and the number of prisoners in the already existing camps rose sharply. Henceforth the six or eight big camps numbered from 50,000 to 100,000 inmates each, counting all their outside details, while smaller camps seldom fell below 2,000 inmates.

(3) Quarterly and semi-annual reports from certain prisoner hospitals show that mortality in the "regular" camps was about ten per cent annually, though even by 1938 and 1939 it had risen higher. It kept on rising during the war, ultimately reaching thirty-five to forty per cent of average strength.

(4) There was constant turnover and exchange of prisoners among the camps. These shipments were purely internal matters and did not directly affect total strength, except as they hastened the death of prisoners. They can therefore be ignored in the kind of statistical tabulation here attempted. Prisoners either died, or were executed, or were released. All others remained in the camps. As a matter of fact, discharges may also be ignored because they were so few in number.

(5) The tabulation made by the SS Main Economic and Administrative Office showed that during six months in 1942 sixteen camps had, in round figures, 110,000 new admissions and 85,000 deductions (77.3 per cent) in the categories described. On an annual basis this would mean 220,000 admissions and 170,000 subtractions.

(6) Three main periods can be distinguished in the history of the German concentration camps:

(a) From 1933 to the outbreak of the war, approximately 3

large concentration camps with about 20,000 inmates each, 65 smaller concentration camps with about 1,500 inmates each. Total: 85,000 inmates

(b) From the fall of 1939 to 1942, approximately 16 large concentration camps with about 20,000 each, 50 smaller concentration camps with about 1,500 inmates each. Total: 395,000 inmates

(c) From 1943 to the spring of 1945, approximately 20 large concentration camps with about 25,000 inmates each, 65 smaller concentration camps with about 1,500 inmates each. Total: 600,000 inmates

Subsidiary details of the base camps have been taken into account in this calculation. They often included no more than a few hundred men. If they were all counted as separate camps, the total number would of course be much higher, even though prisoner strength would remain the same.

After 1940 there were concentration camps in the east which can only be described as extermination camps. Chief among these was Auschwitz, with at least 3,500,000 victims, probably 4,500,000. About half a dozen smaller camps of this description accounted for perhaps 1,500,000 to 2,000,000 victims, chiefly Maidanek, Treblinka, Skarzisko Kamienno, and the ghettos of Warsaw, Lemberg and Riga.

An estimate on this basis leads to the following approximation of the total picture:

Year	Base Strength	Additions		Deaths		Increase or Decrease
		% [1]	Number	% [2]	Number	
1933	50,000	25	12,500	10	6,250	+ 6,250
1934	56,250	30	16,900	10	7,300	+ 9,600
1935	65,800	20	13,200	10	7,900	+ 5,300
1936	71,000	20	14,200	10	8,500	+ 5,700
1937	76,800	20	15,350	10	9,200	+ 6,200
1938	83,000	100[3]	83,000	20	33,200	+ 50,000
1939	133,000	150[4]	332,500	20	93,100	+ 239,500
Totals......	536,000		487,650		165,450	+ 322,550
Ann. Av....	76,550		69,650		23,650	+ 46,100
1940	372,500	440	149,000	25[5]	130,400	+ 18,600
1941	391,100	60[6]	234,600	25	156,400	+ 78,200
1942	469,300	60	281,600	30	225,300	+ 56,300

254 EUGEN KOGON

Year	Base Strength	Additions		Deaths		Increase or Decrease
		% [1]	Number	% [2]	Number	
Totals......	1,232,900		665,200		512,100	+ 153,100
Ann. Av....	411,000		221,750		170,700	+ 51,000
1943	525,600	70[7]	369,000	25	223,650	+ 145,350
1944	670,950	70[8]	469,650	30	342,200	+ 127,450
1945[9]	798,400 } −223,550 } 574,850	20[10]	159,700	40[11]	383,250	− 223,550
Totals......	1,771,400		998,350		949,100	+ 49,250
Ann. Av....	590,450		332,800		316,350	+ 16,400
Gr. Total...			2,151,200		1,626,650	

Deaths at Auschwitz................... 5,500,000
Original Base Strength................ 50,000
Total Death Victims................... 7,125,000
Total Admissions, "Regular" Camps.... 2,200,000
Base Strength, Extermination Camps.... 120,000
Additions, Extermination Camps....... 5,500,000
Total Concentration Camp Inmates..... 7,820,000
Survivors [12]........................ 700,000

[1] Of base strength.
[2] Of base strength and additions combined.
[3] Mass arrests of Austrians, Sudeten Germans, and Jews.
[4] Mass arrests of Germans at outbreak of war, also of Poles.
[5] Starvation and epidemics.
[6] Mass arrests of Yugoslavs, Ukrainians, Russians.
[7] Mass arrests of French, Belgians, and Dutch.
[8] Mass arrests of foreign workers in Germany, and of Hungarian Jews.
[9] First quarter.
[10] Per quarter.
[11] Mass liquidations and death shipments in camp evacuation.
[12] Includes prisoners discharged before the end.

Chapter Twenty

THE UNDERGROUND STRUGGLE

Camp headquarters was never able to control the tens of thousands of men whom it held in subjection except by primitive methods, based mostly on the element of surprise. The SS men never actually knew what went on behind the barbed wire. They sensed it—and grew to fear it in the dark hours of the gradual decline—but they could never put their fingers on this anonymous spirit. They tried, by means of informers, to gain insight into the internal situation in the camps, especially opposition sentiment and organization. Even SS officers occasionally went into the camps in prison garb, a puerile endeavor to collect information, for they remained in ignorance of countless trifles of daily camp life. They were always recognized at once and kept under surveillance. The only result was to heighten the prisoners' vigilance and distrust.

Nor did the Gestapo and the SS gain much from the employment of Nazi stool pigeons among the prisoners. If a newcomer had any record of Nazi or similar affiliations, his dossier would be known to the underground leaders among the prisoners before he even set foot in the compound proper.

From the first moment eyes and ears that were hard to fool were turned on the new men, who for hours and days had to run through stages during which their true mettle could be tested by their fellows. Nazis in camp remained isolated until they had either been rendered harmless or had proved that they could be relied on—something that happened in only a very few cases.

The only successes the SS scored with informers were with those recruited right in camp—convicts, "asocials" and even political prisoners. Such "squealers" usually drifted into collaboration with the SS of their own accord, by virtue of positions that brought them into constant touch with the SS, or from motives of personal vengeance. The urge for power and prestige also played a prominent part. A handful of prisoners were pressed into service as informers against their will.

Buchenwald saw the most famous and notorious case of voluntary denunciation. This was in 1941 when the White Russian émigré, Gregory Kushnir-Kushnarev, allegedly a former general, who had spent months insinuating himself into the confidence of wide circles in camp, began to betray his fellows, especially Russian prisoners of war. This Gestapo agent became responsible for the death of several hundred prisoners. He did not shrink from denouncing anyone with whom he had ever had even the most trivial dispute. As already mentioned in another connection, his main job was to ferret out Russian prisoners of war according to the secret directives of the Reich Main Security Office. For a long time it proved impossible to catch him alone, which would have meant his instant death. The SS kept him under its special protection. In the end he was actually made foreman of the prisoner Orderly Room. In this position he not only eliminated everyone in camp who ran afoul of him, but in many respects prevented utilization on behalf of the prisoners of the machinery of self-government.

At last, early in 1942, the informer had a slight indisposition. He was unwise enough to report to the hospital, thus placing himself at the mercy of his enemies. With the permission of Camp Medical Officer Hoven, who had long been worked on in this matter and sided with the leading functionaries among the prisoners, Kushnir's ailment was at once diagnosed as infectious and he was put in the isolation ward. Soon afterward he was killed by means of a fatal injection. I well remember the sigh of relief that passed through the whole camp when the news spread with lightning rapidity that Kushnir-Kushnarev had died at 5:10 P.M. in the hospital.

The danger of serious consequences to all the prisoners from informers and denunciations was so great that preventive measures were taken even against the mere possibility of treachery. Anyone who came into contact with SS confidants, even without knowing the whole picture, endangered his very life. Only in rare cases could the nature of the contact be immediately known, nor could it be foreseen in what direction it would develop, even against the will of the innocent prisoner. This led to errors of judgment which taken by themselves seem inexcusable, though they become comprehensible when the whole atmosphere of danger is taken into account. On occasion it took the most painstaking and incriminating mediation to extricate a man who was really innocent from the deadly network. A few became squealers only as a result of unfair persecution among the prisoners. In their despair and inexperience they saw no way out except through the SS, which, of course, sooner or later dropped them when they had served their purpose.

There were a number of effective means by which the prisoners could assert their interests. They were all based on two essential prerequisites: power inside the camp, and a well-organized intelligence service. The pre-eminent task was always to place reliable anti-Fascists in all important positions. When self-government in the prisoner hospital was discussed in this book, it was mentioned that political rather than technical qualifications determined who was to assume the key positions in camp, in the barracks, and in the details. Outsiders and men forced on the prisoners by the SS were seldom able to maintain themselves for any length of time. The machine built up by the old concentrationaries was far too strong for undesirable elements to escape it in the long run. The harsh realities of the merciless struggle for survival, the group interests of the prisoners and the individual's own pursuit of power and relief, all combined in the same direction.

Functional cohesion was insured by the prisoner intelligence service. Such a system was built up in every camp from the very outset. Reliable key members of the ruling group—or the group seeking power—were systematically wormed into all the important posts, sometimes only after bitter and complex maneuvering. There they were able to observe everything that happened in the ranks of the SS and the prisoners, to obtain information on every personnel shift and policy trend, to overhear every conversation. Everything that seemed of the slightest significance was under constant scrutiny. Reports were made not merely at night, when all the prisoners returned to camp from their work, but in important cases immediately. Every detail had its official "runners," ostensibly appointed in order to maintain liaison with the numerous scattered SS offices. Actually three-fourths of their time was taken up by work on behalf of the prisoners.

Posts of paramount importance, such as in the Political Department, the prisoner hospital, camp headquarters, or the adjutant's office were often assigned to capable orderlies of disarming appearance, who were in constant touch with the runners from certain details. A prisoner orderly might be unobtrusively sweeping out an office or a hall, apparently minding only his own business, the SS men never dreaming that his attention was focused on anything but the broom in his hand. It is no exaggeration to say that nothing of any importance happened in a concentration camp, including even secret information, that did not come to the attention of the prisoners either immediately or else in a very short time. All reports converged on the underground leaders and the circles around them. But only a very few prisoners saw the picture as a whole. These few learned of every internal camp detail, while the mass of the prisoners subsisted on slogans, rumors and gossip.

The elastic wall that separated the SS from the prisoners could be maintained only if the prisoners themselves kept the camp under strict organization and uniform leadership. This alone made it possible to control and even protect those elements that remained outside the organization, knew nothing of it, refused to submit to discipline. It was the German Communists who brought the best qualifications to the accomplishment of this task. In contrast to men of liberal views, they had always been inured to absolute party discipline, and in methods and means they were almost the only ones who were the enemy's match. In addition they had the most extensive camp experience. It is to be regretted—and was actually the cause of certain setbacks—that especially in the early years the Communists excluded anti-Fascists of persuasions other than their own, but in practice it could not be helped. The reasons for the Communist claim to exclusive power must be in part sought in old habits and convictions, in part in the special circumstances under which the struggle was waged. Because of their lack of contact with the realities of the outside world, most of the German Communists clung to the time before 1933 in their political and tactical thinking. They had their nineteenth-century concepts, inherited from the positivistic bourgeoisie; their traditional maxims which they regarded as articles of faith of the old party line issued by Moscow; and their so-called dialectical approach which permitted them to proclaim as the immediate demands of reality any views and changing opinions they happened to hold. In this way they oversimplified the highly complex situation in the camps. Another factor was their need to concentrate their resources.

Within their own ranks the Communists were by no means unanimous, though they suppressed dissent with an iron hand, occasionally even by the murder of dissenters. Distrustful of anyone not of like mind, they were out to support only unconditional followers of the prevailing Communist party line. Only gradually did they come to accept selective collaboration with others. Such instances were always rare, remarkable as they sometimes were. The middle group of Communists in camp, the rank and file, refused to learn and never really approved such individual or collective solidarity. The lowest Communist group consisted of opportunists and hangers-on. In keeping with people of such character, they were usually one hundred and fifty per cent extremists.

The positive achievement of the Communists on behalf of the concentration-camp prisoners can hardly be overrated. In many cases the whole camp literally owed them its life, even though their motives seldom sprang from pure altruism but rather from the collective instinct for self-preservation in which the whole camp joined because of its positive results. The main reproach to be made against the Communist party in the concentration camps is its reluctance to purge its own ranks, quick as it always was to lend a hand when men of different convictions were to be excluded. Only in very rare cases did it eliminate certain outright criminal types of Communists who got to be Senior Block Inmates or Prisoner Foremen—in any other way, that is, but by sending them into outside labor details, where they were able to do their dirty work with even less control. They were simply shunted out of the base camp and entrusted with authority over hundreds and even thousands of fellow prisoners whose situation was bad enough as it was. This policy forfeited the Communists much of the sympathy due to them for their unrelenting fight against the SS, darkening, if not altogether overshadowing, the credit earned by those in their ranks who were neither arrogant nor brutal nor corrupt.

Many of the convicts did not recognize the basic political principle of the reds—namely, that there was a sharp line beyond which a prisoner could not go without himself becoming an enemy and an oppressor. All they wanted in any case, was to do away with control and clear the way for their customary practices—corruption, blackmail, profiteering. At Buchenwald during 1938–39 the situation slowly improved because most of the convicts were shipped out to help in the construction of the Flossenbürg concentration camp. But at the outbreak of the war the German police began to round up criminals on a huge scale, and thousands of convicts were admitted to the camp. In 1942, under the regime of Senior Camp Inmate Ohles, they once again won the upper hand at Buchenwald. This brought drastic consequences.

Before being appointed Senior Camp Inmate, Ohles had been foreman of the construction office. He instituted a diabolically clever scheme, using seventy-six green stool pigeons. It worked in this way: a short-wave receiving set was secretly installed in a sewerage duct under the prisoner Orderly Room. Night after night it was monitored by the electrician in the construction office. The next morning he would pass on the foreign broadcasts to Ohles's agents. They would see to it that the news spread among the political prisoners.

When Ohles had collected enough material, he reported to Officer-in-Charge Plaul that the political prisoners were passing foreign radio reports through the camp and therefore must be illegally listening to foreign broadcasts. The Political

Department, which for reasons of its own was also monitoring foreign broadcasts, made an investigation and found that reports current in camp corresponded closely to the broadcasts. Since the illegal receiver was not located, Plaul simply removed fifty of the best-known red functionaries from office, sent them to the penal company and zealously fostered their liquidation in the quarry.

But meanwhile a political prisoner in the electricians' detail had uncovered the scheme of the greens. He reported the situation to a few key people. The Commandant's barber took advantage of an opportunity to inform SS Colonel Pister. At the same time Officer-in-Charge Florstedt, who was opposed to the greens, was told of a trifling arrogation of authority by Ohles, who had certified a posted headquarters directive with his own name. The pressure on the two officials sufficed to bring the green interregnum to an end. Ohles was relieved and transferred to the quarry. He was dead the very next day. Even prisoners who wore the green triangle helped in the job of finishing him off, for Ohles's clique had not shrunk from sending to the penal company any convict who did not play ball with them. Once the Senior Camp Inmate had fallen, the remaining members of his group followed in quick succession.

The tragic interlude had still further after effects. It was impossible to restore a Communist to the job of Senior Camp Inmate at once. The candidacy of a former German Army officer named Wolff was therefore promoted, because no SS suspicion attached to him. Wolff, however, was a homosexual. He soon got into trouble with the camp underground. To gain support among the prisoners, he tried to establish liaison with the Poles through his "Doll Boys."

At the time, a few prisoners with very bad reputations had come from Auschwitz to Buchenwald, and they were deep in intrigues for power. The German Communists were afraid that another internal upheaval was in the making. Their suspicions were fortified by open threats voiced by the new Senior Camp Inmate. Wolff knew that a certain German Communist from Magdeburg was about to be released. He let it be known that he proposed to forestall the release by reporting the man for political activity in camp. This was answered with the counter-threat that the SS would be informed of Wolff's homosexual practices.

The situation grew more and more tense and in the end the camp underground denounced Wolff to the SS, charging him with organizing a political plot! The consequences were disastrous for a number of Poles who, in my opinion, were quite innocent. They were given fatal injections by Dr. Hoven. Gustav Wegerer, an Austrian Communist who was foreman of the Pathology section, and I, managed to save the Polish physician, Dr. Marian Ciepielowski (later placed in charge of serum production in Building 50), by intervening with Dr. Hoven and Dr. Ding-Schuler. But Wolff himself was transferred to an outside detail on the Baltic Sea, where he soon perished.

Henceforth there was no further attempt to break the absolute hegemony of the political prisoners at Buchenwald. It was tantamount to the hegemony of the Communist party which now, true enough, ceased to reject altogether political prisoners of other shades of opinion. There had been too many instances of individual acts of solidarity, and news had slowly trickled through from the outside that Moscow had proclaimed the slogan of the "Popular Front." For a long time, however, this change in policy did not prevail among the bulk of the Communists in camp.

To survive, collectively and individually, we had to apply to the SS the same policy it used on the prisoners: "Divide and Rule!" The underground camp leaders always had as one of their main purposes the demoralization of the SS, chiefly through corruption. This, of course, often resulted in immediate material benefits to the prisoners, though the dangers were disproportionately great on their side. But among the more alert SS men, corruption could also lay the basis for shaking any ideals they might have or for uprooting them altogether as the situation at the fronts grew worse. The essential purpose was always to gain sufficient control over them to keep them silent and even to have them tolerate certain actions, especially those involving rescue from mortal danger.

More and more, in those camps where the reds held sway, actual power, insofar as it affected the internal workings of camp life, passed into the hands of the prisoners. This development was aided by wartime conditions, by the problem created by the influx of non-Germans and by the tight network of common interests that grew up. True, the influence of the political prisoners was never strong enough to forestall general directives issued by the SS—mass liquidations and actions of a similar character. It extended largely to the ordinary minutiae of camp life, which here and there offered opportunities for preventing the worst and even improving certain conditions.

During the final year, self-government among the prisoners in a number of camps had reached a point where the SS was no longer able to gain a true picture of the internal situation. The SS men were tired; they had become used to the fact that the camps ran by themselves; by and large they let the prisoners have their way in many respects. There was many an SS officer who could no longer relinquish his many personal extravagances—extravagances that were impossible without the connivance of prisoners. Such officers were almost entirely at the mercy of the prisoners.

There were instances in which a delay in delivering a sausage on the part of the prisoner clerk in the SS canteen, or the excuse that no alcohol could be procured at the moment because the Second Officer-in-Charge had forbidden the issue—where such stratagems might induce the First Officer-in-Charge to rescind immediately orders by his colleague that were unfavorable to the prisoners. Such methods were used to secure cancellation of disciplinary measures, to induce Camp Medical Officers to intervene either for or against certain individuals, to invalidate controls of all kinds. True, the greatest beneficiaries from this policy were the ruling group among the prisoners, which in the more important camps was more or less identical with the active anti-Fascist forces.

Occasional success also attended efforts to make higher SS officers subservient to the purposes of the prisoners, not merely by corruption but by direct political influence. Such cases were very rare and involved great danger. They were most likely to succeed with a certain type of SS physician. Unquestionably one of the most impressive instances of this kind was the role played by SS Major Ding-Schuler at Buchenwald.

In 1943 I was to be sent to my death at Auschwitz. At that very time a clerk was being sought for the dreaded chief of Ward 46—Building 50 was about to be opened. I was selected. In agreement with Wegerer, the Capo, I decided from the outset that I would not adopt a passive attitude but would meet danger by direct attack, by taking the bull by the horns. Within a week's time, after Ding-Schuler and I had carefully felt each other out, I began to show a cautious interest in his private concerns, including his family affairs. A month had not yet elapsed when I began to engage in political discussion with him. He had initially asked me about my convictions and, dangerous as it was at the time, I had frankly replied that he could hardly expect a man with my past and in my situation to be friendly toward National Socialism.

This answer impressed Ding-Schuler. Two months later there was no political or military event about which he failed to consult me. Step by step I made it clear to him that Germany must inevitably lose the war and that National Socialism was bound to fall. I told him that he, who was responsible for Ward 46, could expect only to be hailed into court and that his sole chance for mitigating his situation lay in doing as much as he could for the prisoners even now. On many nights he sat in his room until eleven or twelve o'clock, talking with me, accepting my counsel, listening to what I told him about that other world—our own world of the spirit, of morality, of humanitarianism and of human grandeur.

(True, I could never get rid of the thought of what my enemies in the barracks might have said to such secret discussions with a major in the *Waffen SS*, and I was always intent on maintaining that "elastic wall" that had to remain intact even between him and myself.)

Ding-Schuler subsequently did do a great many positive things for the prisoners—or at least allowed them to be done. If there is anything of which I am proud during the time of my concentration-camp detention, it is the fact that I succeeded in this very difficult task which no one else had dared to undertake. I can say that never once did I use my very considerable influence to the disadvantage of a fellow prisoner, even though I might have lived in bitter enmity with him. I employed it solely to help those who were in danger or on behalf of the group in Building 50 or the camp as a whole.

Sometimes the difficulties were extraordinary, for Ding-Schuler was a man with a dismal past[1] who was full of whims

---

[1] Heinz Poller, hospital clerk in 1939–40, when Dr. Ding-Schuler was Camp Medical Officer, discusses this aspect in his book, *Medical Clerk at Buchenwald*.

and moods. I always informed and consulted my friends: Heinz Baumeister, a Social Democrat and old concentration-camp hand; Werner Hilpert, a member of the former Catholic Center party in Saxony; Franz Hackel, a poet of sharply leftist orientation; Walter Hummelsheim, who came from the Rhineland; and Ferdinand Römhild, a Socialist poet who was First Clerk in the prisoner hospital. Baumeister sometimes remarked that Ding-Schuler was not worth the nervous energy, the patience and the attention I wasted on him. But I am glad I stuck it out. It is not merely that several dozen valuable human beings owe their lives to this closely maintained association between myself and the SS physician. In the final days of the Buchenwald concentration camp, this work "with and against" Ding-Schuler paid off in a way none of us could have dreamed.

I tried to extend my influence over Ding-Schuler in a purely human way as well, with the aim of getting him to accept the consequences of his guilt with moral dignity and a sense of catharsis after the collapse should have come. "I don't think I could endure the kind of life you have been leading for years," he sometimes said, and he always toyed with the idea of suicide. Then again he would frivolously skip over the gloomy aspects. "You can't deny, Kogon, no matter how opposed to National Socialism you are, that it's quite an accomplishment to have put the Thousand-Year Reich under the sod in a mere five years!" He would laugh and leap on his motorcycle to pursue his wonted round of activity. Arrested as a war criminal in September 1945, he did commit suicide, without awaiting my unbiased testimony or the statements of the rescued secret-service officers.

It must not be glossed over that such privileges as were gradually wrested from the SS benefited in the main only the German-speaking prisoners of the various nationality groups. These Germans, as soon as they got their bearings in camp and if they managed to survive the internal struggle for power, almost invariably moved up into the better jobs, for the SS never succeeded in solving the problem it had created for itself with the admission of non-Germans. Buchenwald, for example, comprised no less than thirty nationalities in 1945!

Except for certain cases of traitors and brazen profiteers,

the power wielded by prisoners in the concentration camps over individual SS officers and noncoms was always employed for the relief and protection of individuals and of the whole camp. The present report has shown enough instances of this. But two other methods that were used to a considerable extent remain to be discussed.

The first consisted of utilizing the selection of men for shipment. As has been mentioned, the prisoner-manned Labor Records Office directed the utilization of manpower in the camps, under the orders and supervision of the Labor Service and Manpower Utilization Officers. In the course of time the SS staff found itself less and less equal to these requirements. In Buchenwald, SS Captain Schwartz on only one occasion attempted to make up a shipment of one thousand prisoners himself. For almost a full day he kept the whole camp standing in the roll-call area to muster the ranks, and in the end he managed to round up some six hundred men. The men chosen had been ordered to step out of ranks, but they simply disappeared in the other direction. No one lent Schwartz and his two SS assistants a hand. They simply could not get the huge job done, and it was impossible to keep on asking headquarters and the Commander of Troops for help for such purposes. Henceforward the Manpower Utilization Officer left all questions of work assignment to the prisoners in the Labor Records Office.

That work was guided by the principle that anti-Fascist forces—which meant, in the main, Communists—must be kept in camp while elements likely to sabotage the common effort, as well as the physically weak, had to be smuggled into the shipments to be got rid of. Undesirables included chiefly men who had shown a lack of solidarity in camp—bread thieves, racketeers, hoarders and the like. They were signalled out by the Communist representatives from the various nationality groups, who also nominated the "positive elements" that must under no circumstances be placed on shipment.

To insure that such selection was properly carried out, a special section was created inside the Labor Records Office at Buchenwald. It assembled shipment lists on the basis of the recommendations from the various nationality groups. On certain occasions, especially when German firms required skilled help, engineers might actually come to camp to pick whom they wanted. In such cases it was almost impossible to scratch any given person from the list, though it was managed in very important instances. When the firm in question complained, the prisoner was simply reported unfit for shipment or dead.

There were two classes of prisoners who, on orders from headquarters, could not be sent to an outside detail on any account. These were the so-called DIKAL prisoners (the word being composed of the initials of the German phrase for "not to be shipped to any other camp"), and the so-called "target men"—prisoners with a record of attempted escape, or suspected of planning to escape. Nevertheless, even such prisoners were placed on shipment when it was a matter of saving their lives. In the case of the "target men" this was not without its difficulties. One day eighty-five of them were called up. They were all to receive twenty-five lashes. But only some twenty of them were still in camp. The rest had been smuggled into outside details in well-calculated anticipation of such an eventuality. A storm burst on the whole camp, but luckily this too passed and sixty men were spared the beating.

The second possibility of exploiting the regime of corruption was personal or collective enrichment at the expense of others. Sometimes this attained downright shameless proportions in the camps. Certain prisoners profited from their positions of power to such an extent that they lived like kings, while their comrades died by the hundreds. Surely there was no justification when whole boxes of camp victuals, with fat, sausages, canned goods, flour and sugar, were smuggled out of camp by SS accomplices and sent to the families of the prisoners in question. At a time when not even the rear-echelon SS any longer wore riding boots but merely ordinary army shoes, there were such provocative sights as members of the tiny goup of prisoner big shots stalking about like dandies, in fashionable tailored clothes, sometimes even leading a dog on a leash! And all of this cheek by jowl with misery, filth, disease, hunger and death! Here the "instinct of self-preservation" transcended all reasonable bounds, resulting in a ridiculous though quite intractable form of hypocrisy that ill befitted the social and political ideals proclaimed. These things were not precisely typical of camp life, but unfortunately they were part of it.

From mere self-defense the concentration-camp prisoners occasionally proceeded to active resistance against SS measures. The most notable instance was occasioned by the attempt to impress into army service those inmates who were German citizens. A certain Dirlewanger, a fellow with a long criminal record who had fought on the Fascist side in Spain, offered his services to Himmler during the war for the purpose of "indoctrinating" concentration-camp prisoners with a view toward their "volunteering for front-line service." Dirlewanger was later invested with the Knight's Cross and the rank of SS major-general. He was one of the worst bloodhounds in the Lublin district, and personally committed atrocities which cannot be described here because of their bottomless depravity.

In some concentration camps, such as Sachsenhausen, political prisoners were simply detailed to the Dirlewanger program against their will. In other camps, such as Buchenwald, the campaign went no further than an appeal for volunteers. Only an infinitesimally small number of prisoners wearing the red triangle responded, in contrast to quite a few greens and blacks. The last campaign of this nature was directed at the homosexuals in 1945, but they never got to share the honor intended for them.

The convicts who evinced this solidarity with the *Waffen SS*—there were as many as five hundred at Buchenwald—contributed their share to enhancing the reputation of the SS as butchers. They were used in the fight against the partisans in the eastern regions, and in 1944 to help put down the Polish uprising in Warsaw. Some of the survivors, after extended periods of such "front-line parole," were sent back to the concentration camps where their fate was not a happy one.

The remaining prisoners were a good deal more amused than the SS men when such convicts who had donned the uniform sent army postcards, signed "fraternally yours," to the very men who but recently had taken the whip to them. The political prisoners observed maliciously that by rights the Dirlewanger men ought to wear a green triangle on their SS uniforms as a distinguishing mark of their fellowship.

In 1942 Russian volunteers too were trained at Buchenwald.

They had volunteered in the prisoner-of-war camps for service against the partisans.

Such resistance as was practiced here and there in the case of the Dirlewanger campaign was possible only on the basis of years of building up the power of the prisoners inside the camps.

Many a privilege acquired in the course of the years by "old concentrationaries," however, was time and again endangered by the ever-present chance of being sent "on shipment." More and more slaves were needed in the outside details, and more and more prisoner functionaries were needed to man the new camps. The chance of evading such a dreadful pilgrimage, with the necessity of starting all over again in some other camp, grew smaller and smaller. Anyone who was not absolutely indispensable in the base camp or who failed to have the most influential connections, might find himself on shipment at any moment, in imminent danger of losing whatever privileges he enjoyed. Toward the end of the war, newcomers had very little chance of remaining in any of the base camps. As the confusion among the SS grew, power slipped more and more into the hands of the "old-timers" among the prisoners, and new prisoners were naturally the most likely material for shipments. Another factor that helped to dispatch them to one of the new camps as soon as possible was the serious overcrowding in the base camps.

Anti-Fascist activities proper among the concentration-camp prisoners extended to political organization and training and to sabotage.

There was a wide-spread notion throughout Germany that concentration-camp inmates received Nazi political instruction and were then returned to the "racial community" as men who had "seen the light." This is sheer nonsense. After the initial phase at Dachau, the SS never even instituted, let alone carried out, any program of political indoctrination or the like. The only thing that could have been even remotely interpreted in this sense were the radio broadcasts over the German network. In the beginning the prisoners had to listen to Hitler's speeches while standing in the roll-call area. The speeches were as endless as the rain that often poured down on the shorn polls. Their effect was the same. They were simply shaken off. Later on the prisoners were permitted to listen to the speeches in barracks. But by that time repeated defeats had shortened Hitler's speeches and made them less frequent, something the prisoners regretted since most of them were able to take a healthy nap during the oratory.

Party organization by the prisoners was well developed on the left, with the Social Democrats as well as the Communists. Indoctrination took place fairly regularly, though only in tiny cells. At times when there were no informers at large and when power was unequivocally organized, there was an enormous amount of political discussion in the camps. Newspapers were available. In the course of time news broadcasts from abroad got to be somewhat more widely known in camp. It was of the greatest importance that the prisoners should succumb neither to needless discouragement nor to vain self-deception. Some knowledge of the situation in Germany and throughout the world was essential. Actually the monitoring of foreign broadcasts was only an effective supplement to the kaleidoscopic intelligence brought into camp by newcomers from every nation and every walk of life. All this news was collected by the political leaders, carefully evaluated and transmitted to the appropriate men, often resulting in a picture that was more accurate than that available to most Germans on the outside.

The organization of this illegal intelligence service was fraught with great difficulty and danger. The central agencies in most camps were the construction offices and electricians' shops. Prisoners who assumed the job of radio monitoring were in constant danger of their lives. In Buchenwald no one was ever actually executed for "black listening," but in other camps like "Dora" and Sachsenhausen dozens of prisoners were hanged on this account. One protective device for the monitors lay in the policy of having them pass on their news to but one or two fellow prisoners who in turn took care of transmitting it to larger groups.

During the last critical weeks in camp, when it was all-important for us to remain well informed about the situation at the fighting fronts, so that we could take appropriate measures in time, I myself spent many nights at a five-tube set, the property of Dr. Ding-Schuler, which I had been able to wheedle into camp "for repair." There I heard "The Voice of America in Europe" and the "Western Broadcasts for Soldiers," writing down important dispatches in shorthand.

Curiously enough, there was probably no place in Germany outside the concentration camps where politics could be discussed so frankly! Something like an unofficial propaganda ministry developed, which collected and transmitted obscure dispatches of significance, sometimes permitted to be published by Goebbels only in certain frontier papers. Astute political minds analyzed the situation, presenting a clear picture to those prisoners who were interested, especially at times when Hitler seemed to fail in nothing he undertook, spreading deep gloom among them.

Permanent lines to and from the outside world were carefully cultivated. Sometimes these lines were strung by prisoners who had won release, sometimes they ran by way of outside details and civilian employees. In this way the picture of conditions throughout the country which was sketched by the reports of new arrivals could be constantly corrected and supplemented. Important news from the camps was also sent to the outside.

Anti-Fascist celebrations were repeatedly held at Buchenwald. Appropriate security measures were always observed and naturally only absolutely reliable long-time inmates were invited. These occasions usually consisted of a serious and a humorous program, the latter offering barbed political satire. There were even anti-Fascist literary readings. The volumes in the camp library were carefully searched for suitable material, especially from the German classics, and the effect was always impressive. These programs were greatly enriched by material salvaged from the wastepaper collection. Heinrich Heine's revolutionary and satirical poems were restored to honor from this source.

The morale of most of the prisoners might have been buttressed by some form of religious observance to a far greater extent than by these occasional celebrations. I think it is appropriate in this connection to mention the utter lack of any religious work in the concentration camps. Naturally the SS permitted nothing of the kind. Prisoners of the political left who were otherwise of high character would have regarded religious observances as absurd and reactionary, because of outdated views and old and deep-rooted prejudices. True, in later years a few of them began to show more understanding, lending their authority time and again to keeping priests from being shipped out. But the influence of these few clerics was only clandestine and thus extremely limited.

There can be no question but that the merest rudiments of spiritual care, especially among the Poles, could have prevented much moral disintegration, much brutality, much unhappiness. It might have reassured thousands, succored hundreds in their last minutes, given countless sick and maimed new inner strength and the will to recover. But instead, these blessings remained confined to an infinitesimally small circle of men who were unusually courageous and already endowed with strength of character. Only among the Dutch and French at Buchenwald, and then only during the very last period, did an *ecclesia abscondita*, an underground ministry, become possible, shedding at least a ray of light on the dying on their way to the crematory. The Dachau concentration camp formed a real exception, likewise illegal. As already mentioned, thousands of Catholic priests and a considerable number of Protestant pastors of the Confessional Church were there quartered in special barracks. Some of them unfolded vigorous pastoral activity among their fellow prisoners. But by and large religious work in the camps was without practical significance.

Direct sabotage, such as damage to machinery or weapons, was possible only in isolated instances. Generally speaking, sabotage had to assume forms that were hard to recognize. The primary possibility was manpower utilization. Naturally the prisoners preferred to assign skilled workers only to plants that were not directly concerned with arms production. The latter were sent mainly unskilled help. Reliable anti-Fascist experts, however, were wormed into positions where they could practice systematic sabotage.

The German civilian foremen and engineers in charge of production were poor in technique and organization since they were almost without exception regular Nazis. They often had to depend on their prisoner experts. As a result it was possible to conduct a comprehensive program of sabotage by means of faulty planning and building, delays in procuring machinery, tools and materials, fostering internal jurisdictional disputes, applying official regulations and test standards to the letter and similar methods.

Such sabotage was by no means confined to the armament

plants. It pervaded the whole structure of the concentration camps. Insofar as it consisted of slowing down the work, this was quite in keeping with the understandable disinclination of the prisoners to do any more work than was absolutely necessary. Some quite impressive records in loafing and dawdling were hung up.

To maintain and carry out this entire program of illegal activity an effective defense organization had to be built up. When power had been consolidated, this also served to prepare for the end of the camps. All the larger nationality groups created formations of this kind—the Czechs, the Yugoslavs, the Poles, the Russians, the French, the Belgians, the Dutch. For every conceivable reason and pretext, additional auxiliaries to the Camp Police or other institutions that might be of value in emergencies were called into being—special fireguards, in addition to the permanent fire brigade, a first-aid unit, an emergency unit and similar outfits, until in the end Buchenwald numbered more than one thousand carefully disciplined men at the disposal of the camp underground and only waiting for its orders.

The SS never succeeded in obtaining a clear picture of this powerful organization, its growth and its significance. The courage, the ruthless assumption of responsibility even against conflicting forces inside the camp, the skill and infinite patience required of the anti-Fascist forces to build up this effective system of self-protection in constant underground struggle—all these can be imagined. The example that was set, the influence that was gained were so great that political prisoners in other camps terrorized by the greens sent appeals for help. Organizers were dispatched by Buchenwald in outgoing shipments, and although they were unable to work any basic changes at their destination, they were able to help bring relief.

When the end came, it was not in the way that had been anticipated. But the preparations at Buchenwald proved so effective that the situation there in 1945 was brought under control in better fashion than in most of the other concentration camps.

Chapter Twenty-One

THE END OF THE CAMPS

At an early date the leading minds among the prisoners in all the concentration camps endeavored to prepare for the various contingencies that might arise when the camps were evacuated or liberated. The average prisoner anticipated this event, which always loomed in the background, with a sense of fear that bordered on panic. It was generally assumed that Himmler would issue a timely order for the liquidation of all concentration-camp inmates and, as time went on, that he might use Allied air attacks as a "cover-up." Poison, gas, machine-guns and air raids by German planes were considered possibilities.

But whenever such possibilities were examined in detail, the conclusion became inescapable that they would not be easy to put into effect successfully. Without a doubt any plan to poison all the inmates could have been forestalled, though that would have jeopardized continuance of the food supply. Any attempt to mow down the prisoners from the towers by means of machine-guns or flame-throwers would have provoked uprisings in many places. The electrically charged barbed wire would have been razed. Hundreds and perhaps thousands would have fallen, but still more would have escaped, though their further fate throughout the country would have been extremely uncertain.

The least protection seemed to be available against a German Air Force bombardment. Fear of such action was moderated, though not completely banished, by such general considerations as the temper of the population and the command situation in the air force, which might not permit such a thing. The camps were even more defenseless against mass liquidations by gas, whether on the spot, where gas chambers were available, or by shipment to other places. Concerted and individual escape en route, resistance immediately outside the gas chambers—these seemed to be the only possible defense measures, and their effectiveness was not considered great.

The argument that ultimately proved correct was at first ignored altogether and even later put forward by only a few. This was that a central liquidation order was quite unlikely since in the final stages of dissolution the concentration camps would have become no more than a marginal concern of Himmler and his staff and the chain of command would no longer be functioning at full efficiency.

It had become clear that progressive demoralization had long since deprived the rear-echelon SS of effective striking power against masses of men. But this realization seemed too uncertain to depend on. With the turning of the tide of war against the Nazis, the situation of the SS in the camps grew increasingly chaotic, especially as more and more of their armament plants were bombed by the Allies. The industrial installations adjoining Sachsenhausen, Dachau, Buchenwald and Auschwitz were all seriously damaged in 1944. In most cases the United States and Royal Air Force bombers really did precision work. Though the SS men were already bitterly complaining about their own leaders, and most of them no longer believed in a Nazi victory, they might, in typical German fashion, pull machine-gun triggers and throw hand grenades to lay us low if the appropriate order were issued with sufficient vigor. Definite and reliable precautions, however, against such an eventuality could be taken in only a few camps—as far as I know, only in Buchenwald, Sachsenhausen, Dachau, Mauthausen and Lublin.

The first concentration camp to fall into Allied hands was

Lublin. From incoming prisoners we learned that with the approach of the Russian front the SS had taken to its heels, leaving to the enemy some six thousand prisoners who had not been evacuated and who had evidently succeeded in creating a defense organization. There were wild rumors that on taking the camp the Russians had strung up prisoner functionaries guilty of offenses against their fellows or that they had surrendered them to prisoner vengeance. Some of the big shots among the Buchenwald prisoners began to worry seriously about their own fate. Men who were enmeshed in incriminating circumstances quietly made plans for putting out of the way reputable witnesses who might testify to their sorry deeds.

Soon after the liberation of Lublin, a huge stream of evacuees from the eastern camps to the interior of Germany began to take place. Camp after camp was evacuated by the SS. The surviving inmates were driven westward on foot whenever transport facilities in the general exodus had become inadequate. As much of the physical evidence of atrocities as possible was blown up. Prisoners of so-called "German blood" were issued arms to keep their foreign fellow prisoners in check, for of course the SS staffs were the first to take flight by rail and car, and the remaining SS troops were as a rule inadequate to keep under proper control the thousands of concentration-camp prisoners to be set in motion.

In endless columns the wretched host rolled over the countryside, day after day, often for weeks, without food or adequate clothing. Those who could go no farther were shot down by the SS or their armed prisoner minions, or simply left by the wayside. Many fled and hid but were picked up by the German military police or by fanatics among the population, to be detained elsewhere or executed, as the case might be. Others made their way into Germany or Poland or behind the Russian lines. More centrally located camps had to make room for thousands upon thousands of evacuees who reported stories of unrelieved terror. The picture was one of chaotic disintegration, studded with harrowing incidents. One had only to look at the wretched figures pouring into the narrowing interior from every side to believe them.

Orders had meanwhile been issued in the west, as well, to

withdraw subsidiary camps and outside details. Construction brigades were the first to be withdrawn, from the Atlantic coast to eastern Belgium. During the summer of 1944, together with the inmates of the western camps, they retired behind the right bank of the Rhine. In the winter and spring they drew back farther, step by step, until they collided with the evacuees from the east at Dachau, Sachsenhausen, Neuengamme, Buchenwald, Flossenbürg, Mauthausen.

Beginning in February and March 1945, the situation in every concentration camp grew increasingly tense. Wherever appropriate preparations had been made, the political prisoners were now at long last able to reap the fruits of years of effort. The story of the end of the Buchenwald concentration camp may serve as the best example, since Buchenwald was more unequivocally under the rule of the political prisoners than any other.

The defense formations at Buchenwald have already been discussed in the preceding chapter. Steps to procure a supply of arms began to be taken during the air raid of August 24, 1944. Advantage was taken of the general confusion that reigned, and as many rifles, pistols, carbines and hand grenades as possible were removed from the SS divisional replacement depot. The weapons were carefully concealed in camp. Some of them were buried, others walled up, and the locations were known to but a few key people. Insofar as was possible, these supplies were steadily augmented. This aspect of the preparatory work alone would have been impossible unless the internal organization had functioned smoothly, all questionable and treacherous elements having been systematically purged as the result of a sustained campaign.

The possession of arms for the first time created a sense of security. At least the prisoners would not have to die without putting up a fight. They could no longer be simply butchered. This was reassuring, though there could be no illusions as to the extraordinary difficulties of the situation. On the one hand the fight was against the SS, but almost equally, at the crucial moment, it would have to be waged against weaklings, cowards and the inevitable panic.

When the first large shipments from evacuated camps reached Buchenwald, a curious intermediate state of affairs arose. The SS, sensing the beginning of the end, was afraid of the anonymous masses of tens of thousands of prisoners. The masses of the prisoners were afraid of the SS. During this period the surrounding population, especially the people of Weimar, feared the camp like the plague.

Unquestionably the group which worried most were the civilians employed in the SS plants—who often enough had behaved abominably. They feared they would be slaughtered outright when "the day" came. Among the political prisoners there was an unbridled thirst for vengeance, especially against the city of Weimar to which money and benefits of every kind had flowed through hundreds of channels from the Buchenwald charnel house and where no one had shown any sympathy or pity, let alone any active help. But the forces of order in Buchenwald were concerned with their own political reputation and sought to prevent the camp from becoming a focal point of chaos, for the sake of the country and the future. Efforts were intensified to retain control during the impending events.

Months before the actual end, when the situation matured more and more, the question arose whether to organize an armed uprising or to pursue a further policy of waiting. After considerable controversy it was decided to continue avoiding all provocation. Resistance was to be offered only when the situation really grew critical. Preparations were still further intensified, to the accompaniment of constant difficulties, not only with respect to the SS but also to the masses of prisoners who were not in on the plans. Trustworthy representatives of the various nationality groups were placed in every barracks. The defense formations were elaborated. Everything finally pointed to the one great question: what orders will Himmler issue? For it had long since been made certain that the SS units in the camps would no longer take action on their own.

There were two groups in camp which, independently of each other, were preparing a definite plan for taking over the camp after the defeat of the SS and the entry of the Allies: the Communist party, and a non-Communist group under the leadership of the British Captain Burney. As developed after the liberation, the plans did not differ very much, for both were based on the same camp background. The main difference was that the Communist party, proceeding from the fact of its actual control of power in camp, for understandable reasons of secrecy and from old habit, had slated only its own men for the seizure; while the other group proceeded purely on the basis of individual qualifications, assigning no less than a good third of the proposed new functionaries to the Communists. Both groups worked on an international basis.

As early as mid-March 1945, it was beyond doubt that the western Allies would reach central Germany. Hope in camp was primarily centered on aid from the air when worst came to worst. In the event of an aerial landing operation on the plains north of Buchenwald, active intervention on the part of the camp was decided on, no matter how difficult the situation might grow. Everyone expected, however, that the SS would first attempt an evacuation. Early in April, preparations pointing to such a plan were in evidence. The SS divisional replacement installations were evacuated. A complete state of alertness had been ordered among the prisoners, though the situation had not yet developed to the point where an unequivocal solution was possible.

We knew that the Commandant, SS Colonel Pister, was a bureaucrat by nature, who would do nothing on his own initiative and was fond of procrastinating. Through SS Major Ding-Schuler we learned that on April 2, Himmler, in a telephone conversation brought about by the Weimar police chief, SS Colonel Schmidt, had left it up to the "discretion" of SS Captain Oldeburhuis, Commandant of the Ohrdruf camp, to liquidate his convicts and political prisoners regarded as "especially dangerous."

Himmler, however, expressly ordered that nothing should happen to the Jews—a paradox that can be explained only by the curious expectations entertained by the top leadership of the SS on the international level. The remaining Ohrdruf prisoners were to be evacuated. This death march of 12,000 Ohrdruf inmates to Buchenwald actually took place, thousands being shot down en route. On April 5, on the last brief leg from Weimar to Buchenwald alone, seventy-four prisoners wallowed in their own blood. Hundreds had been indiscriminately shot down before by fanatical Hitler Youth and even by women. The victims at Ohrdruf itself ran to more than 1,500.

There were now 47,000 men herded behind the barbed wire

of Buchenwald, their food supply doubtful, their misery passing all bounds. The thunder of cannon could be heard from west of Erfurt, where American armor was waiting to complete its deployment. These were days of extreme nervous tension.

On the afternoon of April 4, all the Jews in camp had been suddenly ordered to assemble. Not one appeared in the roll-call area. Nothing like this had ever before happened in a concentration camp. It was unimaginable that the SS should no longer dare enforce its orders by brute violence. Yet all it did was to announce that the Jews were to be transferred to an exchange camp for shipment abroad, about which Himmler was negotiating. No one believed a word of this. It ran directly counter to the SS mentality. (Later it developed that there was an element of truth in the story after all. In his pathological belief in "Jewish world power," Himmler had put out certain feelers in Sweden as to whether some "deal" involving the lives of the Jews could not be concluded!)

The hesitation on the part of the SS brought a valuable night's respite, during which hundreds of "Old Guard" Jewish prisoners were afforded a chance to submerge. Names, numbers, markings, details were swapped, barracks assignments exchanged. The next morning the SS lined up the camp inmates by barracks and ordered: "Jews, front and center!" Some of the Jews complied, but the rest had to be picked by the SS "by sight," for since the bombardment of Buchenwald there were no longer complete records. There were chaotic scenes. The Buchenwald noncoms proceeded indiscriminately. Some butchers from Auschwitz went to the Little Camp and, armed with clubs, picked out men as they pleased. But it was impossible to do the work without the Camp Police, which did nothing to aid in the proceedings. Men who were nimble enough to act on their own initiative simply disappeared into formations that had already been combed out. In the end some 1,500 of the 6,000 Jews in camp were assembled, their number to be swelled by the Hungarian Jews arriving from Ohrdruf the next day.

On April 5, a warning was received from an SS source that there was a plan to liquidate the eighteen Britons and two Americans in camp. A few trustworthy men at once helped the four officers among them, Southgate and Burney in the lead, to submerge. They were secreted in a space two feet high under Building 56, in the Little Camp.

To relieve the extremely tense situation, four important personalities among the non-Germans in camp had been persuaded as early as April 3, to address a letter to the Commandant. They were the Belgian cabinet member Soudain, the French under-secretary of state, Marie,[1] Captain Burney and the Dutch naval officer, Cool. The letter, in clever fashion, certified the Commandant's loyal and correct behavior and expressed the hope that the four signers, once they had returned to their countries, might find the opportunity to call this to public attention. The Commandant's barber transmitted the letter, which had its effect. Pister took it to be a safe-conduct for himself and his family. "One can always delay carrying out an order!" he remarked. Neither side, of course, actually called things by their proper names.

Pister hesitated—that was the main thing. The sounds of battle could be heard and American planes were circling the countryside. Time was being gained. Had it been known that another eight days would have to pass before liberation, these delaying tactics would probably not have prevailed, especially since the Commandant by no means adopted an attitude unequivocally favorable to the prisoners, but, on the contrary, vacillated further in the direction of the SS.

The crucial test came on April 5. During the preceding days the SS officers had destroyed the most important records left in camp. SS Major Ding-Schuler returned to camp once more and told me he had learned from Dr. Schiedlausky that the Weimar Gestapo had issued orders to execute forty-six political prisoners the next morning before the camp was evacuated. There was to be another Ohrdruf! Ding-Schuler knew only four of the names—the Hospital Capo and his deputy, the Capo of Ward 46, and myself. The warning was of inestimable value, for it afforded almost eight hours' leeway. The entire internal camp organization was instantly alerted. It was decided to meet the issue head on, to refuse to surrender the forty-six, at the risk of an open fight. But who were they—in addition to those already known?

That night the list reached the Orderly Room from the Roll

---

[1] To become for a short time Premier of France after the war.—*Tr*.

Call Officer. It required the men named to report to the gatehouse the next morning. It was a rather uneven list. Important names were not included, while others, of no importance, were. It was a typical Gestapo measure, and its obvious source was a denunciation already known in camp. Months ago a certain Duda who had joined the Dirlewanger group had squealed. It now developed that he had reported all the names that seemed important to him, partly with justification, partly without. In all likelihood his list had been augmented by the Camp Medical Officer Schiedlausky, who two days before had been observed giving a hand-written letter to the Weimar Gestapo chief at the gatehouse. And Schiedlausky had been Ding-Schuler's informant! The fact that almost none of the newer underground leaders were on the list shows at least that secrecy had been rather well maintained.

That same night all the men on the list, except the French manufacturer Bloch whose inclusion baffled everyone, slipped into safe hiding places. When the men were summoned the next morning only Bloch appeared at the gatehouse. He was sent away after a while, probably for tactical reasons, to lull the suspicions of his fellows. Following this second challenge, the Commandant summoned the Senior Camp Inmate and demanded that the Camp Police locate the missing men. The Senior Camp Inmate proceeded with an eight-hour "search," of course without finding a single one of the men who had submerged.

The danger of a general roll call now loomed. The underground leaders decided that such a formation would be boycotted, if called. A concentration camp without roll call! This meant that the most important SS control measure had vanished. Henceforth no one any longer reported to the gatehouse when danger was anticipated. It was an open declaration of war. When night fell, the SS dared enter the camp only under heavy arms. They realized that the political prisoners were determined to fight.

The responsible men in camp had no illusions about their prospects of success in the event of an armed clash between the SS and the prisoners. Within a few hours at the most, the fight would necessarily end in favor of the SS. But they took into account the impending arrival of the liberating troops,

expected almost hourly. To check the danger of a last-minute
evacuation, it was decided to smuggle an emissary out of
camp who should head for the Allied lines from Weimar in
case the Americans by-passed the strategically important Ettersberg where the concentration camp was located. He was to
address an immediate message to the Buchenwald Commandant. The police radio had reported—and the camp intelligence service had passed on the news—that in the
preceding night forty parachutists in civilian clothes had been
dropped on either side of the motor highway south of Weimar
without being captured. The letter to the Commandant was to
be attributed to one of these parachutists. It read:

> *Commandant!*
> *Shipments are leaving Buchenwald—death shipments
> like that from Ohrdruf!*
> *The ghastly tragedy of Ohrdruf must not be repeated.
> We have seen with our own eyes the victims of the escort
> units and of the incited populace.*
> *Woe unto those who are responsible! Woe unto
> Thuringia, if such a thing is repeated! We understand that
> you—like the whole country—are in difficulties, which
> you believe you can master only by sending thousands on
> their way. An end to it! An immediate end! Our armored
> commanders are approaching to settle your account. You
> have one more chance!*

> JAMES MCLEOD,
> MAJOR,
> WAR OFFICE, LONDON

On April 6, more than three thousand Jews were scheduled
to leave Buchenwald on foot. At this juncture the camp
emissary could make good his escape in but one way, since no
one could leave camp except with the shipments. This was by
way of Building 50 and Dr. Ding-Schuler. I therefore emerged
from my hiding place, though SS patrols were searching the
camp, met Dr. Ding-Schuler who had been notified by SS
Sergeant Feld, already mentioned in this report as a courier,
and made arrangements for the hazardous undertaking. The
next day, April 8, the Weimar police was to send a truck to

pick up valuable instruments and serum for SS Colonel Schmidt's combat group. I was to squat in one of the boxes, to be taken to the Weimar home of Ding-Schuler.

The Commandant had ordered another shipment of 14,000 men from Buchenwald for April 7. After protracted delay, the SS was furnished 1,500 prisoners, and when 200 heavily armed SS men with machine-guns marched into camp, another 4,500, in order to facilitate the impending battle. For among the greatest difficulties were the food situation and the masses of men in camp—convicts, asocials and others—who might menace the rear of the fighting ranks or otherwise impede them. There was no other way. The two shipments departed, for an unknown destination.

We have learned meanwhile what happened to them, and the story, typical of those days, is here briefly reported. The smaller shipment was scheduled for the Flossenbürg concentration camp, but only about 170 men arrived there. The rest succumbed to the hardships en routs, were shot down or escaped. The larger shipment set out for Dachau, but by way of Saxony! Provisions for but one day were taken along. The forty railroad cars with 100 to 120 prisoners each were shuttled over rail lines that were not yet destroyed or had been hastily repaired. They got as far as Czechoslovakia, and thence by way of the Bavarian Forest to the vicinity of Passau, where they got stuck in the little village of Nammering which had extensive rail sidings because of the local stone industry.

There is a report by Johann Bergmann, a minister of Aicha vor dem Wald, who between April 19 and 23, with great courage and Christian charity, looked after these half-starved Buchenwald prisoners. Among other things he went out among the farmers in his district, who were horrified at the turn of events, and immediately collected some twenty tons of potatoes and several tons of bread and other food, and saw to it that the food actually reached the prisoners. According to the minister, some 270 bodies of men who had perished were inadequately cremated by means of a wood fire kindled under a makeshift grating of rails. The bodies of 700 others who had starved to death or had been shot were thrown into a ravine. SS First Lieutenant Merbach of Buchenwald, an escort officer, began to shudder at his own handiwork and made little effort to interfere with the work of the minister and his associates. The lieutenant finally got drunk, in order to "forget the misery at least overnight," as he put it. On April 23 the cars with the remaining 3,000-odd prisoners moved on in the direction of Munich to be routed to Dachau. . . .

On the morning of April 8 there was a protracted air-raid alarm at Buchenwald, after which the entire camp was ordered to assemble for evacuation at twelve o'clock noon. The expected truck from Weimar which was to take away the medical supplies from Building 50 had not yet arrived! At last, around 12:45 P.M., it rolled up, with four SS men who had no idea of what was afoot. The boxes were loaded aboard without incident, under Feld's supervision. Four hours later the letter to the Commandant was posted at Weimar. It had its effect. Pister vacillated even more. Another 4,800 prisoners were evacuated on April 9, and 9,280 on the morning of April 10, mostly from the Little Camp. Some of them had volunteered for shipment, while others were brutally rounded up. It was on this latter day that the Commandant found himself no longer able to postpone even more drastic measures, for SS Lieutenant-General Prince Waldeck-Pyrmont came to Buchenwald in person to "whip Pister into line," as he put it. Despite his duplicity, the Commandant had so far countenanced ruthlessness on only a partial scale. He had failed to take thorough-going measures for carrying out the orders he had received. Now that Prince Waldeck himself intervened it was already too late, for April 11 was to bring the issue to a head.

The action directed against the remaining Jews and the forty-six political prisoners had meanwhile been dissipated in the general confusion. Had there been a general evacuation, the remaining forty-five men might have been intercepted at the gatehouse and shot down—if they had appeared, that is! For like the sick and the administrative personnel, who were scheduled to remain behind, they were determined not to leave camp. They had decided to guard against the danger of being cut down at the very end by hiding out in safe underground shelters—Prince Waldeck had actually voiced the intention of blowing up the camp.

On Wednesday, April 11, 1945, there were still 21,000

prisoners in Buchenwald. At this point conditions would have favored armed action. But the SS were no longer in a mood to attack. At 10:30 A.M. the First Officer-in-Charge announced that the camp would be surrendered. Some credence was given to the statement, though it was known that the SS had requested low-flying bombers from a near-by air base, on a mission to destroy the camp. All the forces inside the compound remained in a state of complete alertness. About an hour and a half later the loudspeaker called on all SS members to report to their stations outside the enclosure immediately, and tension mounted to its climax. Soon afterward the SS began to withdraw.

The die was cast. Only the guards on the watchtowers remained behind, and shortly before three o'clock in the afternoon, when the sounds of battle drew closer and closer, they retired to the surrounding woods. Members of the camp defense formations, who had been in cover fully armed, at once cut the barbed wire, occupied the towers and the gatehouse and broke out the white flag on the main tower. Thus the first American tanks, rumbling up from the northwest, found a Buchenwald that had already been liberated. Aid from the direction of Weimar had become unnecessary. The city was taken by the Americans that same night.

There was tremendous enthusiasm among the 21,000 men who had been saved. The organization prepared by the Communist party for taking over the camp was immediately put into effect. An international camp committee was created, with sub-committees for the various nationality groups. There were some 5,000 Frenchmen, 3,500 Poles and Polish Jews, 2,200 Germans, 2,000 Russians, 2,000 Czechs, 2,000 Ukrainians, 600 Yugoslavs, 400 Dutch, 300 Austrians, 200 Italians, 200 Spaniards, and some 3,000 members of other nationalities. The job of the committees was to co-operate with the officers of the Third U.S. Army who were arriving. What remained to be done was the formal restoration of liberty to men who, on April 12, 1945, for the first time assembled in the roll-call area not as slaves of the SS, but voluntarily, as free men! After eight years of slave life, the Buchenwald concentration camp, stinking site of barracks eloquent with misery and suffering, had ceased to exist.

But while the men who had been liberated made the air ring with their rejoicing, a remnant of the 26,000 men who had been shipped out of Buchenwald during the final weeks were starving and suffocating in fifty railroad cars on the outskirts of the Dachau camp—nameless, immortal victims. . . .

Chapter Twenty-Two

THE PSYCHOLOGY OF THE SS

Psychologists are likely to find the story of the concentration camps studded with many strange phenomena, both among the SS and the prisoners. On the surface, the reactions of the prisoners appear far more understandable than those of their oppressors. The prisoners, after all, are recognizable as human beings; but there is something inhuman about the whole character of the SS. Actually the psychology of the SS is by far the simpler of the two. It differs little from that of the Praetorian Guard in ancient Rome, the followers of Mohammed's immediate successors, the Mongol shock troops of Ghengis Khan, the Janissaries, the dervishes of the Mahdi, and similar bodies of men known from history. Only in the matter of social origins did the SS bring a modern note into the picture.

Whether they were consciously attracted to SS ideals or not, the men who volunteered for Hitler's Elite Guards were without exception of a type in whom a primitive psychological mechanism was at work. Their minds were enclosed by a hard shell consisting of a few sharply fixed, dogmatic, effortless, simplified concepts underneath which lurked a flood of inchoate emotionalism. They suffered from no internal conflicts between instinct and reason. They acknowledged no universally valid standards of conduct.

The only form of soul-searching to which they submitted was in full accord with the primitive scheme of their minds. It amounted to no more than a check-up as to whether the direction of their instincts actually corresponded to the prescribed SS goals. In keeping with a certain tradition of Prussianism, they called this "licking the inner son of a bitch" (*Schweinehund*). It did not by any means imply resisting their own inclinations. And what a gulf there was between Herr Himmler's "ideals of consecration," and the parasite life of his Death-Head elite!

Nearly all the SS officers were married and had children, but they were quite fond of promiscuity as well. It was not always easy for the prisoners, whose fate often depended on the whims of this gentry, to tell who was having an affair with whom or a feud with someone else. Kurt Titz, one of the orderlies at Buchenwald, was often in serious difficulties on this account. No sooner had he awakened the Koch children at the prescribed hour, washed and dressed them and taken them to toilet, fed and walked the dog, brewed the coffee and brought it to Madame's bed, on which she liked to lie uncovered, than Camp Medical Officer Hoven, nick-named "Handsome Waldemar," would put in his appearance—that is, if the Commandant was absent. And if Titz was not careful, he might be caught unawares at the nightly appearance of Officer-in-Charge Florstedt, who fled his own wife to join the Commandant's. A slip of the tongue in mentioning Florstedt in the presence of Hoven might bring disgrace and death to the orderly. Titz actually did fall into disfavor, but managed to survive the camp prison and Flossenbürg concentration camp.

It will occasion no surprise that the permanent beneficiaries of such a system showed not the slightest desire to give up their life of plenty, of drinking and whoremongering, in order to go to the front and fight for the vaunted German fatherland. The concentration camps became a paradise of shirkers from the Death-Head elite. The SS heroes never tired of thinking up new stratagems to keep them from shouldering rifles and entering the trenches. Agency after agency was created for the sole purpose of certifying that these gentry were absolutely indispensable.

As early as October 1941, for example, when the German armies had not yet reached their peak penetration of Russia, an elaborate "SS Building Inspection Office for Russia" was drawn up on paper. It included a host of regional offices located in cities that were not in German hands at the time or that were never captured at all (such as Moscow). After the battle of Stalingrad these locations were simply changed. Even when the German forces had been driven far back across the Dnieper, the rear-echelon SS officers refused to surrender their posts, simply moving their offices closer to Germany.

Prince Waldeck created an "Office for the Germanization of Eastern Nations"—in Cassel! It's real purpose was to offer refuge to SS shirkers and their harems. Prisoners who came to Buchenwald from other concentration camps told stories of similar SS practices. The Nazi apostles and warmongers fought a tenacious battle to escape the fate they had prepared for the nation.

A show of honor, loyalty, a clean family life within the consecrated SS fellowship—these "virtues" by no means excluded open vileness, treachery and sexual dissipation with regard to those outside the group and especially to groups regarded as inferior—if it appeared appropriate to SS purposes. Indeed, the SS almost demanded such a double standard, as we have come to call it. The constant references to "high ideals" that appear in SS writings and speeches do not disprove its existence. These ideals shared only their names with those of mankind and Christianity generally. They had but a conditional validity, as a code for the "Master Race" applicable only so long as it appeared useful.

It is not my thesis that the individual SS members were aware of these contradictions. Most of them were far too uncritical. They harbored a deep hatred of purely objective intelligence—every kind, that is, except that which was purely a means to an end. They were quite simply attracted to the SS idealogy as the mode of life that appealed to them and agreed with them. And because this mode of life made no intellectual demands worth mentioning on them, while permitting their instincts free play, they accepted more or less willingly the harsh and inexorable disciplinary limitations designed to channel those instincts. This actually afforded them the additional gratification of seeking compensation for the compulsion which drill occasionally imposed on them by "taking it out" on others, even on their own kind, with a great show of strength and virility. Here at last the "inner son of a bitch" could be projected to someone else and "licked" with an enthusiasm that ranged all the way to sadism.

It is in the very nature of such a fellowship that from the outset, and more and more so in the course of its growth, it is composed of members whose cultural deficiencies prevent them from occupying a satisfactory position in normal society. Any inquiry into the origins of SS members will show that in almost every case they were men who were maladjusted and frustrated, whom circumstances had deprived of success, whose innate endowment was slight, who often enough were total social failures. In this respect the SS was almost the epitome of National Socialism. This applies to its founders, Himmler and Heydrich, whose deep-rooted sense of inferiority was overcompensated by boundless ambition, and all the way down to the Death-Head cadres. In the course of time the black SS uniform—all but the *Waffen SS*—came to be the voluntary rallying point for all the kindred spirits among the German people, the Nazi party and the ranks of the professional and avocational soldiers—men of like mental and social make-up. It is this core that was the SS proper. All others either gradually returned to normal life of their own accord or were expelled—they were usually those who had been merely detailed to the SS against their will. As for the members of the *Waffen SS* who streamed in during the war, most of them were limited to the realization of a single SS ideal—a tough recklessness. To them this was the epitome of the SS. After the Polish campaign when the army submitted to Hitler a whole volume of documents about war atrocities committed by the SS, the *Waffen SS* replied with several volumes in kind about the army. But they knew little or nothing concrete about the SS super state or about SS aims. Those among them who in the light of our own standards were the worst, ultimately reached the Security Service and the concentration-camp complements. Only a Nazi victory could have shown how many of the hundreds of thousands of members of the *Waffen SS* were, or would have remained, true SS men in the fullest sense—primitive representatives of a caste whose mental reactions always took a typical, never an individual form.

Without doubt there were SS members who *were* idealists, unselfish and high-minded. But as a rule their political sagacity, their general capacity to see and think in context were in inverse proportion to the intensity of their idealistic convictions. It took a good measure of folly to keep on believing in the general ideals proclaimed by Herr Himmler, in the face of the constant living evidence to the contrary. The true SS idealist, who at least gradually came to see the situation in its true light, necessarily yielded to despair. There were only three roads open to him; to get out of the SS, even if in the end it meant suicide (there were a number of such instances); to engage in a quixotic fight for his ideals, which inevitably joined the issue and brought death; or to go to the front and find death there. It is certain that by 1944 there were no old SS members left who were still convinced and enthusiastic SS idealists.

The natural sense of inferiority that afflicts those who have been dragged down the social scale created a strong predisposition among SS members toward hatred of men of real social prestige, of firmly held political convictions and of substantial education. With many SS men this sense of inferiority was deepened by their own illegitimate antecedents, a matter that should otherwise have been of no overwhelming importance but that denied them precisely the one thing arrogantly demanded by SS ideals—a long, stainless pedigree. Even the "intellectuals" in the ranks of the SS—men who for some reason had never been able to finish college and also a disproportionately large number of dislodged grade-school teachers—all too frequently took out their sense of failure in arrogance, which is but the veneer of hatred.

Let a few case histories, from hundreds upon hundreds that resemble each other like rotten eggs, serve to illustrate what has been said.

SS Captain Hoven: Born in 1903, the son of a postal official. Failed to graduate from high school. At sixteen went to Sweden, where he worked on a farm. Emigrated to the United States at eighteen, where he became foreman at a dairy farm. At twenty-one the lover of a wealthy woman, who got him a Hollywood contract at five hundred dollars a week. In 1925 he returned to Germany, helped out in the office of the Freiburg sanatorium established with great success by his brother, later becoming social director of this fashionable institution. In 1930 he went to Paris with a certain Baron de Maier, for whom he wrote society news at a salary of two thousand marks a month. When National Socialism came into power, he hastened back to Germany and joined the General SS. Now aged thirty-two, he quickly absolved his high-school graduation and began to study medicine, for his brother had died and he wanted to become his successor as medical head of the sanatorium. He passed his preliminary examination only on the second try, but enlistment in the *Waffen SS* enabled him to obtain his state license on an emergency basis, for it was 1939 and the war had broken out. He was now a doctor and within two years had attained such "maturity" that he was able to become Deputy Chief Medical Officer for all the concentration camps. Another two years later the verdict of experts during the Koch trial was to the effect that "from the viewpoint of his knowledge and skill Hoven hardly deserves to be described as a physician."

SS Major Fassbender: Origins unknown, adopted child of the owners of the famous German chocolate firm of Fassbender. A ne'er-do-well, drunkard and wastrel. Married to a Countess Stollberg. Made the acquaintance of the head of the so called Mounted SS, SS Major-General Fegelein, whom he financed, becoming battalion commander in the First SS Mounted Regiment, and together with Fegelein one of the worst SS criminals in Warsaw. Among other things, he "Aryanized" the world-wide fur company of Apfelbaum, in concert with Slava Mirovska, secretary to the owner, who had fled. Fassbender marked down the value of the firm from around 40,000,000 to 50,000 marks. Responsible for the pregnancy of his mistress, he had Fegelein and the Gestapo arrest her husband, a Polish officer, and a few days later, again in concert with the Polish she-devil who obtained a general power of attorney to his fortune at the last moment, shot him down in his cell. Transferred to France, he committed . . . etc., etc.

SS Colonel Koch: Born at Darmstadt, in 1897, the son of a registry official. Commercial apprenticeship from 1911 to 1914, then until 1916 a bookkeeper. War service, with two tours of duty at the front, the first time for two weeks, the second for six. Returned to clerical employment in 1920, holding at least seven jobs in succession during the years from 1922 to 1930, with a record of petty larceny in 1928. Married in 1924, he had a son Manfred who later spent some time in an institution because of marked feeble-mindedness but was still later assigned to the Brunswick music school of the *Waffen SS*. Koch's marriage was dissolved in 1931 with himself as the guilty party. That same year he joined the Nazi party and soon afterward the SS. In 1932 he was expelled from the Party because of an affair that was never cleared up. He was soon re-admitted and in 1935 was the subject of proceedings for malfeasance and embezzlement. Nevertheless he became SS Commandant of the Columbia House concentration camp in Berlin, later of the Esterwege concentration camp. In 1937 he married his second wife, Ilse, and that same year embarked on his notorious career at Buchenwald.

For reasons of personal antipathy, Prince Waldeck and Koch were not on good terms. As long as Eicke was inspector of concentration camps—like the "incorruptible" SS Lieutenant-General Pohl of the SS Main Economic and Administrative Office, he collected "considerations" of up to ten thousand marks from Koch!—Prince Waldeck had no chance to bring his enemy to book. But in 1941 Eicke was transferred to the front as a general in the *Waffen SS*.

That same fall the Thuringian tax authorities suddenly manifested an interest in the financial affairs of the Buchenwald canteen, alleging that no taxes had been paid on transactions running into the millions—which was quite true, of course. An investigation was imminent, and it would certainly, at least in part, have uncovered the SS graft system headed by the Commandant. All records in camp were therefore burned and there ensued a tenacious jurisdictional dispute as to whether outside agencies had any right to intervene in the concentration camps.

As a high SS and police official, and the supreme legal

authority in the district, Prince Waldeck, who was probably behind the sudden interest of the tax office, had the right to intervene. He carried the matter further, but soon encountered resistance on the part of the SS Main Economic and Administrative Office and the SS Operational Main Office in Berlin, until Himmler himself advised him that no further action was desired, since the charges against Koch were unjustified.

In February 1942, nevertheless, Koch was transferred away from Buchenwald, becoming Commandant at Lublin. His adjutant, Hackmann, accompanied him. When these two mass murderers embarked on their journey, they had rapid-firing automatic weapons mounted on either side of their cars, since they feared partisan ambushes in the east. During the departure, the camp band had to strike up marches, while the prisoners were drawn up in a double line.

Prince Waldeck felt that this settlement of the Koch case constituted a disavowal of himself. He sought to prove to Himmler that his attitude toward the Buchenwald Commandant had been founded on fact. He therefore proceeded to examine various Buchenwald records. Among other things he scanned the death rolls in camp. There he came upon the names of Walter Krämer and Karl Peix—"shot while attempting to escape." Krämer, at the time Capo in the Hospital, had once treated the Prince for a case of boils, to his entire satisfaction. It did not take the Prince long to discover the true reason for Krämer's death, and that of his deputy. Like many SS officers, Koch preferred to be treated by prisoners rather than by SS Medical Officers. Krämer had treated him for syphilis. Krämer also knew of the "contributions" from wealthy Jews who had passed through Buchenwald in 1938 during the Vom Rath program—monies that Koch had embezzled. Naturally the Commandant did not wish these two damaging incidents to come to light in the course of the investigations which the SS courts were conducting of him. In November 1941, he had therefore ordered SS Master Sergeant Planck to take the two inmates—who had been suddenly arrested and thrown into the camp prison—to the outside labor detail at Goslar and there to shoot them "while attempting to escape." This was promptly done.

Prince Waldeck took up this matter in vain, for the threatened men proceeded with the systematic liquidation of every possible witness, not only from among the prisoners, but also in the ranks of the SS. There was much wire-pulling throughout the concentration-camp system between Buchenwald and Lublin. The purpose was to destroy all witnesses and records that might have documented the numerous murders, larcenies, embezzlements, orgies, and adulteries that had taken place.

Not until 1943 did the situation reach the point where Himmler permitted an official investigation. Evidently Koch's misdeeds at Lublin and Belgrade had meanwhile made him a public liability to the SS. Envious SS informers, moreover, had meanwhile accumulated a mass of material on SS corruption. On the occasion of a mass escape of Russian prisoners from the Lublin concentration camp, it was shown that Koch had completely neglected his assigned duties in order to indulge his private vices and personal avarice without let or hindrance. Whenever prisoners showed up missing on his rolls, he simply had civilians arrested in the vicinity who were kept as a "black reserve" for contingencies. (A similar procedure was followed in other eastern concentration camps as well.)

Koch himself was now arrested, together with his wife, Ilse Koch, and his adjutant, Hackmann, and soon afterward Planck, Sommer and Dr. Hoven. The Buchenwald Camp Medical Officer and Prison Warden were accused of having put out of the way a certain SS Master Sergeant Köhler in the camp prison, when he threatened to make damaging statements.

The two insisted that Köhler had committed suicide, but an autopsy showed the cause of death to have been an alkaloid poison. The specific compound used was not established, and the members of the investigating commission, SS Major Morgen and SS Captain Wehner, in the presence of the Officers-in-Charge, conducted a "little experiment" in Ward 46. They had four unsuspecting Russian prisoners of war fed various alkaloids in noodle soup. When the men failed to die of the consequences, they were subsequently strangled in the crematory. I know of no other incident that serves so well to characterize the special nature of this SS trial.

The investigation and the trial dragged out for nearly two years, with the threads running all the way up to Himmler. The record grew to some ten thousand pages. The results were as follows: Planck committed suicide by hanging. Sommer, it is stated, did likewise. Koch and Hackmann were each sentenced to death on two counts, with the chance of probation by front-line service. But Prince Waldeck, as the supreme legal authority in the district, swiftly forestalled this possibility, by having Koch shot at Buchenwald a few days before the camp's liberation. Frau Koch was acquitted. Dr. Hoven was suddenly released on April 2, 1945, to play the role of a stool pigeon among the prisoners at Buchenwald during the dramatic final week. This role, however, did not reach full fruition because events went out of control and because Hoven was a shrewd man who took no unnecessary risks. He had been in custody for twenty months, a fact of which he thought he might well take advantage with the victors.

There has been much argument as to the motives that could have led the top leadership of the SS to institute the Koch trial in the first place. In my opinion it was not at all a deliberate action for the purpose of realizing certain political purposes, nor did it spring from a genuine feeling that a purge was needed. The tortuous maze of conflicting personal interests among the SS officers simply erupted at a given point—an abscess on the rotten body burst open.

Dr. Morgen, the ambitious head of the investigating commission, was a figure of considerable psychological interest. On the basis of the experiments he made at Buchenwald, Lubin, Auschwitz and other camps, he reached a devastating judgment of the concentration camp system and its practices. But nothing changed in the over-all situation. If any measure of relief was obtained here and there during the last years of the system, it was not as a result of the conditions revealed in the Koch trial, but for other general reasons that have already been discussed. In its origins, its course and its significance, the Koch affair was no more than a reflection of the all-pervading parasitism of the SS, which brooked neither retreat nor remedy.

That such figures as Koch and Fassbender and Hoven

found preordained careers in the ranks of the SS—especially in the concentration camp SS—becomes understandable when the standards in terms of the character and mind demanded of Hitler's black-uniformed Elite Guards are taken into account.

The intellectual development of SS members all the way up to their highest leaders was far below the average. Their factual knowledge rarely exceeded that of an eighth-grader—and not a very bright one at that. If they had any shreds of ambition left to expand their knowledge, it was in the field of military affairs, especially as it might help advance their careers. In examinations for promotion to SS sergeant, "general intelligence questions" included the following: What is the difference between a child and a dwarf? Between a ladder and stairway? How many members of the *Waffen SS* wear the Knight's Cross?

And what did the SS officers read? Rarely a book—at best detective stories—though they were in the habit of exchanging gifts of luxuriously bound volumes. Their SS training manuals? Certainly not—most of them never even read the magazine of the SS, the *Black Corps*. They would skim the headlines in the newspapers, occasionally read part of an editorial—as long as matters were going well.

Knowledge was not essential to the realization of SS aims. What was needed was conscious awareness of being the master class, of being an elite even within the Nazi party, of being the Praetorian Guard—of who was a friend and who an enemy. All this involved prestige, which could be readily increased by a harsh, ruthless, arrogant bearing, by acquiring a reputation for relentlessness, by spreading fear wherever one went. Critical thought would have required the power to discriminate and make comparisons, which in turn meant an expanding mental horizon. This might have impaired striking power. It would have appeared to them as demoralizing, dangerous, disloyal, "Jewish." It was not necessary to self-awareness—that was satisfied by articles of political faith. They never doubted what their leaders told them—it was pleasant and often even convenient to believe. Doubt would have been treason, whereas their slogan said that their "honor was loyalty." They remained true to themselves.

It is apparent that the motives of the SS were never

heterogeneous in character—that is, truly cultural. They always remained within the realm of SS desires and aspirations. The influence of Himmler's own personality is the only element in the SS that is very difficult to grasp. The man was absurdly unmilitary, and the SS knew it. He was copybook exemplar of virtue—neat, a typical "little man," hard-working, pedantic, neither a general nor a statesman nor a thinker nor a profligate nor a fool. What was it in him that impressed the SS? Among themselves they hardly ever referred to him by any name other than "Reichs-Heini." And yet . . .

What joined them to him was, it seems to me, not his personality at all but the measure of his achievement, the intellectual prerequisites of which they did not ponder for a moment—of course not! They accepted the unresolved contradiction, in keeping with their own nature. But Himmler's achievement was made to their measure—a universal system of power. It was a matter of small moment to his adherents whether this instigator of Germany's ghastliest terrors and mass murders was a bureaucrat or a profligate. They did not care that he was able to invest his cold and petty fanaticism with a flicker of mysticism only by his predilection for early Teutonic history, re-enacted in castles and cathedrals to torchlight by night. It was sufficient that their instincts were given free play. In return they accepted certain austerities, such as Himmler's ambition for justice which seems so paradoxical to us. He was inexorable in his imposition of penalties and almost invariably increased the severity of those pronounced by SS courts. He had his own nephew, SS First Lieutenant Hans Himmler, who while drunk had carelessly tattled SS secrets, demoted and sentenced to death, a sentence from which he was paroled to the front as a parachutist. Young Himmler was subsequently again incarcerated for having made certain derogatory remarks and finally "liquidated" at the Dachau concentration camp as a homosexual. Austere punishment with "front-line parole," or dropping someone only to restore him after a while to a position of even greater confidence and respect—these were specialties of Himmler. I rather suspect that he had read somewhere how similar educational methods had been applied by certain leaders of past eras in order to surround themselves with an aura, and that he simply adapted them to his own bureaucratic ways. The method *was* effective—on its own account, not because of Herr Himmler.

The pursuit of power always tends toward certain individual and social forms which attain expression, if at all, regardless of whether the persons from whom they emanate are men possessed or mere bureaucrats. And unquestionably it was the pursuit of power that impelled men like Himmler, Heydrich, Best, Klatenbrunner and Müller (chief of the Gestapa under Kaltenbrunner) in creating their system and in maintaining it. These men sought only power—power over other men, other institutions, over Germany, over other nations, if possible over the world and the future. All was to go according to their will. Perhaps their pursuit of power was instinctive rather than conscious, under the pretext that it was on behalf of Germany; perhaps they presented a nationalist veneer only to deceive themselves, their environment and the public at large, since naked power for its own sake would probably not yet have been acceptable. Actually, this strengthened rather than weakened the effect. Just as National Socialism carved out for itself a state within the republic, so did the SS within the Nazi regime. Concealing its motives and purposes, it achieved an autonomy that ultimately crowded out all rivals for power.

Figures like Eicke and Pohl were of a different stripe, though they were drawn to the others like iron to a magnet. Mighty lieutenants—themselves lords when seen from below, but only vassals from above. It was they who provided everything that was necessary for creating and maintaining the all-encompassing citadel—materials, money, slaves, arms. To a degree unmatched, they combined the opposites of the tradesman and the hero, two types which according to their own *Black Corps* defied combination. No super Jew of Streicher's ever accomplished what SS Lieutenant-General Pohl managed to do—putting the mass utilization of human bodies on an efficiency basis. During his lifetime each concentration-camp slave, obtained without capital investment, represented the following profit value when fully "utilized" from a financial aspect:

Daily farming-out wage, 6 to 8 marks, average		6.00
Minus: 1. Food	0.60	
2. Clothing Depreciation	0.10	0.70
		5.30
Multiplied by 270 (average life span of nine months)		1,431 marks

Efficient utilization of the prisoner's body at the end of nine
  months increased this profit by the return from:
(1) Dental gold
(2) Personally owned clothing (part of which was used in
    other camps, reducing expenses for new clothing, while
    part was utilized in respinning for army uniforms)
(3) Valuables left by the deceased
(4) Money left by the deceased
        (Down to the early war years, money and valuables
        were returned only to the families of the minority of
        prisoners who were German citizens)

From these returns must be deducted an average cremation cost of two marks per prisoner, but the direct and indirect profit per body averaged at least	200 marks

In many cases it ran to many thousands of marks

The total profit per prisoner, at an average turnover rate of nine months, therefore ran to at least	1,630 marks

Here and there a concentration camp obtained additional
  revenue from the utilization of bones and ashes

Let it not be thought that this calculation is my own handiwork. It comes from SS sources, and Pohl jealously guarded
against "outside interference." The SS Main Economic and
Administrative Office forever sent out inspectors to counter
small- or large-scale competition, such as the German police
in the east tried to establish in the form of "labor camps,"
"police detention camps," and the like.

Some day the naked pursuit of power, hand in glove with
avarice, would have become clearly apparent to everyone. In
the early years and during the war, when many ulterior considerations played a part, this was not very well possible. The
system therefore shrouded itself behind a dense camouflage of
secrecy. There was very little in the SS that was not "secret."
Most secret of all was the actuality of the concentration
camps, which served to propagate a terror intended to be
nameless.

To this must be added a degree of organizational
proliferation which a normal person can hardly imagine and
which served to obscure the whole picture. The Gestapo did
not pay the least attention to whether the concentration-camp
system of the SS Main Economic and Administrative Office
was able to cope with the masses of prisoners often dumped

on the gatehouses without notice. It did not care whether there was space, clothing, food, drugs. Conversely the SS Main Economic and Administrative Office rarely surrendered a Gestapo slave once it had begun to exploit him. These two major organizational forms of the terror were linked only by the urge for power and exploitation at the top level of leadership—Eicke-Pohl on the one hand, Müller-Kaltenbrunner on the other, both operating on behalf of their lord and master, Himmler.

Branching out down below like a nerve system was the chain of command, in curious fashion allowing scope for individual judgment and thus for responsibility. The SS leadership expected obedience of its subordinates, but it also expected independence. Later on, when too many had learned that they were not backed up when the inevitable difficulties arose, SS men became reluctant to assume responsibility, and failed to take any action without written authority. But for the nonce a curious mixture developed, compounded of a cult of obedience and complete lack of control. In a sense the subordinate had to feel his way between these two attitudes. As a result he was reckoned the best SS member who "knew what had to be done," who did not wait for long-winded orders but acted "in the spirit of the Reich Leader SS." As a rule this "spirit" was not a matter of grave doubt, especially in the case of measures against "enemies of the state." Eicke, for example, stated that "it is better to shoot a concentration-camp prisoner than to endanger the security of the Reich by his escape." In order to prevent the guards from being made "unsure of themselves" (i.e., to make them sure!) he issued instructions that when a prisoner had been "shot while attempting to escape" guards "were to be excused from investigations as much as possible." Thus a guard who developed initiative in shooting down prisoners was merely carrying out orders, and in addition earned a bonus for the mental and other discomfort he might have undergone.

The great slogan of the SS was: "Miscarriages of justice must be corrected!" What was meant was the "leniency" of "civilian" justice. This too was virtually a challenge to the Gestapo officials to send people to the concentration camps, an invitation to Camp Medical Officers to resort to the fatal syringe. The legal officer of the SS Main Economic and Administrative Office, SS Lieutenant-Colonel Schmidt-Kleve-now, a sinister figure in Pohl's inner circle, once said during an investigation that it was true Himmler had issued an order against unauthorized killings of prisoners, but that there was a question "as to whether he had not implied a mental reservation with regard to sanctioning non-observance of this order!" It sounds almost like a quotation from a scurrilous anti-Jesuit pamphlet. But no—these were the broadly winking Wotan worshipers of Berlin-Lichterfelde, No. 125 Unter den Eichen.

Like master like man. After all, was the situation very much different in the case of Hitler himself? What we are dealing with here are not baffling mysteries of human nature, but violations of simple, basic, psychological laws in the evolution of inferior minds. It was inferiority—whether of mind, reason, will power, imagination or the numerous social aspects of the human mind—that led these men into the SS, where they readily found refuge and an opportunity to assert their superiority, where they were held fast and driven from vice to vice, from crime to crime. The behavior of each individual SS member, whatever his rank, typified the system and its basic orientation.

Chapter Twenty-Three

THE PSYCHOLOGY OF
THE PRISONERS

During the bitter winter of 1939–40 many of us at Buchenwald suffered from dysentery or at least from severe diarrhea. One day, in a blizzard, an émigré who had fallen back into the clutches of the SS sat near me on the latrine pole. Like so many who simply depended on the forethought and good nature of their fellows, he had failed to bring any toilet paper despite the rampant disease. He saw that I had several scraps of newspaper and barked at me from the corner of his mouth, in typical camp fashion: "Gimme a piece!"

I made no reply. I have always hated this way of asking for anything, even in the concentration camp. But when I was done I passed him and placed three scraps of paper on his knees. "The same old story," I said in passing, "the ant and the grasshopper. . . . "

How did the poor devil react? He leaped up as he was, flung the paper into the mud at his feet, trampled on it furiously, and screamed again and again: "I don't need your paper! I don't need your paper!"

Hysteria? Certainly. But a whole world must have first collapsed inside his mind! Here was a sensitive man who, in-

stead of becoming hardened by the humiliations he had suffered in camp, had on the contrary lost his last protective
armor. At the slightest breath of good-natured irony, in the
face of all common sense, he "blew his top," though he himself had been anything but polite. In fact his very snarl was an
expression of the self-same mental upset.

Concentration camps ground the minds of their victims as
though between millstones. Who could survive the process
without suffering injury? No one came out as he went in. It is
quite true that the camps were melting pots tending toward
uniformity, but this uniformity was not mental. The prisoners
were as diverse as possible in origin, personal endowment,
political conviction and intellectual and moral character.

The "shiftless elements" or "asocials" and the convicts underwent the least change in camp. The reason must be sought
in certain individual and social resemblances to the SS. They
too were men who had gone down in the social scale, who
were of limited education, who were predominantly guided by
instinct, who lacked convictions arrived at as the result of
mental effort. The difference lay in the development, by the
members of the SS, of a class so rigid that no individual
variations could even begin to strike root. The SS man
therefore reached an inner standstill.

SS officers frequently allied themselves with convicts, very
rarely with asocials. Why? In his own way the hardened, active, habitual criminal shared a certain "class consciousness."
He felt a certain professional pride and was inclined to derive
from the fact of his expulsion from "normal society" certain
group virtues such as "loyalty," "comradeship," "honesty,"
unconditional allegiance. Whenever circumstances were
favorable, there was an almost inexorable community of interests that led from the outlaw who had placed himself
beyond the pale of society to the desperate host that had
abandoned all the principles of humanity. They were brethren
under the skin, crows of a feather who soon learned to exchange barefaced winks.

But the bond between the men who wore the black uniform
and those who wore the black triangle was on a lower level,
purely materialistic and individualistic in character. The
asocials had no clan spirit, no bent for daredevil action, no
"touch of greatness." It is a question, moreover, whether the

common symbol of black may not have subconsciously repelled the SS. Certainly they could not have known what they were doing when they picked this, of all colors, to mark the asocial category!

Psychological involvement attained significant proportions only among those prisoners who had some claim to superiority, by reason of their individuality or their allegiance to a given group, stratum or class. These were in the main the rational and political opponents of the Nazi regime. Here men of character suffered the impact of subhuman situations and events. The result was a range of psychological patterns that almost defies classification.

Unfortunately I cannot here deal at length with every individual type. I must confine myself to such psychological phenomena as had some degree of generality. It would be fascinating, for example, to write a psychology of Jehovah's Witnesses. As a rule they stemmed from middle-class trades with relatively simple modes of thought and emotion, though in the concentration camps they unfolded a veritable spectrum of mental reactions and outward behavior patterns, ranging from the extreme of lofty anticipation of the hereafter down to thoroughly earthy appetites.

The development of mental types took place by way of the process of adaptation to the new environment. I have already pointed out in my chapter on admission to the concentration camps that every newcomer immediately had to traverse a course of profound personal degradation and humiliation. Naked he was driven through the unbridgeable abyss that separated the two worlds, "outside" and "inside." It was the immediate effects of this terrifying act of compulsion that determined the ultimate destiny of a prisoner. There were two possibilities and within three months it became apparent which one would apply. By that time a man would have gone into an almost irresistible mental decline—if, indeed, he had not already perished in a physical sense; or he would have begun to adapt himself to the concentration camp. He might abandon all hope, seeing nothing to make life seem worth living. Even if remnants of will power survived the smashing of the old familiar world with its values, the mind, deep in the shadows, would cast off the burden of a body that had lost all impetus to rise above the misery of the day. And if the human wreck that was the result of the efforts of the SS somehow managed to keep on vegetating, it would soon run afoul of someone in the struggle for existence and thus be exterminated. If, on the other hand, the initial process of devaluation succeeded only in killing off the positive aspects of character, unleashing sinister forces that had been kept under control, then the newcomer, step by step or in a twinkling, might adapt himself to one of the numerous strains of the camp underworld.

Whether inward adaptation to camp life succeeded or not was not primarily a question of social origin or former social position. In this respect there was a sharp contrast between the development potentials of the SS, the asocials and the convicts on the one hand, and of the political andd ideological prisoners on the other. With the former, social and individual origins at least suggested, if they did not dictate, the complexion of their career in camp; but the latter were quite unable to derive from their former relatively high social position any useful impetus for life in the jungle; indeed, what they brought with them hindered rather than helped them.

Only when the memory of former social standards had been erased could men of high character fall back on their innermost qualities and begin to gain mastery over their present situation, and even so only with great effort. Utter failure met any attempt to apply once valid social standards to a concentration-camp environment that presented the sharpest possible contrast to any firmly organized social order. Such standards might be smashed at the very outset, during the stage of degradation, to such a degree that their complete uselessness became apparent.

Men were lost if they brought to the concentration camp no more than a non-proletarian class-consciousness, a pride in a clique, clan or caste recognized "outside." The whalebone of social stays was irretrievably bent and battered the very first day. If this was all that had been brought along in place of backbone and character, the wearer could be written off at once.

I knew a very high German cabinet official who, on the night of his admission to Buchenwald, after the humiliations he had suffered, no longer dared look anyone in the eye. His fund of personal values gradually gave him back the self-confidence he had lost, but it was a self-confidence altogether different from what he had had before. The two Dukes of Hohenberg, already spoken of, who carried manure at Dachau, because of their steadfastness of character won the respect of many prisoners who would otherwise have been hopelessly prejudiced against them. Many similar stories could be told of men who had once enjoyed social prestige.

But even if a man had not occupied a high social position in pre-concentration-camp times, it took considerable force of character to overcome the difficulties that faced him, especially the hurdle of not having been a "proletarian." A good friend of mine, Willi Jellinek, a pastry baker from Vienna, will serve as an example. At Buchenwald he was a corpse carrier, a nonentity from the point of view of the camp hierarchy. He was a young Jew, a tall man of notable physical strength with marked personal characteristics. During the Koch regime his chances of survival seemed slight.

But what happened to Jellinek instead? He became our outstanding tuberculosis expert, an excellent practitioner and internist who helped countless comrades. In addition, he was a bacteriologist in Building 50. A deep-dyed pessimist, he nevertheless managed to steer safely past the numerous treacherous shoals across which his course lay in camp.

Chance? Yes—but only insofar as "luck" is a component of personal ability. There were plenty of successful businessmen and high officials in camp who greedily scavenged from garbage cans filled with potato peelings even when they were not famished, indeed, who even became bread thieves. In less serious but more numerous cases, such men would selfishly exploit the smallest opportunity for advantage, without consideration for their fellow prisoners. True, such incidents were not quite as common as many protagonists of proletarian class superiority liked to believe in their predilection for propaganda and generalization. But the disintegration of a "high-brow," of a man who had once occupied a respected position, naturally attracted more attention than the failure of someone who had never drawn any special public notice.

Admission to a concentration camp constituted the shock that immediately hurled the newcomer in one direction or the other. The indignation or desperation that followed the initial terror decided whether he would gradually gain inward perspective and thus a chance for individual adaptation to the new life, or whether he would swiftly succumb. In the former case there followed a process of habituation, of transformation of individual character. During this second stage the ease and speed with which a way was found toward "normalcy amid the abnormal" depended on the pluck and determination with which the new goal was envisioned.

This period of initial adaptation was full of dangers. Not only the hands, the soul had to grow calluses. Understandably, though tragically, the "community" was considerate of the newcomer only *after* he had completed the basic process of adaptation, not *during* the initial period when he most needed protection and consideration. But the group attitude was inevitable in the light of the daily, hourly struggle for life against the SS, in which the slightest weak spot resulted in additional suffering.

Within about half a year a prisoner began to become a "concentrationary," i.e., to develop a specific type of mentality which generally grew fully developed in the course of another two or three years. It is no accident that the "old timers" hardly took a man seriously before then. It took a long time for a mind, torn from the anchorages of the outside world and thrust into life-and-death turmoil, to find a new inward center of gravity.

The change in mentality was by no means a simple matter of good or evil, conceived as standards of value. Both aspects pervaded it. Its main characteristic was a process of regression to a more primitive state. The range of sensations was almost automatically reduced. The mind developed a protective crust, a kind of defensive armor that no longer transmitted every strong stimulus to the sensitive membranes. Pain, pity, grief, horror, revulsion and approval, if admitted in their normal immediacy, would have burst the receptive capacities of the human heart. Terror alone, lurking everywhere, would have effortlessly brought it to a stop. Men grew hard and many of them had their sensibilities dulled. It was the same process that takes place in war. A cruel laugh, a brutal jest were often no more than protective devices for minds in danger of becoming hysterical or unhinged. There were many dead martyrs in the camps, but few living saints—though they should have had a field day! We laughed, wretched souls that we were, lest we grow petrified and die.

This regression with its opposites of good and evil pervaded every mental quality. Some grew hard in order to be able to help, just as a physician, in his capacity as a man, has feelings and yet, in his capacity as a healer, has none. Others developed a cruelty that ranged from repressed sexual impulses all the way to sadism. Some allowed an innate optimism to lead them into a credulity that eagerly accepted every illusory rumor. With others the critical capacity was heightened to pessimistic distrust. A determination to fight back might end in quixotic exploits, cowardice in complete assimilation to slave life.

And how would you have reacted, man or woman, had you suddenly been picked out from the protective rank and file of tens of thousands of your kind, to be placed on a pile of stones within sight of all, stripped to the skin and whipped within an inch of your life? Would you have screamed or whined, or would you have kept silent, biting your lips until the blood flowed? On the way back, in filth and tatters, would you have dissolved in shame over the ignominy you had suffered? Or would you have mustered the superhuman strength and pride to ignore even the final kick from an SS boot that hurled you back into the communion of prisoners? In any event, you would have had to regress to a more primitive level if you wanted to survive. Then your comrades would have welcomed you with a coarse joke that concealed compassion, would have secretly nursed you back to health without fuss or feathers.

Behind this protective armor of the mind, however, there developed in not a few cases a refinement of conscience that sometimes rose to extraordinary heights. In some cases the tension between regressive emotional primitivism and growing sensitivity of conscience found its only possible release in a heightened religious faith. Provided a man had any trace of moral sense and true religious devotion, these qualities, at the very core of personality, were, if anything, promoted by the powerful appeal emanating from the humanity and inhumanity of the concentration camp. In keeping with camp conditions, their presence and their effect could be but rarely manifested in the open, especially since the

outwardly predominant groups in the camps acted at best on
political, never on religious motivations and applied the
highest standards of ethical conscience only in exceptional circumstances. Thus there are likely to be plenty of old-time concentrationaries who will deny that religion and moral sense
played any considerable part. But just as the ordinary
prisoner remained in ignorance of the true situation in camp,
so few if any camp functionaries knew anything about the
inner life of the thousands under them.

It was the pure in heart who suffered the least damage—
those men of shining integrity who strove to give their all, who
never took umbrage no matter what they faced, who
steadfastly put evil to one side. There were such men in the
camps, and to them the words of the gospel may be applied:
pertransierunt benefaciendo—their lives shed radiance and
beneficence on the rest of us. But on no account could they be
placed in situations where they had to take part in making
decisions vital to the very existence of the camp! When the SS
demanded that political prisoners select "socially unfit"
inmates who were manifestly destined for death—a refusal
involving the risk of the end of red predominance and the rise
of the greens—it became necessary for the reds to accept the
burden of guilt.[1] And the more tender one's conscience, the
more difficult it was to make such decisions. Since they had to
be made, and made swiftly, it was perhaps better that they
should have fallen to the more robust spirits, lest all of us
become martyrs instead of surviving witnesses.

Every prisoner was dependent on his fellow prisoners, utterly at their mercy. The predominant impulses that governed
their lives were selfishness and common sense, sharpened by
many feelings of aversion. There were, however, outstanding
examples of solidarity to the death, of the unfaltering assumption of responsibility for the whole group down to the last.
When political prisoners permitted themselves to be led to
execution without offering resistance, this was often done in
patent consideration for the fellows they left behind. Had
such doomed groups defended themselves, in order at least to
die fighting, they would instantly have been branded as

[1] In a conversation with the translator the author expressly disavowed any interpretation of this passage that might appear to sanction complicity in the
taking of human life for any reason whatsoever, except self-defense.—*Tr*.

mutinous and the fiercest reprisals would have been visited on the whole camp. This question was again and again discussed in camp.

But such demonstrations of the ultimate spirit of fellowship were isolated acts, sacrifices made in the face of inescapable death. When the fight was not to the death but for daily survival, the opposite applied. Everyone who has been through a concentration camp knows the saying: "The prisoner's worst enemy is the prisoner!" It is not that this was literally true, but that the constant and direct impact of unrestrained selfishness made it appear to be so. The SS struck like lightning, like a storm that passes, like a hurricane that may at worst last a few days. In such crises ranks were closed as well as possible—unless the individual was forced to go it alone. There was mutual aid and protection and rescue, to the limit of available resources. But the ghastly everyday scramble among the prisoners was enacted without a let-up in overcrowded quarters.

The torments of this inexorable pattern were intensified by the unspeakably coarse outward forms that it always assumed. A great many prisoners actually took pride in this special refinement of barbarism. They outdid themselves in giving provocative expression to their lack of culture. Even such minor courtesies like "please," "thank you," "would you like" and "may I"—trifles that make life so much easier even though they have often lost inner significance—were rigidly banned. For months in 1938 the many Austrians who had entered the camps were bitterly hated for their unswerving use of polite phrases that are second nature to the people of Austria. The invariable answer to a "thank you" from them was "kiss my ass." Every "please" drew a plethora of scorn from the primitives.

There were really but three forms of making an adjustment: to remain a lone wolf; to join a group; or to appear in the guise of a political partisan.

The lone wolf, as the term is here used, was not necessarily an anti-social person but rather an individual tending to keep to himself in accordance with his own design and without harm to others. Men of this type were often of high integrity. They had excellent judgment and helped whenever it was necessary, but they did not seek closer association. Their endurance was predicated on privacy, insofar as such a thing was possible in camp.

There were many concentration-camp inmates who disliked this type of fellow prisoner, taunting and tormenting him whenever they could. Part of this may have sprung from the natural urge of the inferior to drag down to his own level anyone who is different. But it seems to me that another motive was an instinctive fear of the living exhortation which such men represented, something their inferiors liked to decry as arrogance. As a result, the lone wolves were always especially exposed to danger, unless they enjoyed the protection of some silent admirer with power and influence. In their isolation from the extraordinary community surrounding them they sometimes developed quirks, peculiar ways of reacting. When such oddities developed into permanent eccentricity, the subject might perish if he had a special enemy to take advantage of the situation (see the story of Johann Stürzer in the chapter "Money and Mail"); or he was tolerated as a harmless freak. He drew verbal abuse but no serious interference. As a type, he had become insignificant, a cheap butt for jokes, a scapegoat for frayed tempers.

Group allegiance meant joining a small circle of friends or co-religionists, men of like mind who brought similar attitudes to their discussions and "club meetings," held in such places as the few privileged rooms of the hospital or even in cellar holes. In such groups men again became human beings, after the humiliation suffered in the toil of the day, after punishment and roll call and barracks life. Despite prison stripes and shorn skulls, they were able to look their fellows in the face, beholding the same sorrow and the same pride, and drawing renewed strength. Hope was revived, helping them to be ready to proceed on the appointed path, step by step. Membership in such a group was perhaps the finest experience in a concentration camp.

Political partisanship, on the other hand, pursued ulterior purposes even in the camps. It was extremely useful for every man of the left, especially for Communists, who found help and support that made adaptation to the new life much easier. There were no parties other than the Communist and Social Democratic in the camps on the German side. The Poles, Czechs, Dutch and a few other nationality groups developed certain party organizations that were not leftist in orientation. But since underground leadership was always in German hands, such organizations either were unable to attain any significant scope or were suppressed after sharp clashes. The leftist parties were the only part of the social structure of the outside world that was taken over unchanged in the concentration camps. Here their adherents found a familiar behavior pattern in which they could seek refuge. It gave them a better start in a physical sense, enabled them to recover their identity more rapidly, but it also involved the risk of unrestrained regression in a primitive direction, of an adaptation that was so thoroughgoing that it meant their undoing rather than protection. There were party concentrationaries who had become completely resigned to camp life, mentally and physically, who no longer knew any other world and sought none. The concentration camp with its opportunities for power and privilege had become their world.

Cutting straight across the groups and parties were new class crystallizations and national allegiances that contributed further characteristics, both positive and negative, to the multiplicity of psychological types among the concentration-camp prisoners.

These classes in the concentration camps were not extraordinary in their social structure, for they developed on the basis of economic position and special function just as they do in the outside world. The prisoners in positions of power formed the camp aristocracy, the "big shots." Some of them were worthless parasites, just as is the case with the nominal aristocracy of all periods and peoples. Below them were the common herd and the pariahs.

The new factor in these classes was not the former class allegiance of a prisoner, though in camps under red sway a former Communist party functionary had to best chance to ascend to the "big shot" class, while men of marked middle-class character had the least prospect. Class position was rather the product of such qualities as militancy or moderation, hardness or softness, adaptability or simple-mindedness and lack of skill, a tendency toward cliquishness or an attitude of reserve. It presupposed the acceptance of a certain responsibility, even if this was often limited to mere participation in some scheme of corruption that drew on the general substance, and it was anchored by means of numerous checks and balances, good and bad, among men on the same level. Clique interests among the Prisoner Foremen, for example, took precedence over solidarity within a detail or a barracks. Because of the positions of its members—positions requiring camp experience—the class had its own "class-consciousness," expressed in various customs, above all in keeping down the newcomer as long as possible.

It was comparatively easy to gain access to a group or party, but the policy of the class was one of hostility. The "greenhorn" was contemptuously rejected. There was much boastful reference to hardships undergone in the days when things were "really tough." "What do *you* know about a concentration camp?" was one of the pat phrases. "Now back in 19—, when we. . . . " "You should have seen Sergeant So-and So!" "Anyone who hasn't been in Camp X hasn't any idea at all!" Thus ran the stereotyped patter of crude conceit, put forward for no other purpose than to deprecate the newcomer and maintain class superiority. The psychological bag of tricks of such men included the attempt to cover up their own moral deficiencies by overemphasis on how hardened they were. But such tricks are not peculiar to the concentration camps. In the complete isolation and the special atmosphere of cruelty of the concentration camps, this feature was merely developed more sharply.

National allegiances likewise ran athwart all other stratifications. Within each nationality group they tended to exert a harmonizing influence, though at the expense of sharpened tension between groups. National allegiance very nearly held the balance to party allegiance, though the latter was perhaps a little stronger. Judged by his everyday conduct, a French Communist was as a rule closer to a German Communist than he was to his own bourgeois compatriot. (Of course it must not be overlooked that in the red camps the German Communists were the ruling group. It may be doubted whether a French Communist or Socialist felt closer ties to a Czech party member than he did to his average fellow countryman.)

Some psychological commentary on the attitudes of the Germans toward each other and toward other nationality groups, whose reactions have already been discussed, would be not only interesting but helpful at this point. It seems to me impossible, however, to do justice to these complex interrelationships in a few words. The picture would necessarily be one-sided, indeed, distorted. Germans as well as Jews were not very popular in the camps, though this was obviously not true of many individuals. Both groups were rather variegated and very contentious toward each other, the Germans despite the fact that, by force of circumstance, they were not infrequently "favored" by the SS (in the matter of penalties too!), the Jews, though they were almost continuously tortured. The role of these two groups, to do them justice, would require a separate book with many case histories, carefully balanced according to their significance. Without doubt it could be shown that the non-German concentration-camp literature that has been published so far literally teems with one-sided statements, over-simplifications and erroneous judgments. In my opinion there were no groups whose role in the concentration camps is so difficult to grasp as the Germans and the Jews. Let this statement at least hint at their significance.

National, class, party and group ties exerted a crucial influence on the individual and collective attitudes of the prisoners toward one another. But all differences were fused into a militant unity with but slight shades of differentiation when the camp stood against the SS—or rather, it was as though the differences retired behind a protective wall. The attitude of the prisoners toward their oppressors was uncomplicated from a psychological point of view. It would have been even simpler, had an active struggle been possible. But since the characteristic feature in the situation of the prisoners was their defenselessness, certain psychological qualities worth mentioning developed.

The concentration-camp prisoner knew a whole system of mimicry toward the SS. This ever-present camouflage ran under the slogan of "everything O.K."—outwardly, and therefore seemingly inwardly as well. No SS member was able to peer behind this wall. The deception ranged all the way from the stereotyped "Yes, sir!" to disarming smiles. In very rare cases, after an occasional SS man had already been demoralized or corrupted, prisoners might in the course of time unbend to a certain extent, but they never wholly abandoned their reserve and under no circumstance went as far as actual familiarity. The basic enmity and the things that had happened and were still happening were never forgotten.

The great majority of the men in the camps were filled with an unimaginable thirst for vengeance—the psychological escape mechanism of helplessness. Tortured men wracked their brains for new, unparalleled, infinitely fiendish torments which they would some day inflict on those who were now venting their cruel whims on them. This thirst for revenge extended to the entire Nazi regime and all its adherents, but it always crystallized around the individual SS man.

Very few were ever able to rise above this psychological escape mechanism. Coupled with the inhuman reality of the concentration camp, it slowly brought about in many old concentrationaries, especially those who were camp functionaries, a curious friend-enemy assimilation. The opposite types retaining their basically hostile orientation, developed similarities in primitive thought and emotion, in outward drill conduct, in tone, in corruption. Paradoxically enough, a curious "gratitude conflict" developed in certain cases of the closest approximation, such as between SS Camp Medical Officers and concentration-camp prisoners, when collaboration resulted in positive aid or even no more than amelioration to individuals or the camp as a whole. The SS member continued to be hated.The inmate knew that a world separated the two partners, yet did not desire that his opposite number should be personally included in the revenge plan.

This mental conflict, if the individual grew aware of it, was generally utilized for purposes of cold calculation in which the partner was regarded as a mere tool, or it resulted, if possible, in an even sharper rejection of all other SS men. Such reactions and considerations might often precipitate the prisoner into profound mental turmoil, but these were only passing camp stimuli, not sustained and not strong enough to give rise to types. When the camps were liberated, there were virtually no instances in which prisoners committed excesses against captured SS men. On the contrary, the SS men were simply, though sometimes triumphantly, handed over to the Allied soldiers. As for the "exceptions"—those SS men to whom a certain degree of obligation was felt—at best intercession was purely oral.

There is one psychological puzzle in the attitude of the prisoners toward the SS that is very hard to explain and that requires discussion because of its general character. With a few altogether insignificant exceptions, the prisoners, no matter in what form they were led to execution, whether singly, in groups or in masses, never fought back! As has already been stressed, the failure of men who felt a sense of political responsibility to do such a thing is quite understandable. Nor is it hard to understand in the case of that relatively large group of men who had long since lost any real will to survive. In the camps they were called "Moslems"—men of unconditional fatalism, men whose wills were broken.

Yet there were thousands of others who had by no means relapsed into fatal apathy. Nevertheless, in mass liquidations they went to their death with open eyes, without assaulting the enemy in a final paroxysm, without a sign of fight. Is this not in conflict with human nature, such as we know it? If at least it had been the spirit of religion that enabled them to accept their fate, inwardly resolute, outwardly serene! In the face of inevitable death, the man of religion, surrendering mortal life to step before his divine master and judge, has no desire for the toils of conflict with the earthly enemy he leaves behind. Nor does he seek, by murder, to enforce the escort of his enemy to the hereafter, where, in the light of faith, other standards apply than in this vale of tears, struggle and guilt. Already consecrated to death, he would feel dishonored by the blood his hands sought to shed at the last moment.

But there is not an inkling that the masses cut down by the SS were religious in this sense. Yet they did not offer resistance. Try to comprehend the following incident: the administration of a Jewish camp in the Lublin district was threatened with an investigation by top SS authorities, because of a far-flung graft scandal. There was the danger that prisoners might offer damaging testimony. The SS officers thereupon in a single day destroyed the entire camp with its forty thousand inmates. According to the statement of SS Major Morgen, the Jews unresistingly lay down in rows on the heaps of bodies of those who had already been massacred and allowed themselves to be shot. They made the job easy for their butchers, and not a hand was raised.

From a psychological point of view, the incident seems

hardly conceivable. The prisoners, after all, were not in a state of hypnosis. But it seems to be a fact that a mass never has any will of its own unless it is imposed from without or by individuals within its ranks. Mental power—insight as well as resolution—is a quality of the individual and unless it is integrated by leaders it declines rather than grows with increasing numbers. In the mass the individual becomes as nothing. He feels no more sense of personal responsibility. He feels dissolved and sheltered as he follows the trend of the whole, even into the abyss. It requires altogether extraordinary personal qualifications to rise consciously above the drift of a mass. Moreover panic, which experience shows appears at the moment of acute danger, has a paralyzing effect on reason and will power. In such emergencies leaders can hardly prevail even among smaller groups. In a concentration camp the complete hopelessness of finding any way out could only reinforce this tendency toward paralysis. The Jewish uprising in the Warsaw ghetto shows that the forces of resistance do awaken and can be organized whenever there is the least leeway and time for planning. But where these factors are lacking the situation becomes inexorably hopeless.

It may be objected that such a mass liquidation as that in the eastern camp must have allowed at least part of the prisoners a few hours' time during which they might have closed ranks. But the counter-argument lies in the partial anonymity of the measure. No one knew whether this was merely another "selection" or whether the camp as a whole was to be annihilated. As a result each individual was able to entertain the hope that he and some of the others might escape, as had happened so many times before. And once a group of victims—200, 500, 1,000, arbitrarily picked out—plodded off to the mountain of corpses that was to become their execution ground, then it no longer mattered whether one leaped out of ranks to be shot down by the SS or whether one lay down in a naked row on rows of naked bodies. What was the value of an act of will that denoted no more than hysterical despair? The very thought of such a thing was stifled. Collective death mercifully paralyzed its victims, froze them to the bone and the marrow.

Men always find it harder to explain death than life. The ever-present closeness of death in the camps had a smaller effect on men who had to get used to it in order to live, than did the relationship to their environment. For death, even when it lurks around the corner every day and we know about it, is a thing that happens but once, while life continues shaping out minds without a let-up in a thousand variations. Even the outside world, from which the concentration-camp prisoner was almost completely cut off, had a greater normalizing effect on him than did the danger of death. This of course is only meant in an anomalous sense, for actually there was no chance for sustained interaction with the outside world.

The prisoner was full of resentment toward the outside world. He had a sense of having been abandoned. Did anyone pay any attention to him on the outside? Ah, they went on living without giving him a thought! What did they know about the bitter reality that faced him every moment? To hell with them and their knuckling under to the regime, their profit-sharing compact! They sang and drank, went on Sunday picnics, to the movies, the theater, the concert. They laughed and made merry, while here—while here . . . yes, here. . . . Such thoughts often rankled with the outcasts. They deeply affected his habitual reactions. This explains many a clash, not only among the prisoners in the camps, but after the liberation within the families and in public.

A hundred different incidents and measures fostered the prisoner's sense of inferiority, intensified the complexity of his reactions toward the "free" outside world. He wore prison stripes and had his head shorn. In some camps he had to wear a coxcomb, an inch-wide strip of hair down the otherwise shaven skull; or a so-called "Pister part," an inch-wide strip shorn out of the otherwise uncut hair. This was the appearance he had to present to the population while working in outside details.

Many prisoners, of course, were able to counter this inferiority complex only by asserting a sense of superiority. When I was en route with a group of from sixty to one hundred men, all of us, neglected-looking and chained with steel shackles, led across German streets and squares, kept standing in railroad stations for half an hour at a time while the people watched us with mingled fear and contempt as though we were criminals—at such times I never gave way to a feeling of shame. On the contrary, I felt a deep pride in having been proscribed by such a regime, in having been cast out of such a society, in being despised by these "law-abiding citizens."

Ours was the path of honor in the midst of political, moral and human disgrace. True we had not chosen it of our own free will—who would ever make such a choice? But we discovered the inherent virtue in necessity. In some prisoners the dishonor of segregation turned into an exaggerated sense of superiority. In their helpless situation they projected their claim to exclusive worth, if not leadership, into the future. Applied to the present, it not only was incapable of realization—it seemed like the sheerest folly. This trend appeared quite independently of any appropriate personal qualifications. On the contrary, it might be said that the frequency and intensity of such claims were in inverse proportion to qualification. From a psychological point of view, all these trends, when placed against the reality of the concentration camp, almost inevitably led to a revolutionary outlook that left no aspect of the outside world untouched in its wishful plans. Experience, the thirst for vengeance, political orientation and habit combined into powerful impulses for the overthrow of the hated order. Among minds that were more self-critical and less optimistic about the course of history, such impulses took the form of serious planning for reforms.

A good part of the special character developed by men in the concentration camps was purely the product of camp life and vanished with the camps. But other aspects had more inherent force and have become permanent traits that now continue to have their effect on the environments to which the surviving prisoners have been returned.

In my opinion it was a terrible blunder that the psychologist who counseled the statesmen failed altogether to foresee this, though so much about conditions in the concentration camps was known abroad. Preparation for a transition to normalcy should have been made. Nothing whatever was done along these lines!

Yet it would have been so easy to enlist the co-operation of those few prisoners who not only had retained their full intellectual power but had actually grown in stature during their detention. With their help the bulk of the prisoners should have been given a breathing space to enable them to make a gradual readjustment to a world from which they had become estranged. Some should have been sent to rest-homes, to recover in mind and body. Experienced counselors might have helped to smooth out the precipitate mental crisis that threatened to disrupt even further the lives of men who for years had been unaccustomed to normal society.

One has only to think of the surviving Jews from the east who, for understandable reasons, had almost completely lost their bearings; or of the thousands of Poles who thought the hour had now struck for them to contribute their share of hate and chauvinistic depravity. And how carefully even the German concentration-camp prisoners needed to be evaluated! Their minds needed healing, their powers disciplining, their essential worth impartial study before the world could proceed in true expiation to give them the chance for social and political leadership they had earned. But as it was, this was done without foresight, at the mercy of chance, with personal connections and the old art of ruthless self-interest the deciding factor. Only a careful program of preparation could have picked from the ranks of the former concentration-camp prisoners those who, on the basis of the evil through which they had lived and the lessons they had learned, had the capacity to serve the cause of democracy in a Germany reborn.

Chapter Twenty-Four

THE GERMAN PEOPLE AND
THE CONCENTRATION CAMPS
—AFTER 1945

The tyranny of the Third Reich has been broken; but no light has come to Germany in the four years that have gone by since then. Too many new shadows lie across the land—shadows of the Soviet dictatorship and shadows cast by other forms of outrageous injustice. World developments have rendered the "re-education" of the German people in part impossible, in part so difficult that no one can predict which forces will carry the day.

This is how the situation appears to me at the outset of the year 1949: Were Hitler to return, many would follow him anew—though with a somewhat worse conscience. The National Socialists would be far more radical and ruthless—quite unwilling, this time, to leave even a single enemy alive. They would have plenty of effective propaganda material against both East and West. The oppositional minority would be stronger and more resolute. There would be an immediate life-and-death struggle, with deeds of bloody violence and mounting assassinations. More young people would be on the side of the opposition—young people who have not yet come to know freedom, but who loathe dictatorships, who are too idealistic to obey blindly, and who reject any form of sacrifice for obscure aims.

Not a few Germans are disoriented. Confronting the sinister facts of the present that seem to outweigh by far the forces of the future—which is the typical state of Europe—they do not feel that the execrated past was quite so bad as it is represented—and as it actually was. True, the attraction of liberty is sensed; but the actual path that leads to it is not yet clearly seen. Hence the country is pervaded by many moods and resentments. Despite undeniable economic improvement, the approach to reality has remained unchanged, compounded of idealism and opportunism—more of the latter than of the former. But in many Germans idealism is frustrated, while with most of them opportunism is aimless and impulsive, ready to enter into any alliance that promises swift success.

The basis of political life in Germany remains seriously defective, a state of affairs that bids fair to continue for a long time, in view of the sins of omission and commission since 1945. Only the fruits of constructive co-operation will be able to overcome this danger. Despite the unspeakable harm which Germans have done, both to Germans and to the world, one of the serious aims of such co-operation must be to cast off the burdens of the past, to strive instead for common justice and the common welfare. Only a policy of reconciliation, with and within Germany, vigilant but not grandiloquent, can pave the way for a better future. The facts must be seen in their true light, if illusions are to be avoided. The background and pattern of the past must be recognized.

Why have the facts about the concentration camp of the Third Reich failed so far to bring about a deep-seated change of heart in the German people? Because it has been shown that the spirit of Hitler lives on in others as well, not merely in Germans; because susceptibility to totalitarian methods has become apparent throughout the world; because hundreds of thousands—indeed millions—of Germans have again fallen victim to them; because the atrocities of the past lose their deterrent effect among the wild horrors of the present; because actions always speak louder than words—especially when those actions persistently fly in the face of preachments.

From 1944 on, especially after the surrender, and in many

instances deep into the year 1946—in Soviet Russia to this day—German prisoners of war were subjected to conditions often resembling the worst features of Nazi concentration camps. If only the world had not insisted that it was conducting a crusade against the organized forces of hell! Arthur Koestler once said that the total lie was combated with only half truths. But the majority of the German people had taken them to be the whole truth, and now they saw only the shortcomings. Their reaction may have been mistaken, indeed, neurotic—but it is understandable.

And the stories that were told by the twelve to fourteen million who were herded from the countries of eastern Europe into the remnant of Germany, often uprooted in the most barbarous fashion, transported singly, in groups, or in whole wretched convoys sealed into railway cars! Try to explain to a mother who has lost her children, to a husband whose wife has been raped, to youngsters who have seen their parents brutally beaten, to all who have experienced death and cruelty in the flesh—try to explain to them that in the vaunted better world these incidents were no more than the melancholy consequences of prior mass injustice, now befalling the innocent and the guilty alike! Try to make it clear to a whole nation that neither hypocrisy nor cowardice were responsible, if this "resettlement" program failed to be carried out in orderly and humane fashion, as was decreed in the declarations of Yalta and Potsdam! Even the Nazis did not shunt more millions across the plains of eastern Europe.

And then the deportations! We do not know the precise number of Germans who are compelled to perform slave labor in Russian or other mines and camps of the East. When it is argued that thousands of these new exiles are not suffering the direst hardships, the German people can reply that neither was this the case with foreign slave labor under the Nazi terror. In any event, the freedom of these deportees, running into the tens of thousands, is ruthlessly trodden underfoot. Until 1947 it could scarcely be denied that the Allies who had waged the Great War against Hitler, Himmler, Sauckel, Frank, and the other great slaveholders formed a common quadripartite Control Council in conquered Germany, at the same time that they sat in common judgment over the war criminals of the Third Reich at Nuremberg.

What could be more plausible than the whispered Nazi propaganda, falling on fertile soil and constantly gaining in persuasiveness, that the trials were merely for show, while in truth events were tragically repeating themselves?

Success might at least have attended the effort to keep cause and effect apart in German public awareness, had it not been attempted to "denazify" the whole nation. In 1945 the Allies prevented a spontaneous, revolutionary purge in Germany. Instead, in 1946 and the ensuing years they went ahead, according to four different preconceived plans, based partly on notions of collective, partly of individual guilt, with a formal judicial process that did profound harm not only to the sense of justice but also to political life in general. The entire nation was driven over hurdles of questionnaires; more than half of all men and women above the age of eighteen were characterized as "liable"; the task of "liberation from National Socialism and militarism" became the concern of a minority of the people, while absolution from denazification proceedings was the concern of the majority!

And what about the "activists" of the vanquished system? The notion prevailed that they must be placed in custody on the basis of "automatic arrest" categories, by rank and office held in the Nazi hierarchy, rather than on the basis of their actual offenses. Hundreds of thousands who had held formal membership in the Nazi party or one of its auxiliaries, or who had held some other office in the ramified machinery of the Third Reich for which every German had worked in some form or other, had to await formal denazification proceedings to prove that they had not been "activists," meanwhile losing their income, often their homes, their furniture, and the right to dispose of their property. Meanwhile tens of thousands of other small and middling Nazis and Nazi adherents were in internment camps under "automatic arrest." It took years before those who were really guilty were picked from their ranks. If the verdicts of the denazification chambers in the internment camps are admitted as proof of guilt or innocence, then at best three or four per cent of those interned up to three years were "activists."

There were scarcely two dozen internment camps in the United States, British and French zones of occupation, but they developed into veritable festering sores in the land. No one knows how it happened that in 1947 an estimated 120,000 suspects were interned in them, about one-tenth of the total in their categories, while nine-tenths in the identical categories were at liberty. A substantial number of major offenders, especially members of the German Security Service (*Sicherheits Dienst* or SD), have never been located. They roam the country unrecognized. Occasionally one of them is arrested. Quite a few seem to have escaped abroad—to Sweden, Spain, South America.

At times a sharp public controversy raged about these camps. Anti-Nazis demanded rapid sifting of the internees by means of orderly judicial process, opportunity for the prisoners to work if they so desired, and a program of genuinely democratic re-education for those willing to learn. Little or nothing was done in these respects. Broad segments of the population were righteously indignant that the camps existed at all, that living conditions in them were less than perfect, and that their inmates were suffering real or supposed "injustices." There was talk about the "new concentration camps," without the slightest distinction being made—which truly meant shutting one's eyes. The internees were described as "politically persecuted," as though internment in an incipient democracy could be compared with extermination and slavery under the Fascist dictatorship. Those who rejected or resented democracy, who closed their minds to the fact and the horror of the Nazi concentration camps, now lent sympathy, compassion, and support to the interned Nazis, storm troopers, and SS men. Under pressure of the charge of collective guilt and the constant official admonitions to atone for the atrocities that stained the name of Germany, this was in a sense, a process of overcompensating for an earlier lack of a sense of justice and humanity.

"Denazification" has now been concluded. The internment camps have been dissolved, except for a few labor camps for convicted major offenders. This end has been attained by virtue of a profusion of often contradictory policy decisions—extensions, limitations, and ameliorations, amnesties and assembly-line proceedings without trial. But it must be stated that there are no signs whatever of the adherents of Nazism and militarism having forsaken their convictions. Inequities are common on every hand, and no one is really in a position to say whether those from whom retribution has been exacted deserve it or not.

The basic error was rooted in the false start. Germans, in the full knowledge of the circumstances, should have initiated and executed the purge against the guilty minority, and it alone—not Allies, no matter how sincere and well-intentioned, to whom the German masses could not but appear uniformly black or grey. The irreparable consequence of this error was the abysmal failure of the Germans concerned—the majority of the German people. Concentration camps of yore—were they still worth mentioning at all? In the confusion most Germans lost all standards of comparison, and those who had never had any failed to gain them.

And then there were the Russian realities in the eastern zone! Buchenwald remained in existence, as did Sachsenhausen-Oranienburg, Torgau and Ravensbrück. A few camps were actually expanded, others newly built. There are now probably six main camps and altogether at least a dozen subsidiary camps and camp-like prisons, with presumably a core of more than 100,000 inmates and at times apparently up to 250,000 prisoners, deportations to Soviet Russia taking place at arbitrary intervals. Is the system directed only against former Nazis? It appears to embrace anyone suspected as an "enemy of the state," an "agent of a foreign power," a "class enemy," a "kulak," or similar categories.

These facts have become more and more widely known among the German people. Until late 1946 the licensed press in the three other zones of occupation was not permitted to write about them. That would have been "criticism of an Allied power." Since 1947, when the conflict with the Russians came into the open, such criticism has not only been permitted but actually desired. But the German people had their own ideas even before then. There was a conspiracy of silence—another enforced silence, so far as they were concerned. They took note of the fact that the Western Allies failed to lift a finger, that their representatives on the Control Council neither demanded an investigation, nor protested, nor intervened actively. At least, if there was any such action, no one learned of it, just as had been the case under the Nazi regime, when there had likewise been protests and petitions, characterized in 1945 as "insignificant," "showing no special sign of courage," "without value."

To any man of good will, concerned with the common welfare, the similarity grew frightening. Late in 1947 and early in 1948 I asked Communists with whom I served for years in Buchenwald, as well as leading members of the Socialist Unity party, dominant in the eastern zone—likewise onetime political prisoners—what they thought of these developments. Some stated that dangerous political opponents must always be put behind bars and rendered harmless. They admitted frankly that on this score their methods did not differ from those of the Nazis. If such be their general opinion, I should like to know why the Nazis are suddenly expected to be horrified over the concentration camps from 1933 to 1945! The difference, I was told, is that prisoner must not be treated badly. But are they treated well in the MVD camps? True, in many respects the system does not appear to be as brutal as it was under the Nazis. There is no gassing, no garroting, no hanging, no wholesale shooting. But it is bad enough. Hundreds of Poles and German prisoners of war who have escaped the hell—for every highly organized system has its loopholes—have brought reports from Soviet Russia. Dozens have made statements about similar camps in the eastern zone. It is argued that these are all exaggerations—an argument that has a familiar ring. The great mass of prisoners is stated to consist of incorrigible enemies of the state—again a familiar argument. Of course there are injustices, but what can be done in the face of the decrees of secret police? This too we have heard before—applied to the all-powerful Gestapo.

It is those who were persecuted by the Nazi regime for their race, religion, or political convictions who are the chosen fighters against such injustice and barbarism. It is they who must raise their voices against the new and glaring injustices throughout the world and in Germany, particularly against Soviet Russia and the eastern zone! Their protests cannot fail to register an impression and bring results. Intervention from this side would be more effective than from any other source.

So many others would be suspect, because of their own prior guilt or weakness, and because ordinary protests so often carry overtones of political propaganda.

But here we touch upon another sore point. German and European opposition to Fascism no longer carries its old political and moral force. Anti-Fascism has failed to develop into a new vanguard in the postwar years. For the most part it has fallen under the spell of contending groups. Such "anti-Fascist action" as is maintained commands little respect among the broad masses of the people, because it fails to oppose the new injustices. Hence it finds little support even in its struggle against the surviving and very real remnants of Fascism in general.

It would be short-sighted, of course, to ignore the fact that political developments throughout the world have made the situation extraordinarily difficult. The conflict between East and West demands personal partisanship on the part of virtually everyone and makes it difficult to fight against injustice, wherever it raises its head. Far worse than that, it serves almost inevitably to spread totalitarian methods—discrimination, distortion, false alternatives, blindness toward the nuances of reality. It drives the Soviet Russians deeper into radicalism and the Western democrats into alliances with semi-Facists. If this process continues, it will not be long before the vanquished Germans are openly drawn into the defensive systems and other deployments of the contending opponents. In the case of the German police in the Soviet zone this has already begun on a large scale.

How can the general evil still be countered?

It is not my task here to examine at length the positive possibilities inherent in the general political situation, contrary to all appearances. I can hint only at the German possibilities.

There can be no doubt that the forces of leadership and regeneration are in the minority, endangering our hope of escaping ultimate disaster. Yet the experience of the four years since 1945 offers proof a hundred times over that there is a latent majority among the German people, especially a considerable proportion of the younger generation, that is in truth prepared to back those men and women who would head a vigorous turn for the better, if only the prospect of common

European solutions can be made more concrete and plausible than has been the case heretofore. It is of crucial importance to Germany to become fully integrated with Europe. Such a development would lessen many of the peculiarly German problems. A visible victory over the narrow nationalism that is in evidence everywhere would create the tangible opportunity for far-reaching improvement in Germany. It must be realized, of course, that the old spirit is doomed and cannot enter into the new Europe. But there is the chance of making a fresh start, because the arguments of the incorrigibles, who today find food for folly on every side, may yet pale into insignificance.

The literature, good, bad, and indifferent, on the old concentration camps, has nevertheless managed to find millions of readers in Germany. It will in the end, render its contribution toward a change, as soon as circumstances begin to change, as soon as the deep shadows that rest on the land begin to lift, as soon as life within the European community again becomes worth living. This is a distinct possibility in this time of decision—an alternative to the possibility of another period of darkness, whether of war or of dictatorship. The time is not far distant when it will become clear whether Europe will follow the path toward freedom or toward slavery.

As for the German people, it is not so much the former slave who has never known freedom who hates slavery, as the man who has lived a free life in a community of free men. This will become a question of new experiences—not of Nazi or other totalitarian policies. Only thus will Germany be able to overcome the remnants of Hitler that survive within it—and they are, on the whole, by no means inconsiderable, in thought, action and emotion. A wholesome revulsion against any form of concentration camp will stand the German people in good stead.

Are the Russian concentration camps any excuse for their German predecessors? No! On the contrary, the system of the SS super state must be recognized for what it is, so that any spread of the GPU super state may be combated, so that any resurgence in our midst, whether by our aid or because of our silence, may be prevented. With all the present knowledge at our command, there is no excuse left for anyone—inside Germany and out.